Collection of
Leonard J. Barr II

CUNARD
WHITE STAR

CONCERT
PROGRAMME

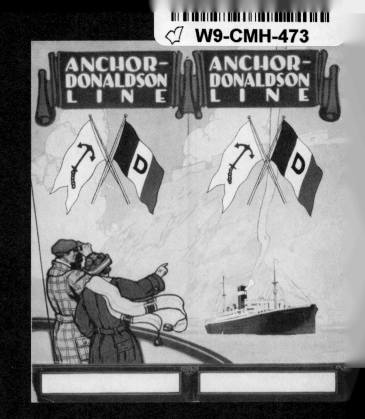

ANCHOR-
DONALDSON
LINE

ANCHOR-
DONALDSON
LINE

LUNCHEON

N.S. SAVANNAH

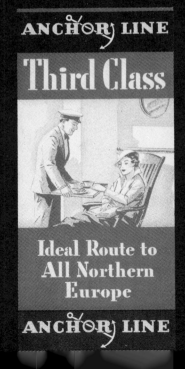

ANCHOR LINE

Third Class

Ideal Route to
All Northern
Europe

ANCHOR LINE

THE MODERN
THIRD CLASS
TO EUROPE

HOLLAND AMERICA
LINE

FIFTY
FAMOUS LINERS 3

The finished Olympia *on one of her early arrivals in New York* (courtesy of Jeff Blinn).

FIFTY
FAMOUS LINERS 3

Frank O. Braynard FRS
& William H. Miller

W · W · Norton & Company
NEW YORK   LONDON

First American Edition, 1988

Library of Congress Cataloging-in-Publication Data

Braynard, Frank Osborn, 1916–
Fifty famous liners 3
Includes index.
1. Ocean Liners—History. I. Miller, William H.
1948–   II. Title.
VM381.B692   1987   387.2'432   87-24060

ISBN 0-393-02551-9

W.W. Norton & Company, Inc.,
500 Fifth Avenue, New York NY 10110
W.W. Norton & Company Ltd.,
37 Great Russell Street, London WC1B 3NU

Printed in Great Britain

1 2 3 4 5 6 7 8 9 0

Contents

Introduction I

It is amazing how much pleasure comes through working on this series. Bill Miller and I have found new friends around the world, people who have answered our requests made in the first two volumes for names of other liners to include in this and future volumes. We now repeat the call.

It might be appropriate to chat a little about how we do decide on which ships to include. What makes a ship famous? A basic factor would be her career, was it long, did she survive many problems, serve many owners? A classic case is the *Medina*, covered in this volume. Another criterion would be whether she participated in some great event in maritime history such as the *Savannah*, the first nuclear passenger/

cargo ship. The centre of much controversy during her short career, her story must be told.

From a practical standpoint the first thing that comes to mind in the picking of a liner is the matter of potential illustrative material. Our combined collections include many thousands of artifacts, but photos are harder to get and we must have good photographic resources as we try hard to offer new pictorial material. One ship that really stumped me was the *Quaker City*, a fascinating vessel which did just about everything in her lively lifetime. Eventually I located reprints of several old drawings of deck scenes in the magazine put out by the International Mercantile Marine called *The Ocean Ferry*. Please bear with us if they are not as sharp as we would like them to be.

Let me add that picking out the ships to cover and searching for illustrations is one of the most fascinating assignments that Bill or I have ever enjoyed. It highlights the importance of having a world-wide photo index of ocean liners, a project begun years ago by the late C. Bradford Mitchell. Here's an idea for some of you upcomers!

Frank O. Braynard
Sea Cliff, New York

Introduction II

On a cold January afternoon in 1986, Frank Braynard and I spent hours, in that treasure chest he calls 'the cellar' at his home in Sea Cliff, poring over several hundred photos, brochures and, perhaps most, interestingly, well preserved newsclips. As always, Frank is the champion of spirit, joy and encouragement. (In later months, as we worked separately at our homes, he would always enquire 'What great progress, but are you having fun?' Yes, even on the very latest nights, it has been great fun!)

For my end of the research, Frank's newsclips have been an incalculable help. They have given 'life' to these famous ships, the third group of 50. They have rendered so much additional information and insight; the details of a collision or wartime exploit, the number of passengers or the berth used on a particular voyage. Also, I want to acknowledge, as always, the superb assistance from 'shipping friends', from the loaned, very rare photographs of the tragic *L'Atlantique* to negatives of the museum ship *Hikawa Maru*.

There are also, of course, some personal recollections of many of these ships. As far as I recall, the *Flandre* was one of the first liners that I visited. I sailed overnight along the California coast aboard the *President Cleveland* (in 1971, for $25) and later spent another night aboard the former *Monterey*, which was lying off the New Jersey shore during a 'cruise to nowhere'. I recall seeing the *Conte Grande* during one of her few appearances at New York in the mid-fifties and also the *Stockholm*, just arrived and minus her bow, following her collision with the *Andrea Doria*. Other recollections include a World Ship Society meeting onboard the *Savannah*, a quiet afternoon tour of the *Hikawa Maru* and a wintery midnight sailing of the *Olympia*.

If the current outpouring of books is any evidence, interest in passenger ships, especially ones from the past, is blossoming further. Frank and I have already begun to think of the next 'fifty famous liners'.

Bill Miller
Jersey City, New Jersey

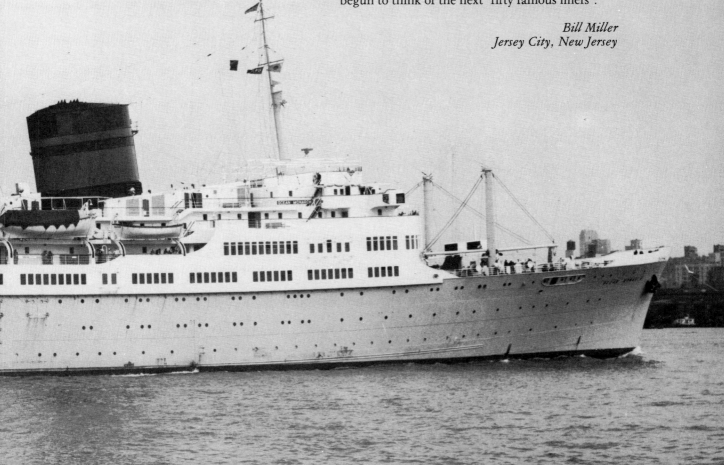

FIFTY
FAMOUS LINERS 3

Quaker City

Quaker City

Few ships have lived such full lives of varied service, excitement and historical importance as the little American Coastal paddle-wheeled steamship *Quaker City*. Her life illustrates how wide a range of activities a passenger liner can experience. Despite her peaceful name, this sturdy vessel survived two periods during which she was a full-fledged man-of-war. Built in 1854, she was to sink only 17 years later. She proved too expensive for her original run between Philadelphia and Charleston and was shifted to a line between New York and Mobile, later extended to New Orleans. Twice she was called on to fill in on two different trans-Atlantic steamer services. Her touch with immortality would come from another very special Atlantic crossing described by Dewey Ganzel in his book on the ship as 'one of the most famous journeys of the 19th century'.

The *Quaker City* looked much more like a modern liner than a sailing ship, although she used sails as well as steam, as all ocean-going steamers of her day did. She had only two masts, instead of the traditional three or four. Only her foremast had square yards. Her stem was virtually plumb. A short bowsprit projected forward, parallel to the raised forecastle but with none of the rake traditional to sailing craft. She had two beautifully-proportioned and perfectly raked stacks. They were widely spaced and gave her a silhouette that was strikingly advanced for that day. Her decorated paddle boxes were placed far aft, being only 91 feet from her stern. Her wheels were 31 feet in diameter. Scroll work at her stem and around the counter gave her class, as did a thin gold band painted at deck level around her wooden hull.

One of the best paintings of her was done when she was operating between New York and Charleston. It showed her flying her name burgee at the top of the foremast and her company houseflag at the main. The houseflag featured a large letter 'L' which stood for Arthur Leary, her principal owner. A bridge connected the tops of her twin paddle boxes, and in the painting an officer is shown standing on the bridge. A raised pilot house just aft of the foremast and a small lounge aft of the second stack were the only superstructure above her one level of deck houses. A covered promenade deck with stanchions supporting the deck above stretched from just aft of the foremast almost to the stern, another reason for the ship's modern look.

The *Quaker City*'s first transatlantic voyage was made early in 1856 when she was chartered as a replacement for the ill-fated Collins Line's *Pacific*, lost without trace after presumably having struck an iceberg. Despite bad storms both ways she made the run to Liverpool in 14½ days and returned in 15½ days, excellent time for that era. Although she boasted only 750 horsepower her hull lines gave her great speed. She set a new record for the run between New York and Havana, averaging 14.2 knots. She also suffered a near disaster off Cape Hatteras. A freak engine accident disabled her completely and she had to be abandoned, her passengers being rescued by a sailing ship. She was towed into Norfolk, her engines were rebuilt and she went back into service.

Then America was engulfed in civil war and the *Quaker City* became the setting for one of the most unusual chapters in naval history. Feelings were running high and a group of New Yorkers calling themselves the Union Defense Committee acquired her, armed and crewed her, all at their own initiative and expense, and sent her off to fight the Confederate States of America, as the seceding southern states called themselves. Without papers of any kind, she took up station off Virginia, examining incoming vessels and detaining those owned by Southerners. Eventually her master, Samuel W. Mather, was given a US Naval Commission, but the crew remained civilians and continued to receive their pay from the private citizens of New York. During this strange period the *Quaker City* captured a Norfolk-bound vessel. Eventually she was chartered to the Northern Navy and served for three years as a fast naval auxiliary. One of her assignments was to search for the Confederate raider *Sumter*. She did not find her, but, as the war dragged on, she participated in many kinds of wartime activity. On one occasion she battled two Confederate ironclads, surviving four hits. On another she captured the cotton-carrying steamer *Douro* and proudly entered New York with her prize steaming in her wake. She served as part of Admiral Porter's squadron attacking

Above Quaker City *as shown in an old print when she flew the 'L' house flag of Arthur Leary* (courtesy of The Mariners' Museum). **Below** Quaker City *with the warehouses and hills of Naples in the background, taken during her famous* Innocents Abroad *cruise with Mark Twain as a passenger* (courtesy of The Mariners' Museum).

Fifty Famous Liners

Fort Fisher, near Norfolk. She chased the *William H. Webb* and forced her on to the beach near New Orleans. She carried troops here and there. When the war ended Arthur Leary bought her at auction for $35,000.

Reconditioned at Philadelphia the sturdy craft was operated between New York and Charleston by the Leary Bros Line. Maritime engine and design technology was advancing at a rapid rate at this time, and, although the *Quaker City* was only 11 years old, she was becoming obsolete. She was fortunate to survive her next bout with fate, a bad hurricane. Her paddle boxes were stove in and her bowsprit was torn off. Although a nearby liner, the *Republic* was sunk the *Quaker City* managed to stay afloat. She even rescued survivors from one of the *Republic*'s lifeboats. Again she was repaired but her owners decided to lay her up. The year was 1867.

'Good morning, sir. There is no hurry' was the caption to this picture when it was used in the first edition of Innocents Abroad *(courtesy of The Mariners' Museum).*

Shortly before the Civil War, William K. Vanderbilt, fur trader, railroad magnate and enterprising shipowner, built a new passenger liner. He named her *North Star*. She was intended for his transatlantic steamship service, but, before putting her into the run, he fitted her out as his private yacht and took a group of his friends on a grand tour of the Mediterranean. This event made a great impression on many people of the day in America. The Leary brothers, Arthur and Daniel, decided to offer a five-month Mediterranean excursion to any American who could afford the fare of $1,250.

Charles Duncan, master of the *Quaker City* at that time, was induced to stay on and to sign the advertisements announcing this spectacular voyage. It may well have been the first cruise from New York to the Mediterranean with paying passengers.

To add glamour to the trip a committee of people with high sounding names was selected to, as it was put, 'pass on the applications' for passage. Some sort of a promise to go was secured from famed Union General W. T. Sherman and popular preacher Henry Ward Beacher which gave credence to the offer. They

"GOOD MORNING, SIR. THERE IS NO HURRY"

Crew members mock the Czar of Russia after Quaker City's *passengers had the unexpected opportunity to call on that potentate during a stop while cruising in the Black Sea. From an old engraving in* Innocents Abroad.

never went but the cruise quickly became the talk of the town.

And here, in one of those unpredictable quirks of fate, the jaunty little ship, well past her prime, came to the attention of a sharp-witted reporter, still unknown but whose star was on the ascendancy—Samuel Clements, whose pen name was Mark Twain. A native of Hannibal, Missouri, he had grown up along the Mississippi, eventually becoming a river pilot. After a short spell with the Confederate Army he had returned to mining in the West and had evolved into a confident and hard-bitten San Francisco newspaper man.

'Who could read the program of the excursion without longing to make one of the party', he wrote.

He imagined a 'great steamship with flags flying and cannon pealing departing from New York loaded with distinguished passengers who would occupy themselves on the voyage by scampering about the decks by day and filling the ships with shouts and laughter, reading novels and poetry in the shade of the smokestacks or watching for jelly-fish and nautilus over the side'. By night, as he saw them, 'they would dance on deck in the midst of a ballroom that stretched from horizon to horizon and was domed by the bending heavens and lighted by no meaner lamps than the stars and the magnificent moon'.

His enthusiasm convinced his editors that he should make the trip. He promised to send home 50 letters. The *Quaker City*'s slot in history was secure.

'I hurried to the Treasurer's office at 117 Wall St and deposited my ten per cent. I rejoiced to know that a few vacant staterooms were still left. I did avoid a critical personal examination into my character by that committee but I referred to all the people of high standing I could think of in the community who would be least likely to know anything about me...' Twain wrote in his first letter. The 74 passengers who did go included three ministers, eight doctors, 'an ample crop of professors and a gentleman who had the title Commissioner of the United States of America to Europe, Asia and Africa after his name'. This august personage turned out to be Samuel B. Parsons, horticulturist, who would win fame in his field as a result of the trip.

'Sailing day was June 8, 1867. The pier was crowded with passengers moping about in a drizzling rain and looking as droopy and woe-begone as so many molting chickens. The ship's ensign hung limp and disheartened by the mast', Twain wrote. As the paddle wheels began to turn and the visitors scampered ashore there were 'two very mild cheers from the dripping crowd. The flag made an effort to wave and failed. The battery of guns spake not—ammunition was out.'

Twain described his cabin as large enough to turn around in 'but not to swing a cat in, at least with entire security to the cat'. His favourite pastime when not drinking, or cavorting with women, or smoking, or swearing was watching the older passengers aboard get seasick. Here's how he put it: 'Playing whist by the cabin lamps, when it is storming outside, is pleasant; walking the quarter-deck in the

HOMEWARD BOUND ON THE QUAKER CITY

'Homeward bound on the Quaker City', *the caption for this engraving carried in* Innocents Abroad.

moonlight is pleasant; smoking in the breezy foretop is pleasant, when one is not afraid to go up there; but these are all feeble and commonplace compared with the joy of seeing people suffering the miseries of seasickness'. We leave the rest of his hilarious romp to those who wish to read his masterpiece of humour—*Innocents Abroad*.

After the cruise the *Quaker City* made one more Atlantic crossing and then resumed her run to Havana and New Orleans. In 1869 she was bought by revolutionaries seeking to overthrow a government in Haiti. Again she became a warship, being renamed *Columbia*. She went into almost immediate combat, attacking two Haitian warcraft, sinking one. Then she shelled Port-au-Prince and her

crew took the city. They executed the country's current president. A year passed and the weary little craft was again sold and renamed, becoming the *Republic*. She was loaded with logs and headed for New York under the command of a Haitian admiral who had bought her as an investment. As might be expected, her engineers were not competent. There was a boiler explosion, and a fire, and the poor ship was abandoned. She slowly disappeared below the waves and on to the pages of history.

Gross tonnage: 1,426 (also reported as 1,800)
Length overall: 234 feet
Width: 35 feet
Machinery: Single side lever steam engine
Speed: 14 knots
Capacity: 200
Built: At Philadelphia, 1854
Demise: Lost in 1867 off Haiti by foundering

Quaker City

Germanic

It was a hard decision to make, to select the *Germanic*, of 1874, over the *Oceanic*, of 1870. The *Oceanic* was the pioneer White Star steamship and made a great impact over all liners in ship design. But the *Germanic* just could not be denied. She was a record breaker. She introduced new elegance to her First Class passengers, although her steerage passengers were still required to bring their own bed, bedding and mess utensils. She sank twice but was raised each time. She had a full set of sails on her four masts and used them regularly, particularly one time when her shaft broke and she had to return to Liverpool under canvas. She was twice sold becoming a Canadian immigrant carrier and then being transferred to the Turkish flag. She fought against the land of her birth as a Turkish naval auxiliary in the First World War and served again in the Second. She lasted longer than any other liner ever has—76 years—although it should be noted that another vessel in this book is closing in fast on this record. We picked *Germanic*. *Oceanic* will have her turn in the next volume.

The *Oceanic*, by the way had three cabins with private bath tubs, the first, it is believed, ever built

on a liner. They were so popular that when *Germanic* came out she was given five 'bathrooms'. She carried 230 in first class, meaning a ratio of one tub per 46 passengers.

The *Germanic* was launched from the Belfast yard of Harland & Wolff on July 15 1874. She left on her maiden voyage on May 20 1875. Evidence of the keen competition of that day may be seen in the fact that two other notable new liners had preceeded her on their first trips—the *City of Berlin* on April 29 and the *Scythia* on May 1. Within 23 days three major new liners began maiden crossings. To complete the circle, so to speak, the *Germanic* survived until 1950, the year when the keel for the superliner *United States* was laid. What an extraordinary era her lifetime covered.

In the years that followed the *Germanic* and her sister *Britannic* got the cream of the passenger trade because of their speed. The *Germanic* set a new mark of 396 nautical miles in one day's steaming on a westbound crossing, averaging 16 knots. The iron-hulled liners were rigged as four-masted barques, with square sails on the fore, main and mizzen, and fore-and-aft sails on the jigger mast. Despite all the elegance in their public rooms, ships of this day were most primitive from the standpoint of lighting. The era of candles was past, but oil lamps were not much better. Experiments were made with gas lighting, but leakage in heavy weather caused these to be given up. Electricity did not come in for another decade. The evolution of the Atlantic liner was proceeding at such a rapid pace at this time that the *Germanic* reigned supreme for only five years, losing the Blue Riband to Guion Line's *Arizona* in 1879. Nevertheless she and her sister remained most popular. In 1889 the *Germanic* made 13 voyages averaging 7 days, 15 hours and 21 minutes, showing a wonderful consistency in speed.

In addition to her two sinkings, to be described below, the *Germanic* was struck by a tidal wave and suffered two major collisions. The tidal wave wrenched the steam winches from her fore decks, stove in some deckhouses and flooded her large dining saloon. The first collision was with the *Cambrae* in dense fog in the Mersey. Captain E. R. McKinstry showed his coolness by not pulling away from the *Cambrae*, but by maintaining a slow ahead

FASHIONABLE TRAVEL IN 1875

Drawing from "Frank Leslie's Illustrated Newspaper," entitled "The new ocean steamer Germanic, of the White Star Line." The costumes and table accessories should be especially interesting to travelers of 1924

An engraving published in 1875 in Frank Leslie's Illustrated Newspaper *showing life on* Germanic.

The promenade deck on Germanic *from an old engraving in the files of* International Mercantile Marine.

A broadside view showing Germanic *at her pier with a huge three arm crane in the background behind her second mast.*

Germanic

until everyone aboard the other craft had been rescued. This was in 1895 at which point the two White Star sisters had completed 800 crossings carrying 100,000 saloon passengers and an estimated 260,000 steerage. 'Such a record is probably without a parallel in the history of steam navigation', wrote Henry Fry, in his *History of North Atlantic Steam Navigation*, published in 1896. So successful had the *Germanic* been that she was treated to a substantial modernization in 1895. She was given new triple-expansion engines and her speed was increased by one knot. A new deck was added and her smokestacks were increased in height. All these changes when she was 21 years old. Little did her owners know that she had another 55 years of life left in her.

In a February blizzard in 1899 at New York disaster struck again. The *Germanic* was being coaled (she consumed 300 tons a day) and her coaling doors were open. Ice formed on her superstructure and she took a list to port. Coaling was progressing on both sides and a fierce wind was blowing up river, pressing hard against her starboard side. The list to port got worse. Suddenly a gust of wind blew her to port and her four towering masts swung toward the pier. Her port side coal ports disappeared below the icy water's surface and she began to settle. By morning she was submerged up to her main deck in 35 feet of water. It was not too difficult to raise her, fortunately. After a cleaning it was found that her engines were in good enough shape to take her home for repairs.

In 1905, just as her sister was being scrapped, the *Germanic* began the second of her three careers. She was sold to J. P. Morgan's Dominion Line and renamed *Ottawa* for immigrant service to Canada. She also carried 250 passengers in first or 'saloon' class. On May 11 1908 she smashed her bow in a bad collision with a tanker bound from Australia to Quebec. The *Ottawa* was heading down from Quebec. Her forepeak and No 1 hold were flooded giving her a draft of 30 feet forward, but she was able to limp back for repairs. The tanker, named *Trold*, also survived.

The author's (FOB) great uncle, Professor H. L. Osborn, took his wife on a westbound crossing aboard the *Ottawa* in 1907 and saved his passenger list, deck plan, September 11 concert programme and September 12 dinner menu. Captain James O. Evans was master. The concert was for the benefit of the seamen's home and £9 8s 2½d was collected.

The menu, although small in size, was decidely elegant, starting with 'Norwegian Lox' and Clear Mock Turtle Soup and ending with plum pudding with hard and brandy sauces, compots of pears, lemon cheese cakes or ice cream.

When built the *Germanic* had cost £100,000. She was sold in 1911 by Dominion to the Imperial Ottoman Government for £20,000 for use as a troopship. Renamed the *Gul Djemal*, she left Liverpool March 15 for Constantinople. In World War I she was torpedoed and sunk by the British submarine E 14 in the Sea of Marmora, one of the striking successes of the ill-fated Dardanelles campaign. She was salvaged and after the war put into passenger service to New York. Flying the houseflag of the American Oriental Line (also known as the Ottoman-American Line), she brought about 956 passengers on a 22-day crossing from Constantinople on her first trip. Quarantine officials stopped her as she was said to have sailed without a clean bill of health. There were 200 aboard in steerage. A report in the *Marine Journal* noted casually that 'with the exception of one case of typhoid, their general health was good'. Things like this continued to happen. The next year she left Constantinople without the consent of the French authorities and again had no 'proper bill of health'. Most of her 1,000 Greek, Armenian and Jewish immigrant passengers were believed to have no passports, the *Nautical Gazette* for October 23 1920 reported. During this period the ship's upper superstructure was again enlarged. She made four round trips in 1921 on the New York run being featured in headlines when she sailed on June 10 as having the 'Inter-Allied Commission' aboard. This crossing, it was said, 'marked an epoch in the development of trade between the United States and the Near East'. It also marked the end of the old ship's trans-Atlantic voyaging.

As a White Star liner the *Germanic*'s smokestacks were the traditional buff with black tops. Under the Dominion Line the black tops remained but the rest of the stack was a bright red with a thin white stripe near the top. Under Turkish colours in 1920 – 21 she had black stacks with a white band featuring an old-style anchor, much like the markings of the modern state-owned Turkish passenger fleet.

She continued to serve the Turks in the Mediterranean and the Black Sea through the 1920s, being renamed *Gulcemal* in 1928. She ran ashore in 1931

Dominion Line, S.S. "Ottawa"

The Ottawa *with red stacks, black top and thin white band near the top of the red. This was the* Germanic *after she had been sold to Dominion Line for service to Canada.*

Dinner menu on the Ottawa, *September 12, 1907.*

in the Sea of Marmora and then seemed to fade out of the shipping news columns. What was done with her in World War 2 is not known, but she again was reported in 1949 as a store ship at Constantinople, with her engines intact and her superstructure reduced. A year later she was said to be serving as a floating hotel but her days were numbered. On October 29 1950, she left port under tow for Messina, Sicily. She arrived on November 16 and was promptly scrapped.

Gross Tonnage: 5,008
Length overall: 455 feet
Width: 45 feet
Machinery: Triple-expansion steam
Speed: 16 knots
Capacity: 220 First (raised to 250); 900 Steerage (raised to 1,500)
Built: Harland & Wolff, Belfast, Ireland, 1874
Demise: Scrapped 1950 – 51, Messina, Italy

Germanic

MENU. DOMINION LINE.

R.M.S. "Ottawa."

Thursday, September 12th, 1907

DINNER

NORWEIGIAN LAX

CLEAR MOCK TURTLE

BOILED SALMON, CUCUMBER   TARTARE SAUCE

COMPOTE OF PIGEON

MACARONI ITALIENNE

ROAST SIRLOIN OF BEEF & YORKSHIRE PUDDING

TURKEY A LA ST. JAMES

CALVES HEAD & BACON   PARSLEY SAUCE

VEGETABLE MARROW   JULIENNE ROOTS

BOILED & DUCHESS POTATOES

PLUM PUDDING HARD & BRANDY SAUCE

COMPOTE OF PEARS   LEMON CHEESE CAKES

ICE CREAM

DESSERT   CHEESE

COFFEE

Campania

The *Campania* was the first Cunard Line steamship to abandon entirely the use of sails. There was no doubt about that and her huge smokestacks, proportionately thicker and taller than any ship before her, may have been designed this way for that reason. They were 20 feet in diameter and their tops were 130 feet above the waterline. Certainly they were most impressive, each with its three thin black bands evenly spaced within the Cunard red funnel section and below the traditional black top. There were no yards on her two very tall pole masts. She had two decks of open promenade space, huge air funnels and a remarkably tall bridge supporting a tiny pilot house six decks above the main deck. It was placed back a dozen feet from the rim of the bridge, leaving space for officers to pace from side to side. It was reached by a two-deck high open stair-ladder, a cold climb on a bad night.

The *Campania* and her sister, the *Lucania*, were Cunard's answers to two equally famous pairs of liners built for Inman and White Star. The Inman ships were the illustrious *City of Paris* and *City of New York*, the first great liners with twin screws. White Star's equally famous pair were the *Majestic*

and *Teutonic*. The adoption of twin-screw propulsion eliminated forever the shipowner's fear of a shaft breakdown with a resulting dependance on sails. Without sails the superstructure need no longer be kept to one deck house above the main. Now deck upon deck could be built with the modern liner silhouette the end result. The great size of the stacks on *Campania* marked her as well ahead of her time from this standpoint. The American Line's pair *St Louis* and *St Paul* had shorter, thinner stacks. The Germans, who were designing larger and larger liners each year, chose to go in for four, thinner and shorter stacks. The *Campania* and her sister could be distinguished for many miles at sea by this great pair of funnels. For a short period they were not only the world's fastest ships, but the world's largest. And they were elegant!

Although the amount of space offered for public rooms on the *Campania* was small when compared to later liners, it was very large in contrast to previous ships and the deck plan reflected this. The athwartship vestibule on the Upper Deck was half filled with a huge stairway going up both to the left and to the right. This area was labelled 'Grand Entrance'. There were tufted couch seats in all four corners. Each of the eight tables ringing the small library forward on the promenade was shown in the deck plan along with two oval-shaped eight-seat clusters filling most of the rest of the room. Three more eight-seat clusters were built, one for the long 'Assembly Hall' amidships on the promenade and two in the first class smoking room aft.

Another break-through for *Campania* was that she had several suites. These boasted a connecting parlour and bedroom. Noted maritime historian Noel Bonsor called them among the first on the Atlantic. They were on the upper deck forward of the Grand Foyer. Henry Fry in his *History of North Atlantic Steam Navigation*, was ecstatic in his praise of the lofty and well ventilated first class staterooms. About 75 per cent of the ship's passenger areas were devoted to first class passengers. Small sections aft on all four decks were for second class and steerage got what was left. The deck plans identified large blank areas on the lower deck and at the bow of the saloon deck as 'steerage,' showing only that there was one

Above Campania *about to be launched* (courtesy of Cunard Line).

Right *An oil painting of* Campania *reproduced on a Raphael Tuck postcard.*

Right *The long gallery aboard* Campania (courtesy of Cunard Line).

Campania

narrow flight of stairs leading up from each steerage space.

'The old wooden coffin-like berth', wrote Henry Fry in 1896, 'has been superceded by Hopkins' 'triptic' beds, which are so constructed that the upper bed folds up against the bulkhead. The lee board is movable, and being only one-half the length of the bed can be fixed at either end or in the middle. The rooms for those in Second Class are all placed abaft the machinery. The steerage is fitted with iron portable berths. Its passengers are allowed to promenade on the Upper Deck.'

The same author's description of the dining saloon is worth quoting: 'It is a vast, lofty apartment 100 feet long, 62 feet broad and 10 feet high, capable of seating at dinner 430...in revolving armchairs. The ceiling was panelled in white and gold, the sides in Spanish mahogany, and the upholstering was in a dark, rich red figured frieze velvet, with curtains to match. There was a central well 24 × 16 feet, carried up from the Saloon to above the Awning Deck, where it is covered by a curved dome of stained glass.'

Any two of the *Campania*'s 18 watertight compartments could be flooded and she would remain afloat. The compartment doors could all be closed from the deck 'by a common rack-and-pinion arrangement with a certainty that cannot be gainsaid', author Fry wrote. The new Cunarder had a crew of 424 persons and was lit by 1,300 ten-candle power incandescent electric lights. The crew wages and food cost Cunard from $12,000 to $15,000 a month. An annual subsidy was paid the company by the British Admiralty of £19,000 for the *Campania* and her sister to insure that they would be held at the

Campania with her second stack whistle blowing (shown by the white steam) getting underway, bound for America.

disposal of the government for service as armed cruisers.

On her trials the new beauty attained a speed of 23.2 knots. She broke the eastbound record on her maiden voyage, averaging 21.82 knots and taking 5 days, 17 hours and 27 minutes. Later she broke the westbound record, but was eventually beaten by the *Lucania*. Both Cunarders were surpassed by the *Kaiser Wilhelm der Grosse* in 1897, the first of a series of German record breakers.

Although wireless was quite widespread on the Atlantic when the *Campania* was new, Cunard retained its old emergency night signal, which called for a blue light and two Roman candles, each throwing six blue balls. The new ship had two wireless operators, while most ships only had one. The wireless/telegraph office was between the funnels atop a domed deck, where the ship's roll was very evident. The *Lucania* was famed as being the first ship to be in simultaneous touch by wireless with both sides of the Atlantic.

In 1897 there were 11 major liners in position at Queen Victoria's Diamond Jubilee. They were the *Campania, Lucania, Teutonic, Majestic, Himalaya, Australia, Victoria, Arcadia, Empress of India, Empress of Japan* and *Empress of China*. Also on hand were 30 miles of British warships. Aboard the *Campania* was a delegation of members of the Houses of Lords and Commons.

With newer and faster ships coming out from yards in England, France and Germany the

Campania *rebuilt as a naval unit and sinking — a sad sight.*

Campania and her sister all too soon fell into the background, although as money earners they continued among the best. Sad to say the *Lucania* suffered a disastrous fire in 1909 at Liverpool, tipping over and sinking at her pier. Her machinery was intact and it was thought she could be saved, but in short order she was sold to Thomas Ward for scrapping in Scotland, being the largest vessel ever demolished up to that point, except, of course, for the *Great Eastern*.

The rapid increase in size of liners around this time meant that the title 'world's largest' passed to a new ship every two or three years. The 12,000 tons of the *Campania* came to seem small in only 15 years, with the arrival of the 31,000-ton *Lusitania* and *Mauretania*. Nevertheless the *Campania* sailed on. A list of 1912 New York-Liverpool sailings showed her scheduled for nine crossings. She carried as few as 42 in first, 135 in second and 279 in third class and her best crossing saw 117 in first, 366 in second and 449 in third. She could still make a 19½ knots crossing in either direction and was well maintained. Near the outbreak of World War 1 she made two voyages under charter to the Anchor Line from Glasgow. Her final crossing for Cunard was made after war had begun. She reached Liverpool on October 15 1914 after this voyage and was sold for scrap. The new four-stacker *Aquitania* was on the scene and a 12,000 tonner looked like something out of a history book. However she was saved by the Navy while at the scrapper's yard and rebuilt as a so-called aircraft

carrier, or more specifically a 'mother ship' for sea planes.

For this new war service she was completely altered. Her bridge was moved far forward and two new smokestacks, each smaller and shorter than the original forward stack, were built athwartships. The after stack remained in its original place. Much of the superstructure was removed 'leaving a clear deck for the seaplanes', according to a news clipping of December 27 1916. She was given new boilers and could still average 20 knots. This same source noted that she participated in the Battle of Jutland and was also in the Dardanelles campaign. At that point she was under Vice Admiral Beatty and attached to the North Sea Fleet.

The *Campania* survived the war, but only days after the Armistice she sank. She was in a storm and broke loose from her moorings in the Firth of Forth. The winds smashed her against a nearby battleship, the HMS *Revenge*. She began taking water at the stern. Although efforts were made to beach her they were unsuccessful and the old lady slowly disappeared beneath the waves, her hull painted in wild streaks of camouflage and her three stacks and numerous tall cranes making her look like a floating derrick barge or dredge. A sad end for a great lady!

Gross tonnage: 12,950
Length overall: 620 feet
Width: 65 feet
Machinery: Triple expansion, twin screw
Speed: 22 knots
Capacity: 600 First, 400 Second, 1,000 Steerage
Built: Fairfield Shipbuilding Co, Govan, Scotland, 1893
Demise: Sunk, Firth of Forth, 1918

Campania

Prinzess Irene

At the close of the 19th century and up until World War 1 there were two German ship lines whose houseflag could be found on almost every trade route. They were the Hamburg American Line and the North German Lloyd. Seven sisters were built for these two lines between 1896 and 1900 known as the *Barbarossa* class. Two were for Hapag (the way Hamburg American is frequently referred to) and the rest for NGL. The last of the NGL seven was the *Prinzess Irene*. She would live for 32 years, well beyond the average liner's 20-year life. She would have four different names. She would do yeoman service helping the Allies defeat the country of her birth. She would miraculously survive a surface gun duel with a German submarine. Her eventful career is well worth a full volume. Near the end she would give up her then current name to one of Germany's greatest liners of all time—all this and much more remains to be packed into a brief 2,000 words.

The first of this historic class of liners was named *Barbarossa*. In outline each was much the same, with graceful lines, two masts and two smallish smokestacks. Each had a raised forecastle and well

deck forward and another well and raised poop aft. All had long and eventful lives. When new, the *Prinzess Irene* served on the NGL's Mediterranean run with her sisters *Königin Luise* and *König Albert* and two smaller company liners. The fare to New York from Genoa or Naples or Gibraltar was $55, first class. The 1904 folder giving this information proudly boasted that since its founding in 1857 the company had carried over three million passengers.

Later the older ships were retired and a weekly sailing to New York was offered with the *Barbarossa, Prinzess Irene, Königin Luise, König Albert* and *Friedrich der Grosse*, five superior twin-screw steamers. Large old-style wall paintings, stained glass ceiling panels, carved mahogany wall panels and rich table covers gave the proper feeling of high class elegance that was demanded of liners at that time. A few lines from a letter written in 1907 aboard the *Prinzess Irene* can be fitted in here:

'It seemed too bad not to be on deck while we were going down the Bay, but I thought I'd better get things unpacked and settle our room before we got outside, so everything would be in place in case we were sea sick. Harry was more patriotic about looking back and seeing the last of our country. After I was through we went on deck until the trumpet call announced that lunch was ready. Such a lunch!!! The boat is remarkably steady. We have made up our minds that a big boat is an immense advantage over a small one, and we began to think we'll actually enjoy the voyage.' The lady writing did not get seasick despite rough weather later in the voyage. Her letter was rapsodic about the table...' Immense variety, everything deliciously cooked. Everyone so attentive and obliging'. She and her husband had begun their Atlantic voyaging on the Anchor liner *Furnessia*, built in 1880 and of only 5,495 tons, a ship with sails and a single stack. They were the author's (FOB) great aunt and uncle.

On April 6 1911, the *Prinzess Irene* ran aground off Saltaire, on Fire Island, nearly 100 miles east of New York. That community, to this day, remembers this event as one of the memorable happenings in its history. Dr George S. King, a local physician with a passion for shipwrecks, pulled a 16-foot oar in one of the surfboats that went out to offer help. Fortunately the liner got off after a brief embarrassment, leaving a record of snapshots and anecdotes that have survived the generations to follow. Her master at the time was a Captain Peterssen, and the *New York Tribune* carried a picture of him in a circle over a view of his ship being assisted by tugs into her Hoboken berth on April 11 1911. The original of this photo is in the author's hands. The ship looks no worse for the grounding.

World War 1 began and the *Prinzess Irene* was seized along with 11 other major German liners in New York when America entered the conflict. On April 6 1917, she was renamed *Pocahontas*. She was commissioned July 25 1917, and entered US Navy service. Her story is told by Vice Admiral Albert Gleaves in his *A History of the Transport Service*. She operated in the Newport News Division and served with the Austrian luxury liner *Martha Washington*, whose name did not have to be changed. Two of her

An old postcard showing Prinzess Irene *passing the lighthouse off Genoa.*

The wonderfully ornate music room on the Prinzess Irene.

Prinzess Irene

23

A *broadside view of* Prinzess Irene *entering New York well before World War 1.*

original sisters were in this same unit—the *Grosser Kurfurst*, renamed *Aeolus*, and the *Friedrich der Grosse*, renamed *Huron*. The old *Rhein*, another NGL Atlantic liner, was there too, as the *Susquehanna*. As first rebuilt the *Pocahontas* had space for 2,400 troops, not many more than she had been designed to carry when in the Mediterranean run. She was rebuilt after a few trips to transport 2,900. She made nine voyages before the Armistice carrying over 20,503 souls and bringing home 221. After the war's end she made nine more trips, returning 20,693 troops and 1,382 sick and wounded.

The most exciting occurrence of the war period for the *Pocahontas* took place May 2 1918. She was proceeding homeward, unaccompanied, under the command of Captain E. C. Kalbfus. The sea was smooth except for white caps. At 10:20 am when about 1,000 miles west of Brest, a large U-boat 'cruiser' came to the surface astern. She had evidently tried and failed with torpedoes. The range was 7,000 yards, well beyond that which the transport's small guns could reach. The submarine lay across the ship's wake and opened fire with two high power guns. Captain Kalbfus ordered full steam ahead and steered a zigzag course, for he knew his guns were useless. The liner's engine room responded and soon she was turning 80 revolutions for an amazing 16.7 knots, as high as she had ever gone while under the German flag. The submarine's

top speed was 15 knots. Meanwhile shells were falling on all sides and ahead of the *Pocahontas*. Incredible as it seemed, there were no direct hits. At 10:40 the fire slackened and at 11:20 the last shot was fired and the submarine disappeared astern. Nearby ships were warned by radio and the engagement was over.

After the war the *Pocahontas* was assigned by the US Shipping Board to the ill-fated US Mail Line, which described itself as '100% American—100% service' in its advertisements. The company was mismanaged from the beginning. The *Pocahontas* was put on her old route to the Mediterranean sailing in company with her old sister, the former Hapag ship *Kiautschou*, later renamed *Princess Alice* (with a 'c' not a 'z'). She made two round trips. She was due to sail on the third on May 19 1921 with 204 in cabin, 220 in second and 200 tons of cargo. The departure was delayed for several days and then the voyage began.

One reason for the delay at sailing time was a series of labour troubles. She sailed with a motley crew and off Long Island began to suffer from boiler troubles. She had to be towed into Newport. The next day she left for Boston arriving there May 27. Repairs were

Aground off Saltaire on Fire Island, April 6, 1911. Prinzess Irene *will never be forgotten by people of this Long Island summer resort* (courtesy of Mystic Seaport).

made and, despite more crew troubles, the ship managed to sail for Naples on June 4. During the crossing an assistant engineer named James Daniel Prendegast either jumped or was thrown overboard. More engine difficulties caused the voyage to end at Naples on July 5. In all probability the crew was not paid. This, plus their evident dissatisfaction and unrest may have been responsible for two boiler fires that broke out while she lay at the Italian port. Debts piled up and the vessel was attached by many different persons and firms. On August 16 1921, the American Consul cabled home that some 1,900,000 lire was owed. The reputation of American shipping was damaged by the whole episode. Needless to say the Italian newspapers made daily attacks on US Mail management and the ship's personnel. The passengers and crew began to drift away.

Finally, after the Shipping Board had paid all the debts, she was able to sail for home. This was on September 8. She got only as far as Gibraltar when more engine trouble forced her voyage to be cancelled, her crew to be discharged and the vessel to be laid up. A year passed and on August 9 1922 it was announced that the *Pocahontas* had been reacquired by the North German Lloyd. The price was not

disclosed but the Washington bureau of the *NY Journal of Commerce* reported it was under $100,000. At long last she was in good hands again.

In 1923 the sturdy old ship, beautifully restored, was renamed *Bremen* and entered service between Bremerhaven and New York. A report of January 15 1923 noted that 'very little of the old *Prinzess Irene* remains and according to officials of the company she is practically a new vessel. She is of 11,000 gross tons, and will be what is termed a one class and third class passenger carrier.' She sailed with the then new *Munchen*, of 14,500 tons. The Germans were reviving their liner fleet with surprising speed.

As the 1920s drew to a close vastly ambitious plans were coming into fruition for NGL. They would have twin superliners (the term was coined by journalists for these two ships) which would sail on the same day. Both would break the Atlantic speed record held by the *Mauretania* both going and coming. In 1928 it was decided to name them *Bremen* and *Europa*. The name 'Bremen' had to be made available so the old *Prinzess Irene* was once again given a new name, this time *Karlsruhe*, famous Rhine port in Baden Wurttenberg. What a contrast the heavy mahogany, classical oil paintings, drapes and Victorian furniture made with the interiors of the grand, modern new *Bremen*. But the old *Karlsruhe* kept sailing, serving on the line to Boston and New York and returning via Galway, Cobh,

Renamed Bremen, *the former* Prinzess Irene *returned to German hands after World War 1. She later gave up the name* Bremen *so it could be given to Germany's new superliner and was named* Karlsruhe, *she is shown here being docked by Dalzell tugs in the 1920s.*

Southampton, Cherbourg, Boulogne to Bremen. Rates for cabin class were from $130 to $140 and up. Tourist third could be had for from $102.50 to $120 for the whole 12-day trip. Finally the Depression succeeded where war and age had failed and the career of the *Prinzess Irene* came to an end. With no fanfare she was sold to a scrap yard and quietly demolished in 1932.

Gross tonnage: 10,881
Length overall: 523.5 feet
Width: 60 feet
Machinery: Quadruple expansion, twin screw
Speed: 15 ½ knots
Capacity: 240 First, 162 Second, 1,954 Steerage (as troopship 2,900)
Built: Vulcan, Stettin, 1900
Demise: Scrapped in Germany, 1932

Fifty Famous Liners

Deutschland

The success of North German Lloyd's *Kaiser Wilhelm der Grosse* in 1897 and the Spanish-American War were factors in the building of the one Blue Riband holder of Hamburg American Line—the *Deutschland*. Although Albert Ballin, the famed president of Hapag, preferred large, comfortable liners of relatively slow speed, he was willing to listen to his Board of Directors when they pointed to the prestige won for NGL and Germany by the sleek *Kaiser Wilhelm der Grosse*. He agreed to make a voyage on her to see what she was like. He came back still not sold on the idea but was overruled by his Board. The Spanish-American War created a once-in-a-lifetime demand for fast auxiliary cruisers and Hapag sold two of its finest express steamers to Spain. They were the *Columbia* and the *Normannia*. The funds earned by this sale helped pay for their ill-fated plunge into maritime history's area of fiercest competition—the challenge for the Atlantic speed record.

As the *Deutschland* progressed emphasis on her vast power plant could be seen in company press releases. Her horsepower would be over 30,000. What a contrast with the 80 horsepower of the *Savannah* of 1819. Other details were awe inspiring. The distance from the lowest level of the engineroom to the top of the high pressure cylinder was to be 45 feet. Her vast power plant would not only be 'ingenious' but it was pictured as being 'colossal'. She would boast quadruple expansion engines with two high pressure and two low pressure cylinders. Each low pressure cylinder weighed 7 tons. The piston rod would be 3 tons, the connecting rod 10 tons. The two huge propellers would go around 78 times a minute. Steam would be obtained from 12 double and four single-ended boilers. The crankshaft was a steel bar 59 feet, 3 inches long which weighed almost 100 tons. Pictures of it with a tiny figure of a man standing under one of its ends were sent out world-wide.

Trouble began early in the ship's career, however. It had been intended that she would sail on her maiden voyage on June 17 1900, but on her delivery trip from the shipyard in Stettin (now Szczecin, Poland) she grounded in the River Oder. Two craft came to her aid, but it took pontoons fastened to her hull to get her off the bottom. She was refloated only to run aground a second time. She did not reach Swinemunde on the Baltic until early in July.

Much emphasis had been put on how she was designed to serve as an auxiliary in wartime. She had a submerged rudder and there was special protection for the rudder stock. Press releases also noted that 'rapid fire guns with their mounts for the *Deutschland* are to be ready at Hamburg and Kiel so that at the briefest notice the vessel can be converted into a warship'.

She sailed on her first crossing July 5, passing Eddystone Light late on July 6. The previous record had been made in 1898 by the *Kaiser Wilhelm der Grosse* with a 5 day, 20 hour crossing at 22.29 knots. The new *Deutschland* averaged 22.42 knots and took 5 days, 15 hours and 46 minutes. After a six-day layover in New York she set another record on her first eastbound crossing, again beating the *Kaiser Wilhelm der Grosse*. The new eastbound Blue Riband crossing took 5 days, 15 hours and 5 minutes and averaged 22.84 knots. In her relatively brief period in trans-Atlantic express service the *Deutschland* broke her own records a number of times, setting three new westbound and three new eastbound marks.

A most unusual development took place in mid-1902 when the *Kronprinz Wilhelm*, newest speed queen of NGL claimed she had made an east-

bound crossing at 23.53 knots, or two-tenths of a knot faster than the best record of the Hapag liner. There was jubilation in Bremerhaven, but that was not the end of it. Two months later a joint announcement by Hapag and NGL informed the world that the captain's calculations on the *Kronprinz Wilhelm* had been found to be incorrect and stated that the *Deutschland* still held the record. The *Deutschland*'s eastbound mark was beaten in 1904 by the still newer and much larger NGL four-

Above *Beautifully framed by the Hamburg American pier and an old Hudson River sloop, this fine photograph shows the* Deutschland *being docked at Hoboken.*

Left *A postcard of* Deutschland *from the Raphael Tuck 'celebrated liners' series, printed in England before World War 1.*

Right Deutschland *passing the Battery outward bound from New York* (A. Loeffler).

Fifty Famous Liners

stacker *Kaiser Wilhelm II* with a 23.58-knot crossing. So from the standpoint of winning the Blue Riband the *Deutschland* did well, but at what a cost.

'It thus appears that the *Deutschland* with her displacement of 23,000 tons and speed of 23 knots, represents a notable advance in fast steamships, and her career in the immediate future, or until her laurels shall be transferred to some new ocean wonder, will be watched with the liveliest interest', wrote the editor of *Marine Engineering* in August 1900. He was, naturally, an engineer, and looking at the ship from the engineering standpoint. But the view almost from the start was different from the passengers' standpoint. The *Deutschland* had a grave problem—vibration! The grounding on her delivery run had prevented anything but the most casual trials in the Baltic. She went to sea like an untried colt and her master drove her all the way, both over and back. She made seven round trips in her first year, running with the *Auguste Victoria*, *Furst Bismarck* and *Columbia* (bought back from Spain). Her best trip saw her carrying 447 in first, 297 in second and 288 in third class. She operated more or less alone, since none of the other three could match her in speed or capacity, a serious handicap to booking agents. And word of her vibration difficulties spread rapidly. Hapag did their best to correct it without success.

The year 1901 saw the *Deutschland* make nine round trips, carrying two and three times the passengers that the smaller, slower and older ships serving with her did. But something had to be done about the vibration and, after two spring voyages in 1902, she was taken out of service and worked on. She did not return to the Atlantic until November, ending the year with one more crossing in December. Despite bad winter storms she was kept in operation. Her January 12 arrival at New York provoked an eloquent story by a local reporter: 'Three days of pitching and lifting over steep acclivities, shipping them green over plunging bows and to the quiver of racing engines; 70 hours of struggle against full blown gales and spray blown seas, and then a shift of wind to the southward and a beam sea whose mile-long rollers almost hid the great vessel as she sunk into their hollows'. Despite all this, the reporter continued, 'the superb vessel managed to complete her journey in 5 days, 23 hours and 28 minutes, a record that is extraordinary at this stormy season, a period when most of the liners have been coming in from one to three days late'.

But her troubles were not over. She found her slip blocked with ice and had to range abreast of the pier 'until the tugs, which were ploughing through the mess, had cut it up sufficiently for her to warp in. Her passengers were enthusiastic in their praise for the

Deutschland

manner Capt. Kaempff handled the ship, so much so that they drew up and presented him a testimonial. This was his first trip on the *Deutschland*.'

She made 10 trips in 1904 and carried the bulk of the company's express service passengers. The three smaller liners only made one crossing each and were then taken off the run. Thereafter the *Deutschland* sailed alone. Her vibration problem continued. There were the customary accidents as well, as when in 1907 she ran headlong into a pier at Dover. Repairs required the replacement of 40 bow plates. The work was done night and day with the aid of electric lights, a big thing at that time, so as not to keep her any longer than she had to be in the dry-dock, a most expensive place to be for a great liner.

After only two trips that year Hapag decided that something drastic had to be done about the continuing vibration problem. The ship was laid up again. The company chartered White Star's old *Romanic* to replace her, a ship which carried largely steerage class passengers. Nothing the engineers could do stopped the vibration, however, and after

Deutschland *with black hull paint extending up to the promenade deck. Note the Hapag flag on her stem* (courtesy of the Cropley Collection, Smithsonian Institution).

much experimentation it was decided to convert the *Deutschland* into a cruising ship. In 1910 she came out with much less power and a new name. She was re-christened *Victoria Luise*. Her appearance remained the same except that she was given a coat of white paint. Her engines were cut down to produce a speed of 18 knots, all that was needed for voyages to the West Indies, Norway and the Mediterranean.

Ballin had been proved right again, and he smiled to watch his large but relatively slow *Amerika* and *Kaiserin Auguste Victoria* sailing year in and year out with huge passenger loads.

During the First World War the *Deutschland* was used as a receiving ship by the German Navy at Hamburg. She was sadly neglected. At the war's conclusion the Reparations Committee examined her and decided she was not worth taking. She was left

Rebuilt and given over to cruise service as the Victoria Luise.

for the virtually extinct German merchant marine to use, their only major Atlantic liner. As if this was not enough, a fire broke out aboard her causing much damage. Late in 1920 it was announced that she would be rebuilt and would begin service with two other German ships operating a joint service with the new company known as the United American Line. The *Victoria Luise* was again rebuilt, with cargo holds fore and aft. Her two forward stacks were removed, giving her a most ungainly appearance. When she began the run in 1921 she could carry 220 in cabin and 664 in third, although she was called a 'One Class' steamer. She sailed from Hamburg on her first trip with 43 in cabin and 331 in third. She had a new name—the *Hansa*, and she would do quite well. In 1923 she carried nearly 10,000 passengers. Her first master was Captain Kier, somewhat of a comedown for him as he had been commander of the *Imperator* before the war. In 1925 she was sold for

scrap, a sad ending and all too soon for one of the most exciting and most admired ships ever built for the Atlantic.

Dr William McLean, veteran of many Atlantic crossings, has fond memories of the *Hansa*: 'That ship really impressed me so much. As rebuilt by Hapag she carried two in first Class, 36 in cabin and 1,350 in third. After a year she was rebuilt again with 224 in cabin and 1,065 in third, so you can see that cabin Class had plenty of space. The following dishes I can remember as if it were yesterday: German style roast goose, Hamburg cold fruit soup, rabbit pie, creamed vegetable marrow...'

Gross tonnage: 16,502
Length overall: 686 feet
Width: 67 feet
Machinery: Quadruple expansion engines
Speed: 23 knots
Capacity: 690 First, 300 Second, 280 Third; 224 Cabin, 1,065 Third
Built: Vulcan, Stettin, 1900
Demise: Scrapped in Germany, 1925

Korea

She was hailed as the largest ship ever built in the western hemisphere when launched at Norfolk, Virginia, in the spring of 1901. She was built for America's oldest and most famous deep sea steamship company of that day. Some 20,000 people were on hand to watch her slip into the James River. The event was described as one of the 'great moments in American marine history'. And yet at this writing both the ship and the company are almost unknown even among knowledgeable ship lovers. She was the *Korea*, and her owners were the Pacific Mail Line, one of the very few US ship lines that can come near matching the record of major British, French or German companies from the standpoint of length of service and number of ships owned.

When new the *Korea* and her sister, the *Siberia*, were the outstanding liners on the whole Pacific. Their public rooms, while small by today's standards, were large and elegant at that time. They offered all the latest features on any liner in the world—wireless, electric lighting, luxurious suites and a fine cuisine. But, try to find them mentioned in many of the finest modern liner books. They deserve more.

As first projected the *Korea* was to have been called *Corea*, but this was altered before the christening. She sailed on June 18 1902, for her home port of San Francisco via Cape Horn. A few months later she would be followed by the *Siberia*. The two new liners had black hulls and all-black smokestacks, a tradition with Pacific Mail. Each had well decks fore and aft and two tall masts. There was no provision for sails. They looked quite a bit like the American Line's twin flyers *St Louis* and *St Paul*, although were a little less sumptuous inside.

The beginning of the use of fireproof material in ship construction is evident with the *Korea*. A minimum of wood trim was employed. Decks were covered with slate and rubber tile. The main stairway was made of solid bronze, including railings and pillars. They were designed to resemble carved wooden stairs. A fine painting of the new liner by Fred Pansing, noted New York lithographer-artist, showed her broadside with the wind coming from her starboard quarter. Her name pennant is flying at the foremast and the Pacific Mail houseflag is at the main. The Blue Peter is forward and a huge American ensign is spread out in the wind aft. A puff of white steam is coming from below half way up on the forward stack, a surprising place for the whistle. Black coal smoke pours out from both stacks. Prints of this picture were spread all over the Pacific and throughout California, being common in barber shops, hotel lobbies and travel agencies.

The *Korea* and *Siberia* rapidly became queens of the Pacific, attracting large followings, although old salts still preferred the yacht-like clipper bows of the three smaller white *Empresses* of the Pacific owned by Canadian Pacific. Pacific Mail ran the *Korea* and *Siberia* with their two other new liners, the *Manchuria* and *Mongolia*. Some of the proud claims in company folders make quaint reading today:

'Each berth in every stateroom is fitted with an independent electric light, nicely shaded for reading purposes. Each stateroom has an electric fan. The ships are divided transversely by 10 complete watertight bulkheads to the upper deck and six to the main deck, thus rendering them absolutely unsinkable.' This was before the *Titanic*.

Another company brochure explains an unusual

feature of the sisters—the promenade-like passage way on the port side of the upper deck. On the starboard side of this same deck the black hull proper, pierced by a row of portholes, gives the ship a very different appearance. Here is why this design feature happened: 'The upper deck is so arranged that all the staterooms are on the starboard side and the galleys, pantries and quarters for servants and crew are all on the port side, along which there runs a working passage, thus enabling all the service of the ship to be performed without intruding upon the passengers' quarters.'

Another brochure tells us: 'The staterooms are all panelled in white, with dark cherry trimmings. Each is provided with a white enamelled iron bedstead, brass trimmed and fitted with upper and lower berths. There is in each room also a convertible sofa and folding lavatory stand with porcelain and cut-glass fittings. Extensive and perfectly appointed

Korea, *fresh and new on the ways, ready for launching* (courtesy of Newport News Ship Building and Dry Dock Company).

toilets and bathrooms are provided for ladies and gentlemen on both the promenade and upper decks. A great improvement has been made in the cuisine which is now of the highest order and under the personal supervision of Mr V. Moroni, one of the world's most famous caterers.'

A 'swimming tank' was made in the well deck aft. Not very large, it was made out of canvas. A folder described it as 'a treat to the lover of out-door-sports—a salt water plunge on deck—in Mid Pacific'.

The *Korea* and her running mates were billed as 'The Big 4 on the Sunshine Belt to the Orient'. Serving with them were three older ships, The *China, Persia* and *Nile*. Linking San Francisco with Honolulu, Yokohama, Kobe, Nagasaki, Manila and Hong Kong, the crossings were scheduled to take 30 days. Mrs Ralph H. Wardall made a trip to Manila on the *Siberia*. She tipped her 'bath boy' and table steward $1 each, and gave $1.50 to her 'deck and room boys'. These were generous gifts then, particularly as most of the stewards and crew were from undeveloped parts of Asia. And here developed the cause of the downfall of Pacific Mail.

Left *A painting of* Korea *by Fred Pansing. Notice that she flys a name pennant on her foremast, an old sailing ship tradition.*

Right Korea *as operated by Atlantic Transport Lines on the transatlantic run before America entered World War 1* (courtesy of the Smithsonian Institution).

Left *3,000 tons of coal were loaded aboard* Korea's *sister ship,* Siberia, *by these women at Nagasaki. The loading cost was 9 cents a ton in 1913* (courtesy of Mrs Eleanor W. Boettcher).

As an American operator it could survive, or so it believed, only if it could use low-cost labour for the less technical work on its ships. This is what French, German and British ships did and Pacific Mail thought nothing about it. Founded in 1847 as a line between Panama and the 'developing territories' on the West Coast of America, it established its trans-Pacific service in 1867 with the help of a US mail subsidy. While other American deep sea lines crossing the Atlantic failed, Pacific Mail continued. But at the turn of the century, just as it was putting its largest ships into service a new trend in American political liberalism was being born in the middle western states. In due course a strong leader emerged, Senator Robert M. La Follette. He took up the cause and began crusading for legislation to require 75 per cent of all crews on American ships to be citizens.

In opposing such legislation Pacific Mail backed itself into a corner by insisting that it would not be able to continue if such a policy became the law of the land. It did and in 1915 Pacific Mail sold its ships and gave up. It blamed 'cumulative Government oppression'. The 'Big 4' went to the Atlantic Transport Co, a part of the combine known as the International Mercantile Marine. The price for all four was $5,250,000. The W. R. Grace company bought the smaller ships and the company name and

continued the line under new management for another decade.

The *Korea* and *Siberia* did not remain on the Atlantic for long. In mid-1916 Phillip A. S. Franklin, operating head of IMM, announced brusquely that they had been sold to Toyo Kisen Kaisha. He was paid double what the ships had cost him a year before, or $2,000,000 each. He explained: 'The Japanese can operate them cheaper than we can and were willing to pay a high price'.

Under Japanese control the ships got new funnel colours which gave them a more attractive appearance. The TKK Line colours called for a buff stack with black top. The names were altered to add the traditional 'Maru' common on all Japanese merchant ships so they became *Korea Maru* and *Siberia Maru*. The twin liners served without serious interruption for a decade and then, in 1926, were acquired by NYK. Their stacks were again changed. The famous NYK stack was a black funnel with a large white band a quarter of the way down and two thin red stripes in the white band. With NYK the ships catered for Cabin and Tourist class passengers. In company literature it was stressed that they were 'converted first class steamers'. The sixth lifeboat on either side was raised to make room for a small promenade and a new lounge on the top deck, but otherwise the silhouette remained the same. The new funnel markings made the ship look sleek, particularly when photographed from their port side. A NYK folder had this to say about service aboard: 'Cuisine is of the highest. English speaking stewards and maids cater to your every want—

quietly and unobtrusively—American menus—while the beginning of your journey over the Victoria-Seattle route of NYK is both picturesque and handy to all parts of the United States.'

Improvements in accommodation were described: 'In the Cabin Class out of the 32 staterooms, 24 are those of the former first class, and these rooms, which previously usually accommodated three persons, were all converted into rooms for one or two passengers. A Children's Play-Room has been newly provided for the benefit of young passengers in this class. The new arrangements and improvements in the Tourist Cabin class are even more remarkable than those of the Cabin class. Out of 24 rooms in this class, 14 are of the former First class, while the remaining 10 are those of Second class, thoroughly improved, of course. Likewise the steerage accommodation was also greatly improved; all open accommodation was abolished and instead comfortable compartments accommodating from six to 10 persons were constructed.'

The *Korea* and *Siberia* lasted another decade on the Pacific with NYK. Then, with new tonnage being added, they were sold for scrap. Both were broken up in 1935.

Gross tonnage: 11,810
Length overall: 572 feet
Width: 63 feet
Engine: Steam, reciprocating
Speed: 17 knots
Built: Newport News Shipbuilding & Drydock Co, Newport News, Virginia, 1901
Demise: Broken up by Amakasu Sangyo, Tokyo, 1935

Carmania

This lovely liner, one of the most handsome ever built, has a unique and sorrowful distinction. She retains the unenviable 'honour' of being the only major passenger ship which attacked and destroyed an equally handsome and important sister liner. It was during World War 1 and she was, of course, under the control of the military, as was the other liner. Nevertheless the battle between the *Carmania* and the *Cap Trafalgar* remains to this day one of the saddest episodes in the history of great liners, a tragedy that should not have happened.

The *Carmania* and her sister *Caronia* were very special sisters, special because much hung on their performance. The Cunard Line had resisted the advances of the American tycoon J. P. Morgan and would not sell out to his vast combine, the International Mercantile Marine. A grateful British government had provided the comany with enough money to build the world's largest and fastest liners by far. The question was should they be propelled by the then-new turbine engine or should they use the traditional reciprocating plant? A special committee of experts decided that two sisters should be built, one with turbine and one with reciprocating engines. The *Carmania* was to be the experimental ship with Parson's turbines. She would have triple screws, the centre one being powered by a high-pressure turbine and the outer ones driven by low-pressure turbines. On her trials the *Carmania* began to prove the value of the revolutionary new system by making 20.4 knots, over three-quarters of a knot faster than her

sister. The *Lusitania* and the *Mauritania* would be turbine propelled, a decision that proved most valid. The two new Cunarders boasted another important first. They were the first British liners to be fitted with a new apparatus for hydraulically closing all watertight compartment doors from the bridge. The first turbine driven triple screw liners on the Atlantic were the *Virginian* and the *Victorian* of Allan Line. They were about eight months ahead of the *Carmania*.

These two Cunard beauties were long known as the 'pretty sisters', a name that does not seem to do their superb lines justice. They were not handicapped by the odd island-bridge design so common on Harland & Wolff ships, and so ugly. Their superstructure was perfectly balanced, strong and simple. They had no raised forecastle, a design throwback that would persist even up to the *Queen Mary*. Instead their bow was long and sleek. Neither was there a raised poop (sterncastle) aft. Two towering pole masts were the only vestigal remnants showing their ancestry in sail. Crowning the massive upper works were two magnificent smokestacks, tall enough to keep the soot from their coal fired boilers off the stern decks and thick enough to satisfy the most ardent ship enthusiast. They really were great looking liners!

Aside from the greater speed the turbine engines of the *Carmania* provided, her fuel consumption was lower than that of her reciprocating-engined sister. In addition there was more space in the *Carmania*'s engine areas for her auxiliary engines. The *Carmania*'s machinery weighed about 5 per cent less than that on the *Caronia*. One fact that impressed the general public tremendously was the great number of turbine blades on the *Carmania*. There were 1,115,000!

Three quarters of the space on these two liners was given to passengers in first class, although only 300 could be accommodated in this top category. The 2,000 who could be packed into steerage, on the other hand, had only one public room—the dining saloon. It was large enough to seat 530. It would follow that a full passenger list would require four sittings per meal in steerage!

The *Carmania* was one of a fleet of ships that

rescued passengers in 1913 from Canadian Northern Railway's *Volturno* on fire in the middle of the Atlantic. She had been the first to arrive on the scene. Others were the *Grosser Kurfurst, Seydlitz, Minneapolis, Rappahannock, Czar, Devonia, Kroonland* and *La Touraine*. An oil tanker also helped. Despite this huge massed mercy fleet 136 people lost their lives while 521 were saved.

A. A. Hoehling, in his book *They Sailed Into Oblivion*, gives a complete account of the battle between the new *Cap Trafalgar* and the *Carmania*. Commodore Julius Wirth, aboard the German vessel, had chanced to meet a German gunboat off Bahia and was given two 4.1 inch guns, six pom-poms and two machine-guns. He also took on several petty officers to teach his crew how to handle the

Right *A postcard view of the* Carmania, *with the* Caronia *to the right.*

Below *A pre-First World War photograph of* Carmania. *The small number of lifeboats suggests that it was probably taken before the* Titanic *disaster.*

Carmania

Carmania *being undocked in New York. She now has a double bank of lifeboats.*

weapons. The three-stacked liner was flagship of the Hamburg South American Line. She was on her way home. When his ship reached Trinidad, Commodore Wirth decided to anchor and try to disguise her. He ordered her third stack, a dummy, to be removed. He had the other two painted red with black tops. He thought she might be mistaken for a Union Castle Line mail ship and to this end ordered her hull painted light grey. The *Carmania*, with Captain Noel Grant on the bridge, was better equipped when she sailed from the Naval yard at Liverpool. She had eight 4.7 inch guns, nests of rapid firing small calibre guns, a range finder, searchlights and secondary fighting equipment. Most important she was manned by naval reservists, while *Cap Trafalgar*'s fewer guns would be handled largely by the ship's musicians, waiters and Chinese cooks. Both ships were of roughly the same size.

The two beautiful lady liners met off Trinidad on September 14 1914. The meeting had not been planned, but once it happened the die was cast. One would survive, only one. The battle lasted two hours and ended with the *Cap Trafalgar* sinking, taking her

master and many of her crew with her. The *Carmania* was hit 79 times, her bridge and stacks were riddled and she had fires raging in many places. Matthew Green, a steward aboard, was later cited for bravery in fighting these fires. He received the Distinguished Service Medal. It was said that the *Carmania* was so severely damaged that she could not stop to pick up any of the enemy survivors. At any rate she headed for Gibraltar. Repairs kept her there until the spring of 1915.

The greater value of the *Carmania* for troop moving duties was eventually recognised and in 1916 she was changed into a troopship. Late in 1916 when she made her first appearance in New York after the engagement with the *Cap Trafalgar*, one newspaper noted that the places where she had been patched up after the battle could 'still be distinguished easily'. Strange to say the big ship was restored to commercial employment in 1917 despite the continued successes of the German underseas effort. On

Carmania's dining saloon, with fixed chairs and long tables.

January 20 of that year she again made headlines in New York papers when she reached port with only 23 in First and 17 in Second. Her master on that trip was Commander J. T. W. Charles. A notice entitled 'Submarine Alarm' was posted between the two doors leading to the Dining Saloon. It contained detailed instructions to the ship's personnel and passengers in case of attack. Part of it read: 'Passengers will go to their boat stations with life preservers on. Seamen told off for the gun's crew will go to their stations; the remainder will prepare the boats for lowering. Firemen and trimmers will double up the watches in the stokehold and engineroom AND RAISE ALL POSSIBLE STEAM, all bulkhead doors being kept closed. Remainder of men will go to their boat stations to put out fires that may occur... The safety of all on board depends upon the faithful observance and obedience to these directions.'

Finally the long drawn out war that killed so many millions came to an end. On February 1 1919, the *Carmania* left Liverpool for New York. She received wide notice because she was the first ship whose stacks were painted the familiar red and black to cross the Atlantic in four years.

In 1923 the handsome liner was taken in hand for a reconstruction. She became a cabin class liner with space for 425 in her top class, 365 in tourist and 650 in Third. Part of the work was the creation of a gymnasium and a winter garden for cabin class passengers. At the same time she was converted to burn oil. The *Caronia* was restored in a similar fashion. Both vessels were assigned to the Liverpool-Quebec run, with a stop westbound at Belfast. The *Carmania* immediately set a new speed record on a homeward passage from Quebec, 5½ days.

Late the next year it was announced that the two old liners would be replaced on the Quebec service by the new *Aurania* and *Ascania*. *Carmania* and *Caronia* would be assigned to the Liverpool-Boston-New York run. In 1926 they were again reassigned, operating between London and New York in company with *Lancastria* and *Tuscania*. Two years later *Carmania* was given another overhaul at

Liverpool. A new port engine was installed and her speed was brought back to its original level. She and her sister were frequently used to attract American travellers wishing to make cruises to the West Indies. In 1930, when 25 years old, she set a new speed record for the run between New York and Havana. Business was very bad, however, and her days were numbered. The abstract of her log for what was one of her final crossings has survived. It showed that she sailed from New York on June 10 and arrived at Eddystone Light, off Plymouth, on June 17 for a sea passage of 7 days, 2 hours and 56 minutes, averaging 18.118 knots. Her master was Captain A. C. Greig, OBE, RD, RNR. The Depression was going full tilt and Cunard was losing at the rate of £533,204 a year. A story out of London, dated August 19 1931, let it be known that the *Carmania*, 'pretty sister' of 1905 and one of the most dependable profit earners in all Cunard's long history, would be taken out of service and scrapped at Gravesend. The New York office

An artist's impression of Carmania sinking the Cap Trafalgar.

stubbornly denied the story, noting only that the ship was to be laid up at her London dock and had not been included on the sailing lists for the rest of the year. She was actually laid up off the Nore. Eight months later she was sold to Hughes Bolckow & Co for the paltry sum of £20,000 and broken up at their yard at Blyth!

Gross tonnage: 19,566
Length overall: 678 feet
Width: 73 feet
Machinery: Turbine, triple screw
Speed: 18½ to 22 knots
Capacity: 300 First, 326 Second, 2,000 Steerage; later 300 Cabin, 250 Tourist, 1,100 Third
Built: John Brown, Clydebank, Scotland, 1905
Demise: Scrapped Blyth, Scotland, 1932

Fifty Famous Liners

President Grant

Many reasons make this ship important. She had four decidedly different areas of service during her long and full life and did well in each. Few liners have exceeded her in overall persons carried. She and her short-lived sister, the *President Lincoln*, were the only major modern liners built with six masts. She had four different names before she entered service, four that is before being named *President Grant*, and would have two more in the years that followed her use by Hapag.

First she was named *Servian* and launched as such for Leyland Line in 1903. They cancelled their contract for her and she lay idle for some time. Bought by Hamburg American she was to have been called *Brooklyn*, then *Chicago*, and finally *George Washington*. Each of these names was dropped for one reason or another. She joined the fleet as the *President Grant* late in 1907. On her first crossing she carried 227 in first, 256 in second and 1,231 in steerage. For some reason she made only four trips in 1908, while the *Lincoln* made seven. She carried huge westbound passenger lists on these crossings. She was a slow (14 knots), comfortable and most successful vessel. In addition to her large passenger capacity she had 11 cargo hatches serving seven large holds.

World War 1 saw her, still with the same name, carry 77,129 souls over and back under the flag of the US Naval cruiser and transport force. In point of numbers she ranked behind the total carried by only four other ships: *Leviathan*, *America*, *George Washington* and *Agamemnon*. She surpassed the number carried by the famous four-stacker *Mount Vernon*, ex *Kronprinzessin Cecilie*, a larger ship. The *President Lincoln* was torpedoed and sunk in 1918. After the war the *President Grant* made two trips repatriating Czechoslovak troops from Siberia to Trieste.

Her war service over, she was delivered to the US Shipping Board in 1921. She lay idle for three years and was then assigned the name *President Buchanan* and sent to Newport News, Virginia, for rebuilding as a liner with plans by William Francis Gibbs, noted naval architect. Her third and fourth masts were removed. The superstructure was enlarged to give better accommodation to about half of her original passenger capacity. The name *Republic* was substituted for *President Buchanan* and she began service for United States Lines in May, 1924. She linked New York with Bremen, via Plymouth and Cherbourg, and made occasional cruises. Captain A. B. ('Rescue') Randall was her master. He would later command the *Leviathan*.

'There are seven decks devoted to public rooms, staterooms and suites for cabin passengers', an enthusiastic US Lines folder noted. 'Twelve cabins and suites have private baths. The majority of staterooms are outside rooms. Each has running water, electric lights, electric fan and call buttons, steam heat and every essential toilet fixture. The berths are provided with fine, deep mattresses to insure a maximum of solid comfort. Modern American plumbing systems are in evidence throughout the ship.' One picture in the brochure showed a small sitting room with one couch and about seven or eight stuffed chairs. The caption read:

President Grant

Sisters together in New York — President Grant on the left and President Lincoln on the right.

'Women passengers will find a restful retreat in the refinement and charm of the Ladies Salon'. The folder went on with gusto: 'Joyous hours upon the broad, sunny decks in the invigorating salt air will surely bring thoughts of meal time and the cuisine for which the US Lines is famous'. Great emphasis was placed on the smoothness of the voyage for those who sailed on the *Republic*, a fact that was really due more than anything to her slowness.

'Accept the endorsement of upward of 30,000 passengers on her smooth, serene sailing qualities. If you could meet many of them they would tell you how they played deck golf on her broad sundeck...and that the ball ran truly...in weather that would have made such diversion impossible on many ships', another company folder explained cheerfully.

All US Lines ships suffered badly because the Prohibition law in America prevented them from selling liquor to passengers. Nevertheless her passenger lists went over 1,000 several times each year. Her best westward crossing in 1926, for example, saw her carry 590 in cabin and 897 in tourist. On the other hand in 1928, before the Depression, she had three eastbound trips with under 100 persons, one of which saw only 14 in cabin and 33 in third. A souvenir log from Voyage No 40, eastbound, begun April 1 1928, showed that she averaged 14½ knots and made only 344.88 miles per day. The trip extended over nine days, although the log showed the 'ocean passage' as having consumed 7 days, 20 hours and 44 minutes. The trip was so leisurely that when the clocks had to be set ahead at midnight they were set only 45 minutes ahead instead of the customary one hour. The food was outstanding as a

42

look at a menu attests; there were eight kinds of Hors d'Oeuvres, four kinds of soup, two fish dishes, two veal and chicken entrees, three roasts, three vegetables, potatoes in four different styles, two salads, four desserts, three cheeses plus fresh fruit, nuts, raisins and 'demi Tasse'. You ate well on the *Republic*!

The Depression was in full swing in 1931 and the old *Republic* made only two transatlantic crossings, carrying 787 people eastbound and bringing home only 343. She made five cruises from New York to ports in the West Indies carrying 1,416, but her days as a liner were numbered. In July her owners were given permission to withdraw the ageing craft. She was traded in for two World War 1 troopships, the *Cambrai* and the *Somme*, to be added to the American Merchant Line service as the *American Traveler* and the *American Importer*. The *Republic*, retaining her same name, was rebuilt as a US Army troopship. She sailed on November 4 1931, for San Francisco, Honolulu, Guam and Manila, carrying 1,033 officers and enlisted men. For a decade she ran between San Francisco and Honolulu until, in July 1941, she was turned over to the US Navy.

Her World War 2 service saw her mostly in the Pacific. She bore a charmed life, plodding along at her customary 14½ knots taking troops and supplies to Fiji, Samoa, Noumea, Guadalcanal, Sydney, Funa Futi, Hollandia and other ports. She had a capacity of 3,500 troops. As the war drew to a close it was decided to rebuild her as a hospital ship. She emerged with facilities to handle 1,271 patients, 49 medical officers, 57 nurses and 237 medical attendants in addition to 281 civilian crew. She was given refrigeration space for 37,000 cubic feet of vegetable, fruit and meat storage. She had two operating rooms with sterilizing areas, X-ray and three surgical wards. All these areas were air conditioned. For the entertainment of the patients a theatre was installed with a radio rebroadcasting system featuring 74 loud speakers. Each berth was fitted with a berth light, a portable food tray, a utility cabinet and a switch connected to the nurse's call system. The conversion was done at Mobile, Alabama. In September, 1945, the rebuilt ship sailed for new duties in the Pacific. While on her last lap to Honolulu, word was received that she was no longer needed as a hospital ship and she was decommissioned while on this voyage. Ordered on to

Her whistle blows a salute as Republic *reverses out of Newport News for her trials* (E. P. Griffith).

Manila she resumed duties as a troopship.

After the end of World War 2 the *Republic* was laid up. She was offered for sale early in 1952 and bought by the Bethlehem Steel Co, along with four other old liners and a cargo ship, for the grand total of $1,383,100. The other ships were the *Wharton*, formerly the Munson Line's *Southern Cross*, the *Seminole*, a coastal passenger ship built for the Ward Line, the Cheseapeake Bay overnight steamer *State of Virginia* and the Great Lakes passenger steamer *Octorara*. The cargo ship was a Liberty named *Carine*.

The *Republic* made news once more. Her 6,200 mile tow to the scrap yard provoked news stories all the way from the State of Washington to Baltimore. It was said to have been one of the longest 'dead ship'

Left *Worden Wood's oil painting of the* Republic, *used for many publicity brochures.*

Right *Late in World War 2* Republic *became a hospital ship. Note how much lower her stack is here than it had been.*

Below Republic *makes her first voyage as an army transport on November 4, 1931.*

Fifty Famous Liners

tows in history. The 'huge ship', as she was frequently described, left the laid-up fleet in Olympia on March 18. Aboard was a riding crew of eight men under F. W. Surgeon. The leg to Balboa in the Canal Zone was handled by two seagoing tugs, the *Agnes Foss* and the *Donna Foss*. Five government tugs pulled her through the Canal to Cristobal. There she was met by the *Kevin Moran* and the *Julia C. Moran* which completed the job to the Patapsco Scrap Yard. It took 54 days of actual towing time, two months by the calendar. Along the way the riding crew supplemented their diet with fish caught. When they reached Baltimore they still had half a dozen large bonita frozen in dry ice. The *Republic* was a sad sight when the tow ended; her hull was reddish, covered with rust-resisting paint, and marred with streaks and grime. Her stack bore

some remnants of the Army transport service colour markings.

R. W. German, manager of the Bethlehem scrap yard, met the ship, welcomed his riding crew and told reporters that the *Republic* was the largest ship his yard had ever broken up. He said casually that the work would be done in 3½ months.

Gross tonnage: 17,910
Length overall: 615 feet
Width: 68 feet
Machinery: Two 4,000 horsepower four-cylinder steam
Speed: 14½ knots
Capacity: 227 First, 256 Second, 1,231 Steerage; rebuilt to carry 605 Cabin and 1,394 Third
Built: Harland & Wolff, Belfast, 1907
Demise: Scrapped by Patapsco, Baltimore, 1952

Adriatic

'As the *Adriatic* approached the Princess Landing Stage (Liverpool), I was impressed by her smart appearance, dressed overall in cruise bunting, and a new coat of paint ready for the first cruise of the season. She was indeed the most elegant and graceful of the "Big Four"—her extra length, slightly wider funnels and part enclosed promenade deck gave a more "modern impressive appearance".' So wrote Peter Roberts in the summer of 1985 in the journal of the *Titanic* Historical Society. The year his memory was bringing back for him was 1934. The *Adriatic* was 27 years old, but still proud and handsome. She is most deserving of a spot in this book, as are all three of her sisters. Their turns will come.

Dropping back to January 1904, this is what you might have read in the *Nautical Gazette*'s column 'Tides of Fifty Years Ago': 'It is reported that the White Star Line has ordered a steamer 755 ft in length, or 30 feet longer than the *Baltic*, the largest ship in the world. The construction of the vessel will begin immediately at Belfast.'

As completed the *Adriatic* boasted 24,541 gross

tons and was, in her turn, the largest ship in the world. She had a capacity of 2,950 passengers, and, on her maiden voyage, carried 365 in first, 335 in second and 1,802 in Third. For some reason her steerage figures were broken down to show Italians and Greeks separately. The maiden departure was from Liverpool, but on the return crossing she entered Southampton where she was received 'with open arms' as the harbinger of a new era. As the *Shipping World* correspondent wrote on June 5 1907: 'Southampton was decked out in her best, gay with flags of nations and decorative festoons, while the people were frantic in their joy, shouting and cheering to the full capacity of their register, making it difficult for the bands, also mustered for the joyful day, to make themselves heard'. On this cheerful note began one of the most successful careers enjoyed by any great liner.

Among the many new features was the first indoor swimming pool on any liner and the first Turkish bath. The pool was a narrow thing and was known as the 'plunge bath'. In her first full year of service, 1908, the *Adriatic* made 14 round trips. She operated with the *Oceanic, Majestic* and *Teutonic*. Early in 1909 the *Adriatic* chalked up a new company milestone, being in direct wireless communication with land throughout her voyage. It was said at the time that White Star was planning 'to fit all their principal steamers with long-distance receivers'.

A July 1913 *Adriatic* passenger list proudly advertised that the company was building the *Britannic*, billed as 'the largest British steamer'. Her tonnage was shown as 50,000 gross. The *Adriatic*'s master at that time was Commander (later Sir) Bertram F. Hayes. Even after war came she continued in service. In 1915, for example, she made eight round trips, operating with the *Arabic, Megantic, Lapland, Baltic* and *Cymric*. Little did her passengers realise it, but on her eastbound crossings this year she was used to bring fuel oil to England in her deep tanks. The *Arabic* did not make it through the year, being torpedoed on August 19 with the loss of 44 lives.

The *Adriatic*, with 3,000 sacks of Christmas mail, was about to sail on December 17 1918 on one of the first post-war crossings of the line. Her 650 passengers were saying their final farewells when a tremendous explosion shook the ship. The low pressure cylinder on the starboard side had exploded hurling its metal cover weighing three tons against the deck above. No one was injured. Repairs were made and the ship sailed only 27 hours late. All her passengers enjoyed an extra day on the company, although they did not reach England by Christmas.

Seven months later the *Adriatic* again made headlines. A pouch of mail was dropped to her from a plane abooout 1½ hours after she had left New York. This was described by the *New York Herald* as the first experiment of its kind ever undertaken. A superb bow view of the liner sailing from New York was published on the April 1922 cover of *The Ocean Ferry*. On August 11 of this same year New York

Below A dramatic photo of the Baltic, *showing some of the rescued passengers from the sunken* Republic, *whose loss in 1909 prompted the first use of the international distress signal SOS. Captain Ransom can be seen on* Baltic's *bridge.*

Above A fine photographic postcard of Adriatic *early in her career. Note the single lifeboats where there would later be nested extra boats.*

A superb stern view of another of the 'Big Four', the Cedric, *with steam shooting off in magnificent fashion.*

maritime circles were shocked to receive a radio message relayed from the Charleston, Massachusetts, Navy Yard, that an explosion in hold No 3 had so damaged the *Adriatic* that she was able to proceed only slowly. Pictures of her appeared in many evening papers in the port that day, followed by word the next day that there had been no structural damage and that the liner was proceeding full speed toward New York.

Four issues of the *Ocean Times*, the ship's newspaper published aboard the *Adriatic*, have come down from her September 1922 crossing. Among the news headlines were: 'Seven Men Sucked Up By a Waterspout', 'Huge Total of Soviet Execution's' and 'McAdoo Candidate for Presidency?'

On January 6 1923 the *Adriatic* sailed from New York on a Mediterranean cruise. All sorts of interesting bits of colour can be found in the information for passengers section of the passenger list, such as the prices of seven different services the barber shop

would perform. They ranged from 1s for shaving to 6d for a 'tonic dressing'. Picture postcards of the steamer could be obtained on board 'gratis'. A Turkish bath could be had for $1.20 or 5s 6d. The plunge bath was free and a 'costume' would be provided at no charge. A 'Concert Programme' for the cruise has survived for the 'Grand Entertainment' in the first class saloon at 9:15 pm on Thursday, January 11. S. C. J. Freeman-Matthews, Purser, opened things on a humorous tone by appearing as the Mayor of 'Slopton-on-the-Slush'. Mrs J. E. Gear offered a reading entitled 'The Mustard Plaster', which was shown as being of anonymous authorship. Miss Elsie Janis, who must have been someone of importance, arranged the programme and ended things by singing *My Country 'Tis of Thee* and *God Save the King*.

Early in 1928 White Star announced that the *Adriatic* would be operated as a Cabin class liner. A news story of the day noted that 'she has been famous

Fifty Famous Liners

in the North Atlantic trade and was well known as the favourite ship of the elder J. Pierpont Morgan, who chose her in preference to the larger liners whenever possible'.

During a nine-month lay-up in the winter of 1929-30 she was 'completely modernised', with hot and cold running water laid on in all cabins not previously so equipped'. An entirely new lounge was built in the tourist section. The old swivel chairs in the cabin dining saloon were replaced with arm chairs of mahogany, upholstered in red leather. As if this was not enough it was made known, in November 1930, that the IMM 'has decided the Turkish, electric and plunge baths formerly used exclusively by cabin passengers, are to be made available at certain hours for tourist third passengers. The cabin gymnasium will also be at the disposal of tourist passengers during the same periods at which the baths are open'.

James Edmond Duffy, young ship news reporter of the *New York World Telegram*, who by the 1950s would be known as the 'dean' of that exclusive fraternity, had a feature on March 6 1932 about the *Adriatic*. She arrived four days late and managed to disembark her cargo, mail and passengers and depart on her return crossing in a record 23 hours. She was late because she had stood by the collier *De Bardeleben*, which later foundered 500 miles east of Ambrose Light Vessel. Although the weather was too bad for her to take off any of the sinking ship's crew, she provided moral support for two days until another rescue vessel arrived on the scene.

By this time the glory days of the 'Big Four' were long gone. The *Celtic* had been lost on the rocks off Queenstown in 1928. The *Cedric* and *Baltic* had been sold for scrap. Early in 1933 it was predicted in the press that the *Adriatic* would make only two voyages to New York and then go to the breakers. On February 15 these stories were 'emphatically denied' at a press conference held by James S. Mahool, IMM passenger manager in New York. He said the *Adriatic* was scheduled and would operate throughout 1933 between Liverpool and New York. But his decisive comments were not entirely correct. The March 10 departure from New York turned out to be her last in the year. As spring 1934 came she was again in use on the New York run, however. Finally after several more short cruises out of Liverpool like the one Peter Roberts remembered, she was laid up

The front page of the September 3, 1922 issue of The Ocean Times, *published aboard the* Adriatic.

for good. On November 17 1934 word came from London that the Japanese had bought her for £65,000 for scrapping. The price of scrap had gone up. The Japanese war machine needed fine steel and they knew where to get it. A *New York Times* despatch making this known concluded with these nostalgic words: 'Although there were many larger and faster ships on the ocean at the end of the *Adriatic*'s career, she always kept her reputation as one of the most comfortable and steadiest vessels afloat'.

Gross tonnage: 24,541
Length overall: 726 feet
Width: 75½ feet
Machinery: Reciprocating steam, twin screw
Speed: 17 knots
Capacity: 450 First, 500 Second, 2,000 Steerage
Built: Harland & Wolff, Belfast, 1907
Demise: Scrapped in Japan, 1934-35

Cleveland

The *Cleveland* and her sister, the *Cincinnati*, were the two medium-sized liners whose completion in 1909 permitted Albert Ballin to remove the unfortunate Blue Riband holder *Deutschland* from express service and make her into a luxury cruising yacht. Both were strikingly handsome vessels with two large stacks and four masts. They were money makers because of their large steerage capacity, but they could also be used for cruising voyages in the winter. They would be pioneers in the world cruise business even before completion of the Panama Canal. And the *Cleveland* would go on to see herself as the 'flagship' under two foreign liner operations before coming back to Hapag to serve out the last of her four lives. A ship well worth remembering!

A third ship, to have been named *Chicago*, was projected by Hamburg American but never ordered. As first completed the *Cleveland* could carry 250 in real opulence as first class passengers, 392 in second, 494 in third and 2,064 in steerage. With a crew of 360 this meant a total of 3,560 'souls'. Travellers in third class had comparative luxury with rooms for 2, 4 and 6. Steerage were berthed in eleven compartments with 'fixed ladders as well as portable ones leading down the hatches for communication'. Each compartment 'had its quota of seats and tables as well as cupboards', and 'large toilets' have been arranged on the upper deck with baths and showers'. For communication from the forward to the after end of the vessel a wide passage led through the superstructure on the port side, also serving the crew's quarters which were along that side.

Noel Bonsor noted in his five-volume liner classic that the *Cleveland* and her sister were innovative in that they had small tables in their first class saloons. They had the traditional four quadruple expansion, coal-burning engines, however, with twin propellers. They ran for their first four years on the Hamburg-New York run in season, and on long cruises in the winter. The *Cleveland*'s first round-the-world cruise ran into an unexpected problem, it was made known on January 26 1910, by the *Shipping World*: 'The Hamburg-Amerika liner *Cleveland* has been carrying 650 American tourists round-the-world, and, according to a report from Washington, she will incur a penalty of $200 for each passenger landed at San Francisco, because she has engaged in coastwise trade by taking her passengers from New York, round-the-world, and back again to their own country. Such an interpretation of the law is simply ludicrous.'

A 1911 64-page brochure announcing the ship's 1912-13 world cruise stated that rates began at $650 for the 110-day cruise, including all 'necessary expenses aboard and ashore'. What a buy! And apparently the coastwise law penalty situation had been cleared up. This was advertised as her third and fourth annual world cruise, the third departing eastward on October 19 from New York and the fourth starting westward on February 6 1913, from San Francisco. Way ahead of the times, Hapag provided free rail-road transportation from

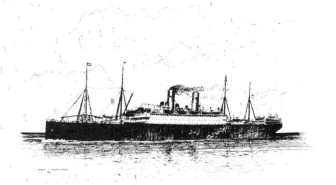

Above *With all her flags flying,* Cleveland *was a handsome sight as she left New York on her pre-First World War world cruises.*

Right *An extremely rare postcard showing* Cleveland *under the United American Lines houseflag with buff stack and two blue bands.*

passenger's home city in the USA to either New York or San Francisco. There were nine cabins at the $650 per person rate. They were far aft on F Deck in what was usually third class. The brochure noted that rooms 190, 192 and 194 'may be sold to gentlemen only'. Suites with bath and toilet sold for $6,600 for the full world cruise. The folder showed pictures of the ship's major public rooms and illustrated what advanced ideas Albert Ballin's interior decorators were using on the *Cleveland*. Gone were all the heavy wall carvings, gilt-framed original paintings and stained glass. Instead there was a simplicity of design and restrained modernity heralding the art deco of the 1920s. The *Cleveland* and *Cincinnati* were pioneers in freshly thought out interior design. And they were innovative in itinerary as well. The

Cleveland

AROUND THE WORLD

THROUGH THE PANAMA CANAL

Two Grand Cruises by Sister Ships

"CINCINNATI," January 16th, 1915

and

"CLEVELAND," January 31st, 1915

From New York to the Principal cities of the world—including a visit to the
San Diego (Cincinnati) and Panama Pacific (Cleveland) Exposition

135 DAYS, $900 UP Including all necessary expenses
afloat and ashore

HAMBURG-AMERICAN LINE

41-45 Broadway, New York

Philadelphia	Boston	Baltimore	Fittsburgh	Chicago
New Orleans	Minneapolis	St. Louis	San Francisco	Montreal

N. G.

Send 25c.
for a double
disc Travel Re-
cord and picture
booklet, "A Day in
Berlin," by the well-
known lecturer, E. M.
Newman. It may be played
on any talking machine.
Other records in preparation.

H. A. L., Travel Record Dept.
45 Broadway   New York

A 1915 advertisement for round the world cruises by Cincinnati *and* Cleveland.

Cleveland's four world cruises carried 2,400 passengers. And the *Cincinnati* was doing equally well with 'Grand Oriental' cruises.

In 1913 the completion of the world's first 50,000-ton liner, the *Imperator*, allowed Ballin to shift his *Cleveland* and *Cincinnati* to the run to Boston, with stops at Boulogne and Southampton. In 1914, as the *Vaterland* was put into service, the two smaller liners were again shifted, this time giving real luxury to the route from Hamburg direct to Philadelphia. When war began the *Cleveland* was safe in Hamburg while the *Cincinnati* was seized in

America. She was sunk while serving as the US troop-ship *Covington*. She had been renamed because the American Navy already had a *Cincinnati*.

The *Cleveland*'s second career began on March 26 1919, when she was placed into commission as the *Mobile*, a part of the US Cruiser and Transport Force. She had been found in Hamburg when the war ended and assigned to the US Navy by the Allied Shipping Controller. She was quickly converted to troop service with a capacity of 4,800, later raised to 5,200, and she made 4½ round trips, returning 21,073 from European battlefields plus 22 sick and wounded. She was decommissioned on September 30 1919.

In 1920, while still named *Mobile*, the liner was assigned by the Shipping Controller to make two round trips for the International Mercantile Marine. Late in the year she was bought by Embiricos Bros for their Piraeus to New York service under the house-flag of the Byron Steamship Co, which operated a joint service with the National Greek Line. A quick restoration job was done at a Greek shipyard and the liner, renamed once again, became the *King Alexander*. She sailed on her first voyage on December 18 1920, carrying 36 in first, 344 in second and 1,846 in third. She flew the British flag. Her houseflag and twin stacks had the same markings as did the Greek Line, but were of a different colour. She made six round trips in 1921, four in 1922 and two in 1923, but the business fell off and she was sold to the new American line headed by W. Averill Harriman and called the United American Line. Her stacks were painted once again, becoming yellow-buff and boasting two thick blue stripes near the top, one of the most attractive stack markings of all time in my opinion (FOB). She was given back her original name and operated under terms of a joint agreement signed by Harriman and Hapag, a pact extremely favourable, as it turned out, to the reviving German line. Her arrival put an end to the short but most interesting careers as 'ships of democracy' of the ex-freighters rebuilt to carry 1,100 passengers and named *Mount Carroll* and *Mount Clinton*. We hope to feature these ships in a later volume.

The *Cleveland* deadheaded it to Hamburg with a cargo of coal and was rebuilt by Blohm & Voss to carry 687 in cabin and 1,002 in third. She was put under the Panamanian flag to permit her to sell liquor when Prohibition was making things so hard for

American liners. United American, also known as the Harriman Line, had moved the ex-Hapag *Resolute* and *Reliance* to the Panamanian flag late in 1922 for the same reason. As Hapag's contribution to the joint service there were the new *Albert Ballin*, the *Thuringia* and the *Westphalia* and the old *Hansa*. The *Cleveland* left Hamburg as a 'one-class liner' on October 21 1923. Why ships which carried two classes should have been called one-class liners is hard to perceive. At New York 500 United American agents inspected her and were entertained at lunch. 'General approval was voiced of the changes which have been made in the steamer.' A new service to Canada was experimented with in March 1924, but quickly dropped in favour of the run from Hambrug to Boston. Captain Conrad Luck, formerly aboard the *Westphalia*, was her master at this time, illustrating how very closely Hapag and the UAL were integrated.

The Harriman Line continued operating *Cleveland* through 1925, but early in the following year word leaked out that she and the *Resolute* and *Reliance* had been sold to Hapag. At first denied, the sale was confirmed on July 23 1926. Again the ship changed flags and funnel markings, her two buff stacks being repainted with black, white and red stripes on their tops, the new Hapag colouring.

Special efforts were made to attract Irish passengers to the *Cleveland*. One folder noted that 'a permanent altar has been installed…and, for the convenience of priests, stewards have been trained to serve Mass'. It was added that 'Irish Matrons are engaged as part of the ship's personnel in order to give personal care and attention to Irish women and children'.

With effect from her May 8 1928, eastbound sailing from New York and her May departure westbound from Hamburg, the *Cleveland* was scheduled to make regular stops at Boston.

The onslaught of the Great Depression in October 1929 changed everything for most ship lines. By then the *Cleveland* was coming to be seen as an old ship. Hapag's new quartet, the *Albert Ballin*, *Deutschland*, *Hamburg* and *New York* were very successful. She was laid up in Hamburg in 1931. In April 1933 a short paragraph made it known that she had been sold for scrap. While the price was not disclosed, it was reported that the demolition would be done by Blohm & Voss, the yard which had built her.

A full page advertisement for the Cleveland *which appeared in the programme for a performance at the New York Hippodrome.*

Gross tonnage: 16,960
Length overall: 587 feet 6 inches
Width: 65 feet
Machinery: Quadruple expansion, twin screw
Speed: 17 knots
Capacity: 250 First, 392 Second, 494 Third, 2,064 Steerage; 687 Cabin, 1,002 Third
Built: Blohm & Voss, Hamburg, 1909
Demise: Scrapped Hamburg, 1933

Vestris

Up until 1928 the name *'Vestris'* meant little to people outside the shipping industry. Some may have remembered that it was the name of a 19th century actress. Since then, however, it came to mean a tragic sea disaster in which one of the best known and most respected ship lines was scarred forever. For Captain William J. Carey, 40-year veteran about to become Commodore of the Lamport & Holt Line fleet, it was the end! What terrible thoughts must have coursed through his mind as he walked into the boiling sea off the bridge of his foundering liner. An editorial in *The Marine News* for December 1928 summed up the thinking of the marine community:

'Any tendency to pile the blame upon the head of one who can no longer speak in self-defence has, in this case at least, been pretty well avoided, although it cannot be gainsaid that Capt Carey failed in a crisis and paid for his failure with his life.' The same source went on: 'The errors in judgement displayed by the master of the *Vestris* cannot be reflected upon the owners of the ship, and up to the time of this writing no evidence has been presented which would show that the owners were cognizant of the situation until the time had passed when any orders or suggestions from them would be of no avail'.

But one paragraph of the Lamport & Holt orders to their Masters did come to wide public attention later, and may have been the crucial influence on Captain Carey's thinking. It read: 'In the case of a serious happening to one of the vessels of the Line...the Master must...carefully consider the actual moment of peril there may be to those under his charge and then judge whether he will be justified or not in fighting his own way unaided. His being able to succeed in this will always be considered a matter of high recommednation to him as a Master.'

Three investigations were held and Lamport & Holt was cleared of any 'specific' blame, but the basic facts of the sinking were so damaging that the line gave up its service from New York to South America. Many questions remain unanswered. Above all why did Captain Carey wait until the ship was listing badly and dead in the water to send out an SOS? Any why were the life-boats on the high port side filled first? A serious lack of discipline, safety planning and direction from the ship's officers particularly the master were all too evident in the hearings. The tragic facts illustrate only too clearly these grave failings. Of the 13 children aboard none were saved. Only 10 out of the 37 women aboard survived. A much higher percentage of crew (153 out of 197) were saved than of passengers (60 out of 128).

Many ships answered the *Vestris'* call for help when it was finally given, and four vessels picked up survivors. The little American Merchant liner *American Shipper* led the mercy fleet to the spot where the boats were finally found and saved 124 persons. Captain Schuyler F. Cumings was on the bridge. He would go on to even greater fame as master of the *Leviathan*. A French tanker, the *Myriam*, the North German Lloyd liner *Berlin* (see separate chapter) and the *Wyoming*, US battleship, picked up the rest of those who survived. The battleship actually saved nine who were swimming in the ocean without even a liferaft to cling to.

*A full page Lamport & Holt advertise-
ment showing* Vestris *as the fourth
largest ship in the company's fleet.*

One contemporary editorial concluded that it was time to 'de-bunk' the tradition that a master should go down with his ship: 'Why should his suicide be accepted as a matter of course? Captain Carey's life was, to him, every bit as sweet as the lives of those in his charge were to their owners. His place was not in the open sea without means of keeping afloat (he had refused a life preserver), but in command of one of the lifeboats, so that he might possibly direct operations while awaiting pick-up by other vessels. Captain Carey's testimony at the hearings would undoubtedly prove invaluable in placing the responsibility—if any—for the disaster.'

For the record the *Vestris* sailed from New York on November 10 1928, with a list and well below her marks. She sailed out into a bad storm and the list got worse and worse until she simply tipped over and sank. She went down on November 12. Everything that could go wrong went wrong. Lifeboats were loaded with children and women and then could not be lowered. In one instance the lines broke and dumped the passengers into the sea. But above all

Vestris

Left *Aboard* Vestris *moments before she capsized and went down. Looking forward over the well deck house towards the fo'c'sle.*

Right American Shipper, *the vessel which found the survivors and rescued more of them than any other ship answering the SOS call.*

Left *The sinking ship pictured from far aft. Her starboard side is already under water and the portholes are filling.*

the SOS was not sent out until the ship was beyond help.

William James Lamport and George Holt founded the line which took their names in Liverpool in 1845. Starting with wooden sailing ships they acquired their first steamer in 1857, named the *Zulu*. By 1895 they had built more than 70 ocean-type steamships and had adopted the distinctive custom of naming their vessels after people famous in the arts. The first of their 'V' class was the

Valasquez, of 7,542 tons, built in 1906. Next came the *Vasari*, of 10,117 tons. In August 1911, the company proudly announced a new monthly service from Liverpool to the River Plate, Argentina. Three new liners of about 12,000 gross tons were being specially built for this run. They were the *Vandyck*, *Vauban* and *Vestris*. The first was nearly ready for her trial trip, and, the announcement said, she would sail on October 5 1911. Sad to say three of the company's 'V' class lines were sunk in World War 1, but

56

three survived—the *Vauban, Vestris* and *Vasari*. They had all done yeoman service as troopers and bringing frozen meat home from South America. Between 1919 and 1921 each of them was chartered to Cunard Line for voyages from Liverpool to New York to permit that company to recover from its huge war losses and handle the post-war demand for passage to the New World. After coming across the Atlantic for Cunard the ships continued on to the Plate for the account of their owners and then returned to Liverpool with passengers and frozen meat. Two new and slightly larger ships were added in 1921 and 1923, the *Vandyck* and the *Voltaire*.

A January 1924, full-page advertisement for the company proudly listed the 50 ships in the company's fleet. A picture of the flagship *Voltaire* was shown as were views of her drawing room, dining saloon, lounge and smoking room. Passengers were 'booked to all parts of the world', the advertisement said, and the same for cargo it was added. The company's first class passenger and mail steamers served between New York and Brazil and the River Plate, calling at Trinidad and the Barbados. Their American headquarters was at 26 Broadway and the company had offices in many large United States cities, a 1926 folder about the sisters *Vestris* and *Vauban* stated. An orange-red map of South America printed on a light green background showed their route. There were stops at Rio de Janeiro, Santos, Montevideo and Buenos Aires. The folder began:

'Two of the prettiest ships leaving New York for South America are the 17,000 ton [they were using displacement tonnage because it was bigger] steamers *Vestris* and *Vauban* of the famous 'V' fleet... which sail regularly from Pier 14, Hoboken... Specially-designed for tropical service, the ventilation of every room being perfect. These magnificent vessels, over 500 feet in length, are unsurpassed in comfort and the menus and service will appeal to even the most fastidious. Each steamer carries an orchestra of accomplished musicians which plays during meals and for concerts and dancing on deck. The public rooms are large and airy, comprising a luxurious lounge, a restful music room and a cosy smoking room, opening on to the Verandah Cafe. The dining saloon extends the full width of the ship...'

As a ship the *Vestris* certainly had class. A massive single stack with its highly distinctive colour markings crowned the ship's silhouette. The stack was blue, with a large black band on the top and an even larger white band in the middle. She operated with her lifeboats swung out over the side, a feature which gave added room for promenading on the boat deck. Two tall, white-painted masts, very tall white air funnels and cargo booms gave a feeling of style to the ship's upperworks. Her forecastle and the full length of her upper deck were white, making the black part of her hull seem longer and her superstructure higher than it might have otherwise appeared. She was a 'smart ship'.

Vestris

Disaster was not entirely new to the 'pretty' *Vestris*. Twice in her short life she had been linked with famous sea tragedies, and even after her sinking, by a strange quirk of fate, her name came to be linked with another major ship loss. The *Vestris* was launched on May 16 1912, a little more than a month after the most notable of all sinkings at sea, that of the great *Titanic*. Just six years later the *Vestris* picked up a routine weather report by wireless from the US Navy collier *Cyclops*. It proved to be the very last time that that unfortunate naval craft was ever heard from. She was lost without trace some days later, taking 293 souls down with her. Finally less than a month after the sinking of the Lamport & Holt liner, one of her crew, John Keown, sailing home on a White Star liner, was awakened by the sound of a fellow passenger screaming. The ship they were on was the *Celtic* and she had run hard aground on a ragged rocky shoreline near Queenstown Harbour, Ireland. All her 253 passengers, Keown included, were safely taken ashore. The famous ship became a total loss.

After the *Vestris* loss Lamport & Holt continued its passenger service from New York to the River Plate but attempted to disguise it as a series of long cruises. Sixty-day cruise voyages to Brazil, Uruguay, Argentina and the West Indies were advertised for the 'luxurious oil-burning steamer *Voltaire*'. Rates began at $975 and included hotels and conducted sightseeing trips ashore. The *Vandyck* also remained in service as a cruising liner but the *Vauban*, sister to the *Vestris*, was laid up and in 1932 was sold for the shockingly low price of £8,500 for scrap.

The last 'V' ship cruise was scheduled from New York for September 15 1939, aboard the *Vandyck*. The destination was Liverpool and the ship was replacing the Cunarder *Scythia*, which had been taken over for war work. The Lamport & Holt liner was described in a cruise poster as 'a favorite of the elite cruising public of Great Britain'. Sad to say the *Vandyck* was sunk off Norway in 1940 and the *Voltaire* was lost to a German raider the following year, forever ending the era of the Lamport & Holt 'V' ships.

Gross tonnage: 10,500
Length overall: 511 feet
Width: 60.8 feet
Machinery: Quadruple expansion, twin screw
Speed: 16 knots
Capacity: 280 First, 130 Second, 200 Third
Built: Workman, Clark & Co, Belfast, 1912
Demise: Foundered off coast of Virginia 1928

Alsatian

To many of the 'older generation' the *Alsatian*, later named *Empress of France*, was one of the finest looking liners of all time. She was the first ever built with a full cruiser stern. Her twin stacks were large enough to match her long, low hull, and tall enough to complement her two fine pole masts, and raked enough to make her look the flyer she was. After seeing two aunts and an uncle sail on her in 1926, this author's (FOB) love of great liners never deviated. It was his moment of conversion.

The *Alsatian* and her trim but unlucky sister *Calgarian* were the climax to a long and successful corporate life for the Allan Line. They were the finest liners serving Canada. All the ships in the Allan Line fleet ended in the letters 'ian', and their black and red stacks with a white band near the top were proud symbols of their fine reputation. As an example of the style with which these twin liners were built, it might be noted that first class public rooms and suites were the responsibility of George Abraham Crawley, interior decorator for many of the great homes of England and the United States. He first was linked with shipping when he did similar work for Canadian Pacific's lovely *Empress of Russia* and *Empress of Asia*. The Phipps estate manion in Old Westbury, Long Island, New York, was also to include many rooms by this talented architect.

The *Alsatian* left Liverpool for St John, New Brunswick, on her maiden voyage on January 17 1914, followed on May 8 by her sister. The two beauties were driven by quadruple screws with four sets of direct action turbines. They immediately established themselves as the fastest ships on the Canadian run. Little did the public realise that they would serve their owners for less than one year. When war came they were both pressed into government service. The *Alsatian* became flagship of the Tenth Cruiser Squadron. During the war she steamed 300,000 miles and was said to be the most successful of all British auxiliary cruisers. The *Victorian*, an earlier-built companion liner, was in the same squadron. The *Calgarian* did duty off the port of Lisbon, and was later assigned to intercept enemy ships that might be entering or leaving New York (the United States was still neutral then). Unfortunately she was torpedoed in March 1918. While the war was in progress the Canadian Pacific Railroad absorbed the Allan Line. When Armistice came the *Alsatian* was renamed *Empress of France*. In February 1919 she was restored to peacetime colours at her builder's yards in Glasgow. On September 26 of that year she resumed her sailings from Liverpool to Quebec, but now with buff smoke-stacks and the red and white chequered houseflag of CPR.

The *Empress of France* made many record passages. She averaged 18.8 knots in 1920 on a crossing from Liverpool to Rimouski, below Quebec on the St Lawrence. Her time was 5 days, 20 hours and 6 minutes. The next year she set a new record all the

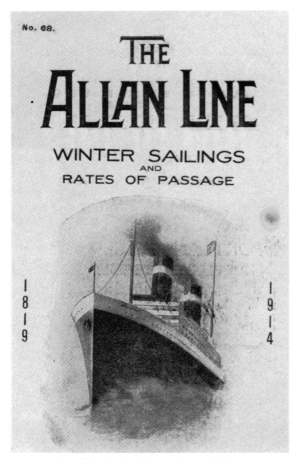

No. 68.

THE ALLAN LINE

WINTER SAILINGS
AND
RATES OF PASSAGE

1819 1914

A promotional leaflet for Alsatian *from 1914.*

way to Quebec of 5 days, 23 hours. Her passengers were rushed to a train and reached Montreal at 6 pm on the same day, making the whole trip in only six days. As one news story put it, her passengers 'had breakfast in London on August 25, completed a morning's business, left by the special train for Liverpool, and six days later were in time for dinner in Montreal'. Two more records were set in 1924, of 19.14 knots eastbound and 19.3 knots westbound.

Early in her post-war career the *Empress of France* came to be well known for her luxury cruises. Frank C. Clark chartered her for his 18th Mediterranean cruise late in 1921. The cost was $600 and up for 74 days. Then in 1922 she made her first round-the-world voyage via the Panama Canal. Again she was

on charter to Clark Tours. She carried 700 passengers, the largest tour group to have visited Panama to that date. In 1924 she was sent back to her builder's yards to be converted to use oil fuel. Again the next year she made a world cruise, but this time had only 284 passengers. She paid $11,153.75 in tolls for this Panama Canal transit.

HRH the Prince of Wales chose the *Empress of France* for a number of his frequent hops across the Atlantic to play polo, and this fact was not neglected in the Canadian Pacific advertisements. In 1926 the company issued one of the most elaborate cruise brochures put out up to that date. It featured the world cruise of their flagship, the *Empress of Scotland*, originally the *Kaiserin Auguste Victoria*, and the Mediterranean cruise of the *Empress of France*. This latter voyage was the one your author's relatives sailed aboard. He well remembers consulting with a cordial old steward about the advisability of his stowing away in a large laundry basket outside their cabin. And he saved a chunk of blue-tinted glass picked up from the promenade deck facing forward under the bridge. A window had been smashed by the rugged Atlantic en route to New York to depart that February 9 1926 for the Mediterranean.

The CPR motto was 'see this world before the next', and the literature prepared for prospective passengers on this trip was eye catching and artistic. The handsome menu for the 'Lincoln's Birthday Dinner' three days after sailing began with fresh caviar on toast and iced honey dew melon. Then came fresh green turtle soup or Ammontillado in a cup or cream of corn Maryland. For a main course the diners could pick from fillet of New York sole Newburg, braised sweetbread with fresh mushrooms or baked Virginia ham, southern style. Then pineapple sherbert. After that: Roast American Quail, Saratoga potatoes, Blackstone salad and a special Lincoln Birthday Cake, or Coupe Georgia, or Mignardises; followed by dessert and coffee.

The *Empress of France* had settled into a comfortable schedule with a long cruise early in the year and then seven or eight trans-Atlantic round trips during the remainder of the year. Her best year on the Atlantic had been 1921 when she carried 10,443 passengers on 11 westbound trips and 7,623 on an equal number of eastbound crossings. After the quota laws put and end to immigration, she

Fifty Famous Liners

CANADIAN·PACIFIC

Above left *As the* Empress of France *she is painted in dry dock, her black hull being turned white for service on the Pacific.* **Above right** *A dance programme issued on a Mediterranean cruise of the* Empress of France *in 1926. The painting shows* Empress of Scotland, *the Canadian Pacific flagship at the time.* **Below** *She later returned to Atlantic service and regained her black hull, as shown in this postcard.*

Alsatian

CANADIAN PACIFIC
Mediterranean Cruise
S. S. EMPRESS OF FRANCE
LINCOLN BIRTHDAY DINNER — FEBRUARY 12, 1926

· MENU ·

Fresh Caviare on Toast
Iced Honey Dew Melon

Fresh Green Turtle, Ammontillado in cup
Cream of Corn, Maryland

Salted Nuts   Celery   Queen Olives

Fillet of New York Sole, Newburg

Braised Sweetbread with Fresh Mushrooms

Baked Virginia Ham, Southern Style
Green Peas au Beurre

Pineapple Sherbet

Roast American Quail with Cress
Saratoga Potatoes
Blackstone Salad

Lincoln Birthday Cake
Coupe, Georgia
Mignardises

Dessert

Coffee

A Lincoln's Birthday Dinner menu from the same cruise. Medina's outboard profile as published in the Marine Engineering *magazine in 1914.*

averaged about half of these totals in the succeeding years. Her cruises, however, were well patronised and the brochures describing them are pieces of fine steamer art today.

In 1929 she was shifted for nearly a year to serve on the Pacific, replacing the *Empress of Canada* that was in for an extended engine refit. She was painted white for this service and it looked so good that she retained it for the rest of her life. The arrival of the great economic Depression did not seem to bother her and her cruises continued to do reasonably well. In 1931, her last year in service, she averaged 304 passengers per westbound trip and 421 per eastbound crossing, most respectable. She left Southampton on September 2 of that year with 486 passengers for Canada, and sailed back with 238 on what was to turn out to be her last crossing. It was her 100th round trip since the end of World War 1. Her career was over.

She was laid up and languished in this sad state for the next three years. In 1934 the *Empress of France* was sold to W. H. Arnott Young & Co, and taken to Dalmuir, Scotland, where she had been built, to be scrapped.

Gross tonnage: 18,357
Length overall: 600 feet
Width: 72 feet
Machinery: Four steam turbines, quadruple screws
Speed: 20 knots
Capacity: 287 First, 504 Second, 848 Third
Built: Wm Beardmore & Co, Glasgow, 1913
Demise: W. H. Arnott Young & Co, Dalmuir, Scotland, 1934

Medina

The story of the *Medina* is one of those remarkable chapters that come along only rarely. Built in 1914, she is still going strong—74 years of age at this writing. It looks highly likely that she will outlive the *Germanic*, which was scrapped at the age of 76. Her's is a story worth telling, and worth remembering, particularly as very few people ever heard of her, at least under her original name.

The *Medina* was built as a straight cargo ship. She was designed by the noted American naval architect Theodore E. Ferris, designer of countless coastwise American passenger liners including the ill-fated *Morro Castle* (see *Fifty Famous Liners 2*). Her owners were a well-known coastal passenger-cargo company—the Mallory Line. Their ships had black smokestacks with a red five-pointed star on them, and they operated between New York and Texas with stops along the way. They had many passenger ships, the last and probably best-known of which was the *Brazos*. The *Medina* was 421 feet long on deck and had a deadweight capacity of 6,600 tons. She could make 14 knots and was described in the September 1914 *International Marine Engineering* magazine as one of the 'most modern and largest freight steamships operating on the Atlantic coast'.

She was of the hurricane-deck type, having a complete steel hurricane deck, main deck and lower deck. Contemporary deck plans show two deck houses on the hurricane deck, with a mess room seating 16 forward and separate mess rooms for seamen, stewards and firemen in the forward house. The after house, separated by a deck passage, contained seven cabins for the Chief Engineer and his staff, cooks, stewards, oilers, carpenter and boatswain. Aft in a small deck house at the very stern was space for 18 firemen and 10 seamen. Another cabin on the boat deck contained the Captain's suite including his office chart-room and bedroom. There were five other cabins here for the first officer, wireless operators, second and third officers, quartermasters and the purser. The purser's cabin was also shown as a 'spare room'. In other words there was room for one or two company guests. The wheel house was above the Captain's cabin. All the rest of the ship was devoted to cargo and stores and to the power plant and shaft alley.

The exterior of the *Medina* was simplicity in itself. Her hull ran in a straight line from bow to stern. She had not raised forecastle or poop. Her stem was sharp and plumb. She had two tall masts and two cargo king posts between the foremast and the superstructure. There were two lifeboats on the starboard side of the Boat Deck and one on the port side. Air funnels rose here and there from bow to stern. Her single smokestack was tall and nicely proportioned. Her hull was black and her name was done in white letters high upon the bows. She sailed from the yard where she was built in September 1914 ready for at least the second longest career in liner history.

The *Medina* survived World War 1 without incident and after the war her owners became a part of the Atlantic Gulf and West Indies Lines (Agwilines) combine, which included the Clyde Line and several other coastwise companies linking America's east coast with the Caribbean. Little or nothing is known of this period and of what she did in World War 2. That she continued to survive is a tribute to her fine hull and excellent triple expansion engines built by

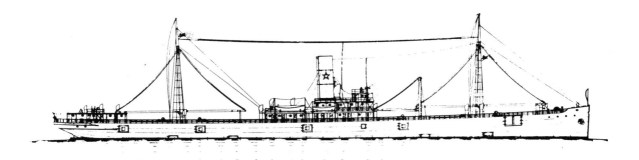

the Newport News Shipbuilding & Dry Dock Co, Newport News, Virginia.

Then her second career began. It was 1948 and waves of immigration were leaving the Old World for Canada, Australia and Israel. Passenger ships were much in demand. A Panamanian concern called Cia Naviera San Miguel SA bought her. She was renamed the *Roma*, but should not be confused with another former American freighter turned aircraft carrier rebuilt as a liner and also named *Roma* at about this same time. This latter vessel was part of the Lauro Line fleet. The *Roma*, ex-*Medina*, was rebuilt at La Spezia, Italy. Her reconstruction included a new superstructure, new bridge, new stack and completely new interior with space for 925 passengers in two classes. She had seven lifeboats on either side and two rows of portholes were cut into her old hull. A

new, slightly slanted prow was welded on her old up and down stem to make her more in keeping with the times.

The rebuilding completed she was taken over by the Genaviter Co, of Rome, for operation. She was sent to New York to make three cruises to Europe with 'Holy Year' pilgrims. She reached New York on June 12 1950. Captain Alfred Landini, her master, told ship news reporters that her reconstruction amounted to rebuilding 85 per cent of her original design. He said that as rebuilt her original engines had easily averaged 14 knots on the voyage from Italy and hit 15 at times. In the transition her tonnage was raised to 6,530 gross and she gained two new decks of well-appointed public rooms and modernised first class staterooms. Her tourist space was broken up into four to eight person dormitory cabins with no

Rebuilt after World War 2, she became the immigrant ship Roma *and then was rebuilt once again after becoming the* Franca C *of Costa Line. This postcard view shows her underway in the Mediterranean.*

more than two tiers of berths in any room. Her hull was painted green and she was flying the Panamanian flag and manned by Italians. Her voyages to Naples were set for June 19, July 12 and August 8. She was under charter to the International Catholic Travel Committee. After the completion of these three voyages the *Roma* made a number of round trips to Australia. It would be interesting to know whether she ever met the Lauro Line's *Roma*. She was then laid up and offered for sale.

Career number three began in 1952 when she was purchased by Giacomo Costa fu Andrea, owner of the now-famous Linea 'C' or Costa Line. She was put under Italian registry and assigned to Costa's two-class service from Genoa to the West Indies. She was, of course, given a new name—one following the company's naming system—the *Franca C*. Having had considerable experience with old ships, Costa knew how important it was to be sure of their ship's power plant. With the *Franca C* it was decided that an entirely new engine was called for. She was given a powerful Fiat two-stroke diesel engine. Her passenger spaces were improved and her capacity cut slightly to 900 persons. She could accommodate 230 on the sun and upper decks. Tourist occupied the rest of the hull, with two, four and six berth cabins for 50 more. The rest of her passenger space was given over to dormitories some having as many as 32 berths. She

Yet another rebuild as Doulos, *'slave of God'.*

was 'completely air conditioned', a company brochure announced proudly. Her new colour scheme gave her a white hull with blue boot-topping and an enlarged yellow stack decorated with a huge capital letter 'C'—the Costa trade mark. Her running mates were the *Anna C* and the *Andrea C*. Her route was the run between Italy and the River Plate. She carried passengers in first, tourist and third classes.

In 1959 Costa anticipated many other cruise lines by putting the *Franca C* into service out of Miami, offering a winter-long series of cruises to the West Indies. This was a somewhat daring step for Costa to take and its correctness has been proved over and over again as Miami grew to be the cruise capital of the world. The *Franca C* proved very popular, convincing Costa of the wisdom of keeping the already very old liner in service. Her accommodation was frequently improved and soon advertisements noted that every room was with private bath/shower. A small, tiled outside swimming pool was built on the upper deck aft. Many coloured beach umbrellas made the area look like a Lido resort. She became a tiny luxury liner—and a very popular one. The rest of the year she cruised on various Mediterranean routes and to Madeira. Late in 1965 it was made known that the *Franca C* would cruise the year around out of Port Everglades, Florida. She would make twice weekly cruises in the summer and fall and longer ones in the winter.

Captain Isaacson and representatives of the 34 nationalities living and working aboard Doulos *(courtesy of Gute Bücher für Alle).*

A brush with the US Coast Guard in May 1966 saw her refused a permit to sail on a Memorial Day cruise because it was stated she did not meet US safety standards. This was cleared up after a 90-day period had passed and the cruises from Florida continued through a technicality in the 1960 Safety at Sea Convention rules. It was true she did not live up to American safety standards, but, since Italy was a signatory to the 1960 pact, the Coast Guard had to accept Italian flag ships if they passed Italian safety laws. It was a case of reciprocity.

Costa again re-engined the *Franca C* in 1970. She continued to be popular, with folders about her cruises put out in many different languages. As Miami developed as a centre for many of the newest and largest cruise ships, the *Franca C* was shifted back to the Mediterranean.

Finally her third career ended and in 1977 she was sold to Operation Mobilisation, a non-profit making German Christian youth project. She was renamed *Doulos*, meaning slave of Jesus, given a new overhaul and a new crew and sent out as an evangelical ship. At the time of writing the Marine Superintendent for this goodwill effort is Captain Mike Poynor, a graduate of the US Merchant Marine Academy, Kings Point, New York. A recent brochure about the *Doulos* and her companion ship, the *Logos*, explained that under the sponsorship of the Educational Book Exhibits Ltd, and the 'Good Books for All' project the two vessels have been welcomed in more than 87 countries and visited more than 200 ports. Some 7,000,000 people have received books and material on board. The two-ship operation has been called the 'Floating United Nations'. We wish them many more years of good works.

Gross tonnage: 6,822
Length overall: 427 feet 8 inches
Width: 55 feet 6 inches
Machinery: Triple expansion, replaced by diesel
Speed: 15 knots
Capacity: None originally; rebuilt to carry 925 in 3 classes; reduced to 570 and currently 450
Built: Newport News Shipbuilding & Drydock Co, Newport News, Virginia, 1914

Fifty Famous Liners

Ebro

The Royal Mail Line was organised in 1839, while the Pacific Steam Navigation Co got its Royal Charter in 1840. For much of their long lives these two companies were operated jointly, even using their ships interchangeably. In 1913 Royal Mail laid keels for two medium-sized passenger liners for their service from Liverpool to the West Indies. They were named after famous rivers, as was the company's age-old tradition, the *Ebro* after a river in Spain, and the *Essequibo* after a river in Guyana. The *Ebro*, whose story we will concentrate on here, was launched in Belfast in 1914. She made her maiden voyage early in 1915. The pair were allowed to make only a few runs as Royal Mail ships before being taken up as auxiliaries. The *Ebro* served throughout World War 1 as a naval troopship. Her sister became a hospital ship and then an 'ambulance transport'. The two vessels were exceptionally good looking. They had the separated island bridge for ship's officers, so typical of Belfast-designed ships of the day. A single stack, both full enough and tall enough to be aesthetically pleasing, and two nicely-raked masts topped a well-balanced superstructure. Both ships would have long lives. Both would write more than their share of history.

A wartime Royal Mail-Pacific Line brochure shows both *Ebro* and *Essequibo* as part of the former's fleet, but does not list them on any of the many different services the company ran. The folder is interesting as it contains in dark-faced type a 'war clause' describing how the routes and schedules may be altered in any way and how the company could not be held responsible. Reading through the small type other odd rules come to light; no gypsies were to be permitted to land at Buenos Aires, Hindoos 'are not booked', and it was thought necessary to spell out that during the war Germans, Austrians, Hungarians, Bulgarians and Turkish 'are not accepted as passengers'.

At the war's end the twin liners were assigned to the Pacific Line during the post-war shipping depression. This meant that instead of buff stacks, they had all black funnels. The *Ebro* was released first and assigned to make a 'Special Sailing' from New York to Liverpool in late May 1919. Then she began a period on the line from New York to South America's West Coast. She first transitted the Panama Canal, southbound, on October 28 1919, and was duly photographed by the noted Canal photographer, Ernest 'Red' Hallen. The *Essequibo* made her first transit on July 10 1920. She became the first vessel to bring fresh fruit from Chile to New York in April 1921. The route of the two fine medium liners linked New York with ports in Panama, Ecuador, Peru, Chile and Argentina. They were known in the company newspaper ads as the 'Luxurious "E" Steamers'. To make them seem larger than they were their tonnage was given as 14,350 displacement. Most liners, of course, used gross tonnage, which for the 'E' steamers was only 8,480 for *Ebro* and 8,464 for *Essequibo*.

As the 1920s wore on Pacific Line adopted the Royal Mail buff-yellow stack colouring. They also stopped using displacement and listed the 'E' steamers with their gross tonnage. The *Ebro* remained 8,480 tons but *Essequibo* became 8,489 for some reason. They served with six handsome 'O' class liners, headed by the *Orduna* and *Orbita*, of 15,503 and 15,492 gross respectively. A 1929 advertisement noted that 19-day tours could be had for $300 and up to Havana or Panama. The ships were then described as the 'palatial oil-burning steamers'. It was added that each had 'all outside

of the Canal on November 14 1930. The twin little liners remained together for five more years, being laid up side by side in the River Dart.

In 1935 both ships were sold and renamed, their paths never to cross again. The *Ebro* was bought by Yugoslavian Lloyd of Split and renamed *Princesa Olga*. The *Essequibo* went to the Soviet Union becoming the *Neva*. While the *Neva* was lost to western ship lovers at this point, the *Princesa Olga* was assigned to cruising in the Mediterranean. Her career is easier to follow. As rebuilt she could accommodate 213 passengers in four classes. First class offered four suites, 36 luxury cabins and 74 regular staterooms. There were only 13 cabins for second class and ten more for third. Part of the rebuilding included cutting off a few feet from the top of the tall smokestack and painting it blue with a black top, the regular Yugoslavian Lloyd colours. As fate had it her running mate was the graceful Royal Mail liner *Araguaya*, which often operated out of New York on the Bermuda run as well as to the East Coast of South America. She had been renamed *Kraljica Marija*. Her Royal Mail gross tonnage had been 10,537. The pair were used on a regular cruise service from Trieste to Dubrovnik, Piraeus, Haifa and Alexandria during the summer only. They were laid up in the winter, according to Luis Miguel Correia, Lisbon maritime scholar.

On March 18 1940, the *Princesa Olga* was bought by Companhia Colonial de Navegacao, of Lisbon. Delivery took place at Split. At first it was planned to rename her *Imperio*, but the new owners decided to honour the memory of a Portuguese Army officer, Captain Serpa Pinto (1846-1900), famous for his voyages of exploration around Africa. An oil painting of Captain Pinto was hung in the first class lounge and draped in CCN houseflags. The lounge, incidentally, was one of the most attractive small public rooms ever put on any liner. Decorative designs on the bulkheads and ceilings, full-sized windows looking out on to the promenade deck on either side, double, eight-paned mahogany doors with decorated four-pane top glassed openings balanced one end. A central staircase, with decorative railings, led below and was centered under a

staterooms—many with private baths', and that they featured 'verandah café, orchestra, swimming pool and deck games'. In 1930 the Depression ended the 'E' steamers joint service. They were pulled off the run. The *Ebro* made her last northbound transit

small round glassed dome opening, centre piece of a low raised ceiling in the middle of the room. Pilasters, fluted columns, brass wall lamps and large rugs, not to mention great arm chairs and sofas gave a comfortable look to the place. The ship seemed to improve with each new owner.

On her delivery voyage to Lisbon the *Serpa Pinto* made calls at Venice and Gibraltar. She entered her new home port on April 19 1940. On her hull was painted her name and her new nationality in large white letters. Her passenger capacity was enlarged to 704. The work was done quickly and just three weeks later she sailed with 258 passengers to West, South and East Africa. Her second voyage took her to Brazil and then, on December 28 1940, she sailed for New York with 631 passengers. Her arrival was greeted as a major news story because she was such a contrast to the drab, camouflaged liners entering the port on war duty. Here, again, was a fine-looking, nicely-painted passenger ship. An *Acme* news photo showing her steaming in through the Narrows appeared in many American newspapers. The *Serpa Pinto* seemed to have a charmed life. Many times she rescued survivors of wartime sinkings. She was used to carry troops to the Azores, Cape Verde Islands and Madeira. Then a long voyage to Buenos Aires, followed by an even longer one to West, South and East Africa. Her closest call came on a May 1944 voyage to Philadelphia. She had 228 passengers aboard and a crew of 157. She was stopped by a German submarine, although Portugal was neutral. The submarine ordered her to be abandoned and set

Above *Renamed* Serpa Pinto, *she is shown here at Lisbon on her maiden voyage as a Portuguese liner in 1940* (courtesy of Luis Miguel Correia).

Right *A postcard showing* Serpa Pinto *restored to peacetime colours and with a new grey hull after service in World War 2.*

Ebro

This is the first class lounge — note the painting of Captain Serpa Pinto with Companhia Colonial de Navegacao houseflags on either side (courtesy of Luis Miguel Correia).

a 20 minute time limit. Captain Americo dos Santos on the Portuguese liner miraculously got his people into boats in the record time of 15 minutes, but not without cost, the ship's doctor and a cook lost their lives in the process of abandoning ship. Then the submarine took as prisoners three of the passengers who held Allied passports. The lifeboats remained in sight of the abandoned ship and the submarine, hoping against hope. An entire night passed, and then the next day, at 5 pm, word was flashed from the U-boat that new orders had been received from Berlin and that the liner could proceed. The lifeboats hurried back. When heads were counted back aboard it was found, to everyone's horror, that a baby passenger was missing! How this had happened has never been explained. At the time the liner was

600 miles off Bermuda and 1,200 miles from the United States.

The redoubtable vessel continued on the run to Philadelphia during much of 1945. On July 29 she was again put on a regular service from Lisbon to Brazil. Again she survived a crisis that might have ended another's ship's career. She nearly capsized when her engine room was flooded in 1948 while she was being repaired at a shipyard in Lisbon. Aftermore rebuilding, she was put into cruise service to Madeira. Then she went back to regular service between Lisbon and Brazil. A suite could be had for $600 from Rio to Lisbon. If you went third class in a dormitory for from 10 to 20 persons the rate was only $160. The round trip with 11 stops took five weeks.

In midsummer 1952 the still handsome and proud

The luxury cabin used by Cardinal Cerejeira who sailed on Serpa Pinto *on her first voyage after the war* (courtesy of Luis Miguel Correia).

liner sailed on a cruise to Helsinki with stops at Stockholm and Copenhagen. The Olympic games took place in Finland that year and the trip was designed to take people to this event. Returning she passed through the Kiel Canal and a photographer snapped a fine view of her passing under one of the colourful bridges over that waterway.

There was quite a movement of immigrants from Portugal and Madeira to Venezuela and Central America at this point. In mid-1953 the *Serpa Pinto* entered on her last assignment. She was put on the route to Leixoes, Vigo, Funchal, Havana, La Guaira and Curacao. The round trip took five weeks and she made 13 voyages. In July 1955 she was laid up at Lisbon. Two months later she was towed to Antwerp and scrapped. She had survived for 40 years. Her

sister lasted even longer. She was converted into a submarine tender for the Soviet Pacific fleet. It is believed she was scrapped in the 1970s.

Gross tonnage: 8,480
Length overall: 450 feet
Width: 57 feet
Machinery: Quadruple expansion, twin screw
Speed: 14 knots
Capacity: 278 First, 328 Third; 213 in one class as *Princesa Olga*; 113 First, 86 Second, 130 Third as *Serpa Pinto*
Built: Workman Clark, Belfast, 1914
Demise: Scrapped in Antwerp, 1955

Ebro

Belgenland

In the August 1915 issue of *International Marine Engineering* magazine there are two photos and a large account of the launching of the *Belgenland*, to be one of the largest ships in the world at that time. She was moved to a fitting out berth and work was stopped on her because of World War 1. As the conflict dragged on, contrary to predictions by the military on both sides, it was decided in Great Britain that the huge hull would have to be put to use. The ship was quickly completed as a combination troop carrier and cargo ship minus her two uppermost decks. Turned over to the White Star Line to operate she was given a new name that fitted into their naming system and yet retained a trace of the original name at the launching—the *Belgic*. She was an oil burner from the start and, at this point, had a gross of 24,547 tons. Her outline was odd, to say the least, with one mast forward and two aft and only two smokestacks. No one knew what to do with her after the war ended.

Ever since the *Titanic* the International Merçantile Marine had been suffering from both lack of direction and lack of spirit. They seemed to be going along largely on momentum. Building coal burners like the *Doric* and *Laurentic* long after they were out of date was one illustration of this lethargy. The case of the *Belgenland* was the supreme example. In 1920 she was still almost a new ship. Her power plant and triple screws made her too fast to operate as a freighter, but in the spring of this year IMM decided

that their Belgian affiliate, the Red Star Line, would build a new and larger passenger liner. She would be of 33,000 gross tons. The contract, it was announced, had been awarded to Harland & Wolff, and the vessel would be laid down in six months. She would be the first vessel of over 20,000 tons ordered by any company since the Armistice. In the autumn of 1920, however, there was an about face. An IMM spokesman let it be known that the freighter *Belgic* would be 'taken in hand' and completed as originally planned and again named *Belgenland* for Red Star. The indecision shown here marked the IMM as not long for this world. J. P. Morgan, Sr, had long since lost interest and the massive combine would flounder on under the uninspired leadership of P. A. S. Franklin for another decade, disposing of one service after another and slowly dying. Perhaps this is why there always seemed to be something lacking in the story of the *Belgenland*, although she was one of the largest ships in the world and flagship of one of the most respected companies on the Atlantic. Word that she would be completed as originally intended, nevertheless, brought great excitement to the old Flemish port of Antwerp, 53 miles up the River Scheldt!

Despite the negative aspects to her story in these early years the *Belgenland* would become one of the world's best known and most famous liners. Possibly it was her magnificent sillhouette, her dignified and distinctive bridge face, or maybe, even, it was because of the superb oil painting done at this time by Charles Dixon. This showed her riding supreme amidst a fleet of Dutch lee-board sailing barges and with distant windmills in sight on the horizon she certainly looked every inch the flagship that she was. Needless to say the company used this painting continuously in brochures, ads and flyers and it became one of the best-known liner impressions of the early 1920s. There were other good things, too. The cover of the *Belgenland* passenger lists was a replica of the frontispiece of the *Biblia Regia* published by order of Philip II, King of Spain. This masterpiece of early printing took from 1568 to 1573 to make and the original was in a museum in Antwerp. There was real quality in the literature about the *Belgenland*.

Ceremonies galore greeted the new ship when she did finally arrive at Antwerp in her completed form. The Mayor congratulated IMM Vice President P. V. G. Mitchell on the ship's showing on her trials. A Cardinal blessed the ship. Preparations for the maiden departure in April were pushed and plans to receive King Albert aboard were made public. She was hailed as the 'finest and biggest liner in the Antwerp service'. Her luxuries were listed as including 'a glass enclosed promenade that allows an unobstructed view of the sea from deck chairs and a complete à la carte service in the dining room without extra charge'.

An early brochure was enthusiastic: 'Every needful comfort of ocean travel and many of the fashionable luxuries of *de luxe* voyages are to be had in the *Belgenland*...public rooms are large and fitted with quiet elegance'. She had no less than 31 suites, several with fireplaces. Her smoking room had a glass dome. She had a good-sized indoor pool and a gymnasium. A three-foot long coloured cutaway was published, today a choice artifact among liner buffs. It was quaint in that it showed people. There was a

RED STAR LINE.

TRIPLE.SCREW "BELGENLAND" 27.200 TONS.

Right *A Charles Dixon painting of* Belgenland *racing along at sea, used as a company postcard.*

Below *With a 'bone in her teeth'*, Belgenland *is shown here to great advantage* (courtesy of Edwin Levick).

man being shaved in the barber shop, a wireless operator sat before his set in his top deck 'chicken coop' just forward of an engineer's lounge. Couples were dancing in the ballroom, and swimming in the 'swimming bath'. Bakers with tall white hats were working in the bakery.

The maiden voyage was marked from start to finish by a steady round of ceremonies. It was April 1923 and the *Belgenland* was the eighth largest liner in the world! Her master was Captain John Bradshaw, who had been to sea for 47 years when he stepped aboard his new command. The Dixon painting was featured on the cover of the inspection and dinner programme held aboard the newly-completed ship on April 14 at New York. As a disappointing footnote, the *New York Tribune* story about the maiden arrival mentioned that she had brought only 250 passengers, one-tenth of her capacity on Atlantic sailings.

Cruising would play a major part in the life of the *Belgenland*. She sailed January 19 1924 on a 67-day cruise to the Mediterranean under sponsorship of Thomas Cook. Her first world cruise brought her wide renown. The job of preparing her for this trip was the subject of a radio talk given by Dr Fred E.

Marble, over New York's WJY on August 15 1924. He noted some of the staples she would load before leaving—there would be 50,000 oysters, 18,000 squabs, 3,700 ducks and a long list of other delicacies. With flags flying from bow to stern she sailed at midnight December 4 1924 from New York, then the cruise capital of the world. A near-capacity for cruises of 475 was aboard. They came from 91 cities in 31 states. At her first port of call, Havana, she anchored with two other IMM ships, the Panama Pacific liner *Finland* on her way to California for the Panama Pacific Line, and the older *Gothland*, en route from Spanish ports to Vera Cruz and New Orleans. No other ship so large had ever entered the harbour of Havana, *The Ocean Ferry* house organ boasted. She was also the largest ship ever to pass through the Panama Canal on December 12. Captain Bradshaw was interviewed by a host of news reporters when the ship reached San Francisco. At Honolulu each passenger got a lei or wreath of flowers around his or her neck. The 28,767 mile

She was the largest ship ever to transit the Panama Canal when she went through for the first time.

voyage ended on April 15 1925. The ship had found her niche! World cruises would become her chief claim to fame.

Captain Bradshaw took her out again on her second world cruise but when it became time for the third he was replaced by Captain Thomas Howell. Her fourth was under the command of Captain William A. Moorehouse who would stay with her for some time. Her long-time Chief Engineer was J. Russell Mackay.

Cyrus W. McCormick, Chicago capitalist, was among the VIP passengers who sailed on the liner's fifth world cruise. She had what was described as a record list. Her sixth cruise will be remembered because of the distinguished passenger who boarded the ship at Antwerp en route to Los Angeles. He was in no hurry so he took the famous cruise liner to get there. His name was Albert Einstein. The noted IMM cartoonist William Seabrook was aboard on this trip and remembered how Einstein was forced to escape from autograph hunters by staying almost continuously in his cabin. The Depression had arrived and, in 1931, the *Belganland* was used for a series of so-called 'booze cruises' out of New York. Americans who could not buy liquor in their own country because of the Prohibition Amendment flocked aboard the ship for one-day cruises to nowhere. With great attendant publicity some 1,647 'thirsty New Yorkers' crowded up the gangplank on that first booze cruise on October 13 1931. A *Daily News* report on the trip noted, with tongue in cheek, that gangsters who controlled the illegal sale of liquor in New York 'speakeasies' were outraged that some legitimate interests had infringed on their business to the tune of '$50,000 worth of serious drinking'. The US Attorney General William E. Mitchell had personally approved the initial cruise.

As the Depression decimated regular trans-Atlantic passenger business, the *Belganland* made fewer and fewer voyages on her regular Red Star Antwerp-New York service. She was withdrawn entirely in 1932. Late in 1934 it was announced that the 27,000-tonner would be transferred to the American flag, renamed and used entirely on short cruises. She was rebuilt for the new service. Two outdoor pools and a lido deck were added and her accommodation was cut to only 900. Amid considerable ceremony the transfer to American registry was accomplished and the new name given. She would

A sad sight indeed — the scrapping of the Columbia, *ex* Belgenland.

be called *Columbia*. She became the second largest ship in the American Merchant Marine, being surpassed in size only by the idle *Leviathan*. To make her cooler in Caribbean climes she was painted white. Her first assignment was a series of 11-day cruises from New York to Miami, Nassau and Havana.

Despite all the advertising and publicity about the new name, new flag and new service, the *Columbia* did not last long in this trade. She was laid up and finally, in 1936, sold for scrap. She sailed for West Lothian, Scotland, and was quickly broken up. One particularly sad picture of her scrapping which showed her second funnel being pulled down into a mass of rubble made ship lovers around the world mourn.

Gross tonnage: 27,200
Length overall: 697 feet
Width: 78 feet 7 inches (90 feet on promenade deck)
Machinery: Reciprocating on two outer screws, turbine for centre propeller
Speed: 19 knots
Capacity: 500 First, 600 Second, 1,500 Third; 900 as *Columbia*
Built: Harland & Wolff, 1914-15; rebuilt 1921-23
Demise: Scrapped in West Lothian, Scotland, 1936

Maui

The *Maui*, of the Matson Line, was the fifth in a series of innovative liners built shortly before and during the early part of World War 1. She was the first major turbine-driven liner built in the United States. Her long career included good service in both World War 1 and 2. She and her class may be best remembered, however, as being the pioneers in engines-aft construction for deep sea service, a feature now adopted for all cruise liners being built in the world up to the present time.

The four earlier engines-aft steamers were the *Lurline*, built in 1908; the *Manoa*, built in 1909; the *Wilhelmina*, built in 1914 and the *Matsonia*, completed in the same year. Each was slightly larger than her predecessor and the *Maui* was an almost exact duplicate of the *Matsonia*. The Matson Line had been founded in the latter part of the 19th century by Captain William Matson, an American of Swedish extraction. The company had grown and prospered serving between the American West Coast and the Hawaii Islands. A weekly service to Kahului and Honolulu from San Francisco was maintained. A round trip took 35 days, with three to five days allowed at each stop. The one-way fare ranged from $65 to $100.

The *Maui* was launched on December 23 1916, being christened by Mrs William Matson. One West Coast shipping news story noted that the new ship would be 'rigged as a three-masted schooner', although the masts were not fitted for sails. They were, however, equipped with heavy cargo booms

and tackle capable of handling weights of up to 50 tons, as the ship had a large cargo capacity.

Much was made of her Westinghouse turbines which drove out-turning twin propellers. The total weight of her machinery was only 146.32 tons, and the ship was balanced with fuel tanks and tanks for liquid cargo forward. This had to be explained repeatedly because the concept of a passenger liner having her engines and stack aft was truly revolutionary. The only earlier liner to have this silhouette was the original *Vaderland*, first Red Star passenger ship built in 1870, but she had been designed to serve both as an immigrant carrier and an oil tanker. A close study of how these Matson liners were ballasted might have served P & O well when their beautiful *Canberra* was built. She had her engines and stack aft. Poor design required several thousand tons of permanent ballast to be added forward to make her ride properly giving her the deepest draft of any modern liner.

There was passenger accommodation for 350 on the *Maui*. All 252 in first class could be taken care of in one sitting in the main dining saloon. Nearly 100 more could be berthed in large staterooms and dormitories aft on the sheltered promenade deck. There were 33 cabins in the first class area on the main deck. They were served by large men's and women's lavatories aft of the cabin area, each with four bath tubs in small cubicles. A variety of cabins on the sheltered promenade deck and the upper promenade deck amidships offered suites with

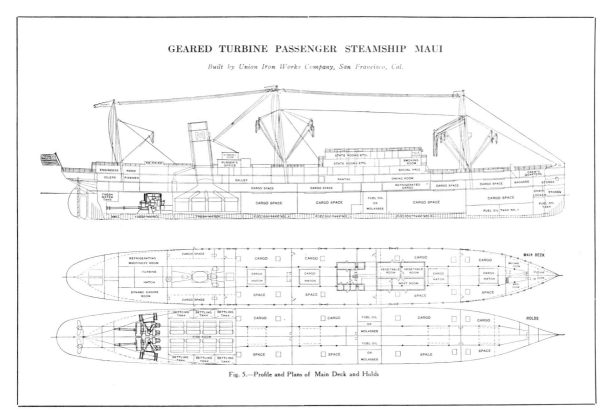

GEARED TURBINE PASSENGER STEAMSHIP MAUI

Built by Union Iron Works Company, San Francisco, Cal.

Fig. 5.—Profile and Plans of Main Deck and Holds

A profile of Maui *and plans of her main deck and holds, as shown in the April 1917 edition of* Marine Engineering.

baths, cabins sharing bathroom with one other cabin and cabins near bathrooms. One special feature unique to the *Maui* was the addition of eight so-called 'bachelor cabins' on the bridge deck aft of the master's cabin and the wheelhouse. These were installed at the suggestion of William P. Roth, vice president and general manager of the line. The *Pacific Marine Review* explained at the time that these cabins were 'referred to by friends of the company as the Roth addition, that gentleman having conceived the idea that some extra compensations were coming to the bachelor as a compensation for his lonely lot'. They were all singles with brass beds.

The ten lifeboats had a total capacity of 500 persons. The ship was also built with a double bottom for her entire length, 11 watertight compartments,

wireless, submarine signals and bilge keels.

Her smoking room was on the upper promenade deck and was done in quartered oak and lit by cathedral-type windows with an ornamental glass skylight. A feature of the forward bulkhead was a handsomely executed Hawaiian coat-of-arms over the mantel of the electric fireplace. A buffet bar was located aft of the smoking room. Forward on the sheltered promenade was a large social hall and smaller ladies' lounge and writing room, with the lobby around the grand stairway. Just below this series of public rooms was the large first class dining saloon featuring tables for two, six, eight or nine persons. The grand stairway ended on this deck in a broad enclosed vestibule from which the dining saloon was entered. The lighting was provided via large false windows inside the side ports and also by light clusters inside large ceiling globes.

An interesting feature of the sheltered promenade deck were the three alleyways that divided the four deck houses and permitted passage from port to starboard. The forward two-thirds of the ship was broken up into four large cargo holds on either side of a centre bulkhead. The *Maui* was fitted as an auxiliary cruiser 'of the second class' under the Postal Subsidy Act of 1891. She had foundations for the carriage of four 6-inch guns.

The *Maui* made her maiden voyage from Golden Gate to Honolulu in 5½ days. When she entered the Hawaiian port a number of Hawaiian outrigger canoes were among the welcoming vessels. She served for only a year before America entered World War 1. Matson immediately contributed three fast troopships to the war effort, the *Wilhelmina, Matsonia* and *Maui*. They were used on the Atlantic as troopers. Later the *Manoa* and *Lurline* were pressed into government service and operated between California and the Philippines. The *Maui* was rebuilt to carry 3,800 troops. She made 13 trips to France and back, transporting 37,344 overseas.

While in war service an odd-looking added cabin was built atop the bachelor cabins aft of the bridge. The ship, like all troopers, was painted a dull grey and her sides were 'festooned' with large rubber life-rafts.

The significance of the turbine installation on *Maui* was demonstrated after a test covering five voyages between her and her companion vessel, *Matsonia*. The five voyages were on the same service and with virtually identical weather conditions and cargo tonnage. The *Matsonia* was powered with old-style reciprocating engines. The test showed a saving in fuel costs on the part of the turbine-driven *Maui* of 23 per cent. The test was widely publicised in a double-page advertisement in marine journals in the United States in January 1920.

After World War 1 the *Maui* was returned to Matson and promptly placed in the hands of the Bethlehem Shipbuilding Corporation's San Francisco yard (the old Union Iron Works) for extensive alterations. Beds were installed in all passenger cabins instead of berths 'with the exception of a few cabins'. All rooms were equipped with hot and cold running water. The smoking room was 'doubled in

Maui *on her speed trials* (courtesy of the Steamship Historical Society of America).

Fifty Famous Liners

Above Maui *enters New York during World War 1.*

Below Maui, *back in peacetime service, enters Honolulu Harbor in 1918.*

A Matson brochure featuring a fine poster style painting of Maui.

gears aboard her had gone 1,000,000 miles in 'excellent condition'. More years of service passed until late in 1938 the *Maui* was chartered to the Panama Pacific Line. This company needed a sixth vessel to supplement the five 'City' boats of their own if they were to maintain a weekly service on the intercoastal run from New York to San Francisco. Another tribute to the remarkable regularity of the *Maui*'s service may be seen in a full page advertisement taken in September 1939 in various American marine magazines. It was sponsored by the Quimby Pump Company. It noted under a fine picture of the liner that a 'Quimby Screw Pump was installed aboard the ship in August 1923. In August 1939—sixteen years later—this customer reports: "The pump is still in service on the *Maui*. Our machinery performance data indicates that excellent results have been obtained by its use".'

The *Maui* was bought by the US War Department just four days before the Japanese attacked Pearl Harbor. She was converted into a troopship by Bethlehem at San Francisco and sailed December 27 for Honolulu on her first voyage in World War 2 grey. In March of the next year she made a round trip to Brisbane, Australia. Two more trips to Honolulu and one to Alaska and the old liner was once again overhauled and repaired. She continued to serve in the Pacific throughout the remainder of the war, seeming to live a charmed life. Her troopship capacity in the Second World War was only 1,650, less than half what it had been in the First. After VJ Day she was moored in Seattle and, in April 1946, was declared surplus by the War Department and taken to a National Defense Reserve Fleet. It was estimated that the 29 year old vessel had steamed 1,500,000 miles during her remarkably successful life.

Gross tonnage: 9,728
Length overall: 501 feet
Width: 58 feet
Machinery: Geared turbines, twin screw
Speed: 16½ knots
Capacity: 252 First, 100 Third
Built: Union Iron Works, San Francisco, 1916
Demise: Scrapped at Portland, Oregon, 1948

size'. New furniture was installed including easy chairs and bridge tables. A barber shop and a beauty parlour were added.

Then there ensued a long period when *Maui* served without incident. A 1930 advertisement boasted that the Westinghouse single reduction

Tirpitz

A 'hero ship', a ship that lived twice as long as most liners, a very beautiful ship, and a ship that had her original name for seven years but never made a single voyage with passengers—here is a remarkable story. The *Tirpitz* was one of a trio of ultra-luxurious medium-sized liners built by Hamburg American Line just after the giant Albert Ballin trio, the first ships to exceed 50,000 gross tons. Her two companion ships were intended for Hapag's South American service but will be best remembered as the *Resolute* (see *Fifty Famous Liners 2*) and the *Reliance*. Like the *Vaterland* and the *Bismarck* of the 50,000-ton trio, these three smaller luxury ships were designed with split uptakes—a feature that marked them apart from virtually every other liner built. Split uptakes meant that the smoke from their boilers came up in two (not one) separate uptakes on either side of the hull so as not to block the passenger areas on the public rooms decks. In other words a clean sweep from bow to stern was physically possible through one great public room after another without any centreline funnel casings blocking the way.

The *Tirpitz* was launched on December 20 1913, but not finished. She was known as 'Ballin's pet', partly because of her great elegance and partly because of a unique engine feature that the famous German shipowner had decided to experiment with her. J. H. Isherwood, in his *Steamers of the Past*, wrote that there is reason to believe the oft repeated story that she was intended as the Kaiser's yacht on which he would accept the British surrender. Work on her was halted early in the war but late in 1916 it was resumed. When peace came she was turned over to the British. She served for a time as a troopship. Then on July 25 1921 she was sold to Canadian Pacific Ocean Services, Ltd, and renamed *Empress of China*. Sir Thomas Fisher, CP general manager, noted that 'she is the only ship afloat with turbines of an entirely new type invented by a German named Fottinger'. In the years to come the company may well have rued the day they took her, for these engines were her Achilles heel. It was decided to use her on the Pacific and she was sent back to Hamburg for refurbishing. She was given special quarters for Orientals, more lifeboats and a general modernisation. The work was completed by John Brown on the Clyde. Again her name was changed and she finally got the name by which she is best known—*Empress of Australia*.

On June 17 1922 it was announced that she would sail from the Clyde to Vancouver. She reached Cristobal on July 1 1922 without any passengers and transitted the Panama Canal in ballast on July 6. When she reached her new Canadian terminus she docked alongside the aged clipper-bowed *Empress of Japan*, then being retired. Many of the old liner's crew moved over to the newer craft. She was black hulled with a white stripe and green boot topping. Her stacks were the traditional CP buff. She was one of the most handsome liners ever built, many believe. Everyone loved her, except her engineers. On her second voyage she had to put back to Vancouver because of what was described as 'an irregularity in her turbine shaft'. It was the Fottinger reduction system and it just did not work. The *Empress* went to Todd Shipyards' Seattle facility for repairs, but her speed continued to be way below what was expected and her fuel consumption was 'outrageous'.

She became a 'hero ship' in late 1923. It was September 1 and she was about to sail from Yokohama. Robert D. Turner, in his splendid *The Pacific Empresses*, described what happened in picture and story. In a sudden catastrophic earthquake the whole world seemed to turn upside down. The pier, loaded with cheering and waving people and linked to the liner with a thousand streamers, was lifted up and demolished. The huge ship bounded around like a

toy boat. Some 143,000 lives were snuffed out. Fires raged everywhere, whipped into a frenzy by 70 knot winds. Captain Samuel Robinson on the *Empress* watched as the gallant old *Korea Maru* (see Chapter 6) bravely made for the harbour's mouth. He was blocked from following by two cargo ships, one of which had smashed into his stern. Somehow he succeeded in pushing one of them out of his way, but his port propeller became entangled in the other's anchor chain. Finally, with the help of a small tanker, the *Empress* was freed and moved somewhat away from the shore. For nearly two weeks she was a rescue centre, her own crew bringing boat loads of burned survivors out for treatment. Captain Robinson was made a Commander of the Order of the British Empire and won many other honours!

Almost continuous engine troubles made it impossible for the *Empress of Australia* to keep up with the three other Pacific Empresses (*Asia, Russia* and *Canada*). It was decided to send her home to be re-engined. The work turned out to be extraordinarily successful and the liner's speed was upped from 16 to 19½ knots, with her fuel consumption dropping from 205 tons a day to 150. The August 1927 *Marine Engineering* magazine contained a feature, with illustrations, on how this was done. New boilers were necessary. The whole job took only five months. It was described as 'a feat which has probably never before been attempted or accomplished in the history of marine engineering'. The work was done even though Great Britain was in the throes of a major coal strike that meant delays in the delivery of many materials. At the same time her passenger spaces were revamped to reduce her capa-

city by one third. She sailed on her 'second maiden voyage' in late June 1927, departing from Southampton for Cherbourg and Quebec. Among her passengers was the Prince of Wales.

An interesting feature of the literature issued by Canadian Pacific to describe her December 1 1928 round-the-world cruise was an entire page giving the length and breadth of every cabin offered. Room 1, for example was 12′ 9″ long and 19′ wide. Room 646, at the end of the list, was 6′ 4″ by 10′ 11″. Wash basins with hot and cold water were in rooms 1 to 487 inclusive. A few cabins had wash basins (known as 'Standard compactum'), with only cold water. A minimum rate of $2,000 was advertised for this 137-day voyage. Suites with bath and toilet cost $7,000 for each of two persons.

In 1929 the *Empress of Australia* was painted white with a dark blue riband and her customary green boot topping. She maintained the company's express Atlantic service with the *Empress of Scotland* and the *Empress of France*. Cruising occupied more and more of the time of these three fine ships, and when not going around the world or to the Mediterranean they often were assigned to make nine- or 14-day cruises to Norwegian waters. A 14-day Norway cruise cost from 21 guineas and up. Deck chairs were free, rugs or cushions cost 3s 6d each. To take a servant with you would cost an extra 16 guineas for a two week jaunt.

As first announced the February 3 1932 73-day Mediterranean cruise was to cost $900—minimum—in first class. Seven weeks before the sailing ads blared new low rates of $550 up in first for just the ship part and $855 for the cruise and standard shore

Fifty Famous Liners

Above *The smoking room and* **below** *how it was changed early in 1939 to became the dining room for King George VI and Queen Elizabeth when they sailed on the liner to Canada for a state visit.*

The white-painted 'Empress' is escorted out into the Atlantic by British Naval vessels.

excursions. Tourist Class passengers were also carried and prices began at $300 for only the cruise or $510 for cruise with shore trips. An 80-page brochure with lots of coloured illustrations and done on slick paper called on the reader to 'escape'. It went on: 'Somewhere in North America! Life... an unweeded garden grown to seed! Humdrum days in a narrow circle! Stale conversations... Escape... from the Nada-on-the-Humdrums to the lands where Cleopatra loved, where Praxiteles wrought his immortal statues, where the Romans built an Empire, where Christ taught and lived...' Passengers had the privilege of returning from Southampton on any Canadian Pacific ship, 'including the new super-luxurious 5-day Atlantic Giantess—*Empress of Britain*' (see *Fifty Famous Liners 1*).

Prices continued to drop as the world remained Depression ridden. A 10-day West Indies cruise on the *Empress of Australia* cost from $112.50 and up in late 1935. This came to about $11 per day. A year

later you could buy an 18-day West Indies cruise for $202.50, just under $6 a day. Rates to Europe from Quebec were $155 and up in Cabin Class, the top category on most Atlantic ships at that time. One way Tourist was as low as $111.50.

The *Empress of Australia* made a 32-day cruise to Rio which cost $310 and up in late 1937. And then a most unusual development took place. News clippings reported that the liner had been requisitioned by the Admiralty. One headline read: 'MYSTERY VEILS TAKING OVER OF SHIP'. Company officials said they did not know why or for how long the ship was being taken over. Soon, however, the real story leaked out. She was being redecorated again and prepared for the Royal Family, who were to make a State Visit to Canada. The year was 1939. It had been planned to send them on the battleship *Repulse*, but war clouds made this out of the question. The *Empress of Australia* was commissioned as a unit of the Royal Navy and listed as a royal yacht for the occasion. At her fore mast she would fly the flag of the King as Lord High Admiral of the Fleet—a yellow anchor on a red background. The royal standard would fly at the main mast and the white ensign at the stern. Twenty British tars would join the liner's normal crew of 500 for signalling and sentry duty. The King would occupy the principal suite on the port side of A Deck; while the Queen would have a matching suite on the starboard. Their Majesties' beds from the royal yacht *Victoria and Albert* were brought to Southampton and taken aboard the *Empress of Australia*. One hundred and fifty workmen were employed making the ship ready. The *Repulse* was delegated to escort the royal yacht half way across the Atlantic and then return to duty. We wonder if Albert Ballin's ghost smiled at this example of history repeating itself with a twist.

The Royal passage proved to be the liner's last Canadian trip as a passenger ship. After it was over she entered on a 13-year career as a British troopship, with more action ahead than most regular naval vessels. Late in 1939 she was severely bombed when participating in the evacuation of British troops from Norway. Her war work took her on all seven seas; a proper book must be written on this period of her life. On January 27 1941, radio reports had her being torpedoed and shelled off Dakar, but the following day the Navy stated that she was 'safe in port', and charged that the torpedoing story was all a German

The veranda of the Royal suite. Queen Elizabeth was known as a 'noted gardener' and it was surmised that this might become her favourite spot on the crossing.

lie! On another occasion she survived a collision, a bad fire and a gale that almost drove her on the wreck of a French ship, all within a week's time. She carried as many as 5,000 troops per voyage. After the war's end she continued trooping through 1951.

In March, 1952, Canadian Pacific announced in London that the grand old lady had been sold for scrap. She had served for 38 years and was still underway bringing troops home from Korea and Malaya. Obituaries for the *Empress of Australia* were carried in marine journals the world over. Her arrival on April 30 with 2,700 British servicemen from the Far East was a triumph, with tugs whistling and stevedores cheering as she steamed up the Mersey into Liverpool. Quickly she was stripped of her handsome fittings and on May 8 1952 began her last voyage. Her bell and the plaque commemorating her rescue work in the 1923 earthquake were removed for preservation. One of the crew which took her around

to the Firth of Forth was Cyrus Strainstreet, who had been at sea for 58 years, 22 aboard the *Australia*. His hobby was making ships-in-bottles. King George VI had sent for him on his crossing to show some of his models. In her career she had steamed 1,700,000 miles and carried 1,200,000 passengers. 'She's a ship with a charmed life', said Captain Jack Dobson, one of her many masters.

Gross tonnage: 21,861
Length overall: 615 feet
Width: 75 feet 2½ inches
Capacity: 400 First, 165 Second, 360 Third, 670 Steerage (as *Tirpitz*); 370 First, 190 Second, 415 Third, 1,000 Steerage; and 500 First, 144 Second, 632 Tourist
Machinery: Turbines
Speed: 16 knots; as rebuilt 19½ knots
Built: Vulcan Work, Stettin, 1913-17
Demise: Scrapped by British Iron & Steel, Inverkeithing, Scotland, 1952-53

President Roosevelt

She was one of the 'work horses' of the North Atlantic in the 1920s and 1930s, and then went onward to give yeoman service during the Second World War. She was one of sixteen vessels built to the same plans during the First World War (at 14,000 tons and 535 feet in length), but none of these were completed to serve and instead were later handed over to civilian operators. All were refitted as passenger-cargo liners—with two going to the United States Lines for transatlantic service, four to the Munson Line for the South American run and the remainder to the American Mail and Dollar lines for mostly Pacific sailings.

Built by New York Shipbuilding Corporation at Camden, New Jersey, located just across the Delaware River from Philadelphia, the intended transport *Peninsula State* was completed in January 1922. She was transferred to the United States Lines, for their service between New York, the Channel ports and Bremerhaven, and in very quick time was renamed *President Pierce* and then *President Roosevelt*. Her twin sister, the *Lone Star State* and which was also given to the United States Lines, was renamed as the *President Taft* and then as the *President Harding*. Large combination passenger-cargo liners, their accommodation was listed first for 320 first class and 342 second class, and then revised (in 1924) to 201 in cabin class and 236 in Third class.

Assuredly the most notable episode in the career of the *President Roosevelt* occurred in January 1926. While outbound from New York to Bremerhaven, she received a distress call from the sinking British freighter *Antinoe*. That smaller ship, with a cargo of overflowing grain, a broken rudder and partially flooded boiler room, was in serious danger that was further complicated by a snow storm. The American liner quickly responded to the call and set course for the *Antinoe*. Once in sight of one another, an attempt to tow the stricken vessel had to be abandoned when the smaller ship's auxiliary machinery ceased to function. The intensely cold weather was then coupled with a ferocious hail storm and soon the *Antinoe* was lost. It took the master of the *President Roosevelt* seven hours to find the troubled ship. The American ship lowered a life-boat, but it was quickly smashed to pieces against the side of the ship and two crewmen lost their lives. A second boat later managed to rescue 12 seamen from the *Antinoe* and, finally after several other attempts, a further 13 were rescued. All were saved, but through endless storms that lasted over a period of four days and which cost the Americans two lives and six lifeboats. This very heroic event was later the subject of one of marine history's most famous paintings. Done by Norman Wilkenson, it depicted the United States Lines' ship flying the now-famous signal flags saying, 'I will not abandon you.'

Another incident in the career of the *President Roosevelt* was reported in an article in *The New York Times*, dated January 31 1932. 'Moving down the harbor through a heavy fog at 3 o'clock yesterday morning, the liner *Roma* of the Navigazione Generale Italiana, outbound on a Mediterranean cruise, crashed into the *President Roosevelt* of the United States Lines, which lay at anchor off Quarantine. The *Roma* suffered only slight damages to her forepost and put to sea last night after temporary repairs had been made.

'The damage to the *President Roosevelt* was more serious. A wide gap was ripped in her port quarter, twelve feet above the waterline. She remained at Quarantine during the rest of the night, however, and was able to proceed later, under her own steam, to her pier at 16th Street, North River. No one was injured in the crash, and though some passengers on both ships were roused from their sleep and dressed and went on deck, they were reassured by members of the crew, and there was little excitement.

'At the time the accident occurred, fog in the harbor was almost impenetrable. The *President Roosevelt*, which had arrived at Quarantine at 7.00 pm on Friday, bringing 155 passengers from

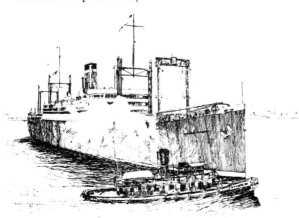

Fifty Famous Liners

Olympic team members travelled to Amsterdam aboard President Roosevelt *in 1928. In a very rare gesture by a ship line, United States Lines painted a salute to the Olympic athletes on the ship's hull.*

Hamburg, Southampton and Cherbourg, lay at anchor with her stern pointed upstream. At intervals, bells aboard were rung simultaneously during five seconds out of every sixty. Suddenly, the lights of two approaching ships loomed close by in the fog. One of them passed within a stone's throw. The other was the *Roma*, though no one aboard the *Roosevelt* could identify her at the time. A warning roar from the *Roosevelt*'s siren caused the Italian ship to swing sharply to port. At the same time her engines were ordered reversed. But it was too late. There was a crash, followed by a sharp snapping of steel plates, as the *Roma*'s bow drove into the side of the anchored *Roosevelt*. The *Roma* backed off at once, and anchored at a safe distance while officers of both ships set to work to inspect the damage. Much of the *Roosevelt*'s plating was found to be badly twisted and a few plates were missing. A six-berth room, usually occupied by stewardesses, but on this trip fortunately vacant, was entirely demolished. Another cabin, from which Edward Wolff, a steward from Saratoga, New York, had moved not ten minutes before, also was badly damaged.

'The *Roma*, which was scheduled to sail originally at 6.00 pm on Friday, and was delayed three hours at the pier because of the fog, was held in Quarantine until 7.00 pm last night as it was necessary to obtain some special papers from the Italian Consulate. Many other ships were delayed by the fog as well. The White Star liner *Majestic*, which was to have left her pier at 12 midnight Friday, did not get away until 10.00 am. The *Ile de France* of the French Line left at midnight Friday but then had to anchor in the fog off Liberty Island. Other steamships delayed by the fog during the night were the White Star liner *Baltic*, the Cunarder *Samaria* and the Red Star liner *Western-*

land. They sailed early yesterday morning, led by the *Ile de France* and followed by the *Majestic*.'

Soon after the outbreak of war in Europe, in the late summer of 1939, the *President Roosevelt* was temporarily used in 'evacuation service,' carrying worried tourists and fortunate nationals away from the troubled shores of western Europe. Shortly thereafter, in other articles in the *The New York Times*, the ship was again in the news. In an article dated November 18 1939, it was announced, 'The New York-Bermuda passenger trade, whose regular British-flag steamship service [with the sisters *Monarch of Bermuda* and *Queen of Bermuda*] was suspended soon after the outbreak of war, will be served regularly by the American liner *President Roosevelt* under a subsidy arrangement [of $1200 per voyage given by the Bermuda Trade Development Board]. The ship is to be specially overhauled at the Robins Drydock & Repair Co at the Todd Shipyard, Brooklyn. She will sail every Saturday from New York and every Tuesday from Bermuda, and will operate as a one-class passenger vessel.' A month later, on December 16, *The New York Times* reported, 'The United States liner *President Roosevelt* will inaugurate an American flag weekly service to Bermuda when she sails at 3.00 pm today with 150 passengers. They include Vincent Astor, Prince and Princess Scherbatow and Morgan J O'Brien.'

This new Bermuda service was quite shortlived, however, as the *Roosevelt* was transferred to the US Army during 1940 and refitted as a troop transport. A year later, in June 1941, she was allocated to the Navy Department and renamed as the USS *Joseph T. Dickman* and used for both trooping as well as hospital work. She was decommissioned in March

Above *Army blimps practise manoeuvres over the liner on October 10, 1928.*

Below *Cots fill her social hall as Americans rush to get out of war-stricken Europe when the* President Roosevelt *sails for home on September 1, 1939.*

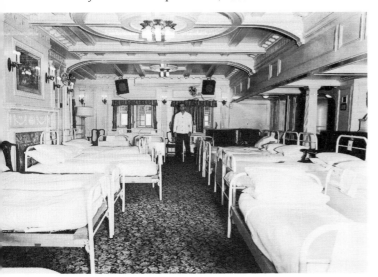

1946, and later turned over to the US Maritime Commission. While she might have seen further service, most likely under a foreign flag, she was declared surplus for any further American needs and sold for demolition.

In a letter to Frank Braynard from John H. Wintersteen of the Kaiser Steel Co, dated January 14 1949, the final days of the former *President Roosevelt* were detailed. The letter read, 'We purchased her from the Maritime Commission early in 1948. She was immediately broken up in Yard 3 [in Oakland, California]. She was floated onto a drydock, wrecking crews removed all of her bright work, furniture, etc and the burners went to work slicing her up into movable sections. These sections were lifted from the hull by whirley cranes and deposited on the same assembly tables which were formerly used for prefabrication of new ships during the war. The sections were then cut down to sizes to fit into gondola freight cars and eventually wound up in the open hearth furnaces of various West Coast steel mills. Those who had developed a special fondness for the *President Roosevelt* can take comfort in the knowledge that her steel may now be serving another useful purpose—possibly as farm implements, railroad cars, automobile components or any of a thousand and one other uses. The *Roosevelt*, incidentally, yielded approximately 5,600 tons of steel.'

Gross tonnage: 14,187 (1922); 13,869 (1924)
Length overall: 535 feet
Width: 65 feet
Machinery: Steam turbines, twin screw
Speed: 17 knots
Capacity: 320 First, 324 Second (1922); 201 Cabin, 236 Third (1924)
Built: New York Shipbuilding Corp, Camden, New Jersey, 1922
Demise: Scrapped at Oakland, California, 1948

Right *In December 1939 she started operating the New York to Bermuda run. Here ticker tape marks her first departure.*

Below *The discharge document for cabin waiter Wendell Herbert.*

Serial No. **F** 876527   BUREAU OF MARINE INSPECTION AND NAVIGATION

CERTIFICATE OF DISCHARGE

Voyage 118   Art. #228   Certificate of Identification No. **Z** 28720

Name of Vessel Official Number	Class of Vessel (steam, motor, sail, or barge)	Nature of the Voyage (foreign, intercoastal, or coastwise)
S.S. "President Roosevelt" 221,901	Steam	Foreign

Wendell Herbert (Name of seaman)	Rating (capacity in which employed)	Date and place of shipment	Date and place of discharge
USA (Citizenship)	Cabin Waiter	January 29, 1939 New York	February 26, 1939 New York

I HEREBY CERTIFY that the above entries were made by me and are correct and that the signatures hereto were witnessed by me.

Dated this 25th day of February, 19 39   *Rashea*   *Wendell R. Herbert*
United States Shipping Commissioner. (or Master of vessel.)   (Signature of seaman)

(Master of vessel)

NOTE.—Whenever a master performs the duties of the shipping commissioner under this act, the master shall sign the certification on the line designated for the shipping commissioner's signature.

Form 718-A   11—11814

Tuscania

In the early 1920s, to replace their losses in the First World War and to reinforce their position on the North Atlantic, Britain's Anchor Line added five new passenger liners—the *Cameronia*, the sisters *California* and *Tuscania*, and then another set of sisters, the *Caledonia* and *Transylvania*. All quite similar in their hull and top deck configurations, the latter two differed in that instead of a single funnel, they had three stacks. The *Tuscania* differed as well, in having the longest and most diverse career of these Anchor ships.

Launched on October 4 1921, from the Fairfield Shipbuilding & Engineering Yards at Glasgow, she was commissioned in the following September. Used in peak season on the Atlantic, between Glasgow, Belfast, Londonderry and New York, and then occasionally transferred to the Liverpool-Suez-Bombay route, the *Tuscania* was rather unfortunately always somewhat superfluous to the needs of the Anchor Line operations. Resourcefully, she became the Company's 'relief', one used wherever needed. Furthermore, between 1926 and 1930, she was chartered to Cunard for their London-New York trade, then laid-up for some months (between October 1930 and August 1931), then used again on the Bombay run and for cruising, and even as a review ship for the launch of the *Queen Mary* at Clydebank, in September 1934.

Her berthing was first planned as 240 in first class, 377 second class and 1,818 in third class, but was rearranged in 1929 as 206 in cabin class, 439 in tourist class and 485 in third class. In his *Ships of the North Atlantic*, first published in 1936, author A. G. Horton-White wrote of the *Tuscania* and her twin sistership *California*, 'Their passenger accommodation is of the type found in all Anchor Line vessels, comfortable and suitable for either of the two routes upon which the liners may run. The *California* is notable in that her public rooms are decorated and furnished in widely varying styles. The Lounge on this ship is panelled and has windows on three sides of the room while the Smoking Room is modern. It extends into the deck above in the centre, and has windows in the sides of the higher portion; the room is illuminated with indirect lighting and is furnished with modernist furniture. On the *California* also

there is a Corridor Lounge and a Cocktail Bar carried out in a modern design, with indirect lighting. The *Tuscania*'s Smoking Room is similar to that of the *California*, her Writing Room is panelled and her Dining Saloon has a large dome surrounded by pillars.'

In April 1939, just months from the outbreak of the Second World War, the *Tuscania* was sold off, rather oddly at such a pressing time, to foreign owners then known as the General Steam Navigation Co of Greece. The Greeks, having run a transatlantic service with older, slower, mostly secondhand ships, were now interested in establishing more of a first rate operation. The purchase of the *Tuscania* was the ideal beginning. Briefly refitted, her passenger configuration was rearranged as 179 first class, 404 cabin class and 1,399 tourist class, she was appropriately renamed *Nea Hellas*—'New Greece'—and departed from Piraeus for New York on her first crossing, on 19 May. The *New York Herald Tribune* made note of her first arrival. 'The 17,000-ton liner *Nea Hellas*, flagship of the General Steam Navigation Co (the Greek Line) fleet, left Piraeus yesterday and will arrive here on 31 May. The vessel will dock at Pier 97, the Hudson River. The first of a projected fleet of vessels to be entered in the New York-Athens trade, the *Nea Hellas*, the former *Tuscania* of the Anchor Line, offers the latest facilities in three classes, including room-and-bath suites in first class.

'Goulandris Brothers of Piraeus, operators of the new line, are among the world's largest operators of cargo ships. The company, subsidized with mail contracts from the Greek Government, has announced that the line would provide Americans

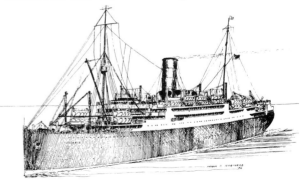

with a direct route to the Balkans and Near Eastern ports, and help to strengthen existing Greco-American relations. The *Nea Hellas* will remain in New York until 10 June, when she will sail on her return trip to Piraeus, the port for Athens. She will be open for public inspection during her stay here. A series of entertainments and dinners will be given for well known members of the Greco-American colony and leading travel agents in the New York area.

Right *A lovely painting of* Tuscania *at sunset by O. Rosenvinge.*

Below *A close up view of her cruiser stern, typical of the ships built immediately after the First World War. The scrape marks and twisted deck railings which can be seen were caused by a collision with the French liner* Rochambeau *when both ships were swinging on their anchors in fog off Quarantine in 1925.*

Tuscania

The tourist third class swimming pool on Tuscania, *1924.*

'The Greek merchant marine has not been identified with the transatlantic trade for several years, the former service having been suspended several years ago. The resumption of regular passenger sailings is another indication that the war clouds are rapidly disappearing abroad, a feeling that is shared by virtually all steamship men.'

Unfortunately, those optimistic forecasts proved incorrect. Within months of her maiden crossing, war was declared and the ship soon thereafter requisitioned by the British Government for trooping service. Sensibly, she was managed by her former owners, the Anchor Line. Over the next seven years, she was dubbed the 'Nellie Wallace' by her mostly-soldier passengers.

She was returned to her Greek owners in January 1947, and then rather hastily returned to commercial service. On August 9 1947, *The New York Times* reported, 'The reconverted Greek passenger liner *Nea Hellas*, on her first post-war voyage from the Mediterranean after a complete overhauling, arrived yesterday with 294 passengers, approximately one-fifth of her new capacity. She docked in Hoboken. Operated by the Greek Line, the ship was not reconverted from troop status in time to allow for

advertising of her first sailing abroad. She came to New York with three more crewmen than passengers. Officials reported that they could have filled the ship easily, from the backlog of passengers awaiting transport to the United States from southern Europe. The ship arrived from Genoa, Naples and Lisbon [her overhaul had been completed at Genoa], omitting the call at Piraeus because of the shortage of time. Leaving here on 15 August, she is expected to take out a heavy list of passengers according to her New York agents.

'The ship was "dressed" in the international code flags when she entered the harbor early in the morning. A few ships saluted her appearance with whistles and the Greek vessel replied. But the harbor was hazy and most vessels missed her arrival. Her master reported that she had been delayed by fog at sea.'

In early 1949, a directive to travel agents from the Greek Line reported, 'Please be advised that the sailings of the TSS *Nea Hellas*, from New York on 11th February and 26th March, have been cancelled. The vessel has been placed on an Emergency Voyage

from Italy to Australia with displaced persons for the benefit of the International Refugee Organization. The *Nea Hellas* is due back in the Mediterranean in time to resume the balance of her 1949 itinerary and is scheduled to sail from Piraeus on 12th April.'

Until 1955, when she was replaced by the brand new Greek Line flagship *Olympia*, the *Nea Hellas* plied the Mediterranean route to New York. Afterward, she was refitted once again, renamed *New York* and placed on a more Northerly course, sailing between Bremerhaven, Southampton, Cherbourg, Halifax and New York. Her accommodation was again restyled, this time for 70 in first class and 1,300 in tourist class. Retaining her popularity, she made deep impressions on some of her passengers. James Kalafatis, a Greek-American, has a very special regard for this liner. 'All of us have moments and experiences in the recesses of our memories that we will always cherish. One of my fondest memories is that of a ship, a ship that passed on to obscurity well

over twenty years ago and which few people may remember.

'On 30 April 1953, my father and I set sail from a pier in Hoboken, New Jersey, to visit my grandparents in Greece. I was seven years old and, as we waved goodbye to my Mom and Grandmother standing on the pier, little did I know that I was embarking on the first and perhaps the greatest adventure of my life. I was onboard the TSS *Nea Hellas*, the pride of the Greek fleet, the ship I had heard mentioned so many times in Greek conversations between my family and their friends. In the 1940s and 1950s, she was the bridge which connected the old world and the new world Greeks. The ship had seen better days. At 31 years of age at the time, she had only eight years to go before being sent to the scrappers, but to a seven year old boy, she was the most majestic ship that sailed the seas.

'We spent the next 14 days crossing the Atlantic Ocean and the Mediterranean Sea, and I learned every inch of that ship from the engine room to the pilot house. Although over thirty years have since passed, it seems more like a month ago that I was leaning over the railing looking at the white foam floating on the ship's wake; or watching the dolphins

A Dalzell tub leads New York *out of port* (courtesy of Jeff Blinn).

race from the prow of the ship; or looking at a speck of a ship on the distant horizon; or hearing the ship's steam whistle blow every few minutes in a soupy fog as we proceeded at a dead slow speed. The steward daily walked the length of the ship ringing a bell or striking a gong (depending upon which class you were travelling) to signal lunch or dinner seatings. I remember the constant rumble of the ship's engine and the creaking of wood as the ship listed in rough weather. I can still picture the waves coming over her bow and drenching the foredeck; the beautiful sunsets and starlit nights; the movies; the horserace games; the lounges with the smell of Greek cigarettes; the rigging whistling in the breeze; the smell of machinery, freshly baked bread and salty air; the other passengers; the Azores, Lisbon, Naples and Piraeus. To me, that summer was as exciting as the Odyssey of Ulysses.

'I spent the summers of 1953, 1954 and 1956 in Greece and would give almost anything to relive those beautiful times of my childhood. Getting there and back was half the fun, and it's sad that travelling the way I did is now part of a bygone era, never to return again. I made four transatlantic crossings on the *Nea Hellas*, two of the most precious

months of my life, living on a ship I will never forget.'

Time ran out for the old ship in the autumn of 1959, when she was laid-up. Two years later, in April 1961, *The Shipping World* noted her final end. 'The Greek liner *New York* has been laid up at Kynossoura since November 1959, and has now been sold to a Japanese shipbreaking firm for what is reported to amount to about £312,000, and is to give October delivery in Japan. The price is looked upon as being a good one, particularly as the delivery is very forward. Bearing in mind that the Japanese shipbreaking industry already have taken two P&O liners, the *Corfu* and *Carthage*, and are showing a lot of interest in the latest P&O ship to become available for disposal—the *Strathaird*—the Japanese obviously see a very great demand for scrap for the rest of the year.'

Gross tonnage: 16,991 (1922)
Length overall: 578 feet
Width: 70 feet
Machinery: Steam turbines, twin screw
Speed: 16 knots
Capacity: 240 First, 377 Second, 1,818 Third (1922); 206 Cabin, 439 Tourist, 485 Third (1929); 179 First, 404 Cabin, 1,399 Tourists (1929); 70 First, 1,300 Tourist (1955)
Built: Fairfield Shipbuilding & Engineering Co, Glasgow, Scotland, 1922
Demise: Scrapped at Onomichi, Japan, 1961

Fifty Famous Liners

Athenia

A. G. Horton-White wrote in *Ships of the North Atlantic*, 'These two ships, the Donaldson Line's *Athenia* and *Letitia*, have proved very popular on their routes, and their steadiness and punctuality have been a great asset to them.' The former would have a special place in maritime history as well— the first merchant ship to be sunk by a submarine in the Second World War.

At approximately 13,500 tons each, these two sisterships resembled some of the smaller Cunarders of that same period, the early twenties, that also sailed the St Lawrence route, between Glasgow and Montreal. Both ships were built at the Fairfield yards at Glasgow—the *Athenia* being launched in January 1922 and then commissioned in April 1923; the *Letitia* launched in October 1924 and then delivered in April 1925. Their accommodation was balanced between 516 cabin class passengers and approximately 1,000 in steerage-third class. Mr Horton-White added, 'The accommodation on both ships is of excellent character. The cabins are well fitted as well as the public rooms. The Cabin Dining Saloon on C Deck is partly two decks in height, and on the *Letitia* is in Tudor style with the usual panelling and beams. On the *Athenia*, this Saloon is in more modern style. On the Promenade Deck is the Cabin Class Smoking Room. Next to the Smoking Room is the Drawing Room, which has a skylight. In front of the Drawing Room, the engine casing divides the long Writing Room from the Corridor Lounge. Both of these rooms lead to the large Entrance Hall.

'The ships are distinctive looking and always give the impression of being fine sea boats, for the superstructure is central, and the funnel is also amidships. They have straight stems, no forecastles, but a small deckhouse with four boats, and supporting the foremast, which is rather nearer to the bridge than to the bow. The bridge is of the island type. The Boat Deck aft of the bridge has 12 lifeboats. On the Boat Deck is the single funnel, slightly raked and rather high. At the forward end of this deck is a small deckhouse forming a landing for passengers coming up from the deck below. The Promenade Deck is continued further than the Boat Deck and on the open space thus formed are the mainmast and four boats. A Deck, which is continued past the

Promenade Deck, is divided by the small well-deck and then continued, and on this deckhouse thus formed there are four more boats. Following this deckhouse is a large uninterrupted space to the cruiser stern.'

The accommodation was restyled aboard both sisters in 1933. Aboard the *Athenia*, it now read 314 cabin class, 310 tourist class and 928 third class. Two years later, the Company's title was changed to the Donaldson Atlantic Line.

The *Athenia* was outbound on a westward crossing to Canada when, on September 3 1939, she was torpedoed by the German submarine U-30 in a position some 200 nautical miles west of the Hebrides. Tragically, 112 lives were lost. The sinking of the *Athenia* was a horrific incident, especially as it had been agreed that no action, in the wake of the Nazi invasion of Poland and imminent declaration of war, should be taken against unarmed passenger

Above *A fine threequarters view of* Athenia. *Can you see the line from her bow down to the lifeboat? Perhaps someone is retouching the hull.*

Left *A bow-on view.*

Above right *Printed by Marcil Cross of Aberdeen, the brochure of which this is the cover is a beautiful example of the fine art of liner literature.*

Below right *A full page from an old Anchor-Donaldson Line folder showing an artist's impression of the* Athenia *approaching a bell buoy.*

ships. The German High Command in Berlin denied responsibility for the sinking.

Ten days later, on September 13, a newspaper article described the arrival of the survivors. 'A weary but wildly cheering throng of *Athenia* survivors jammed the decks of the tiny freighter *City of Flint* this afternoon to greet a pilot and photographer in a press plane, which flew 230 miles to sea for the first pictures of the rescue ship to reach North American shores [at Halifax]. All was apparently well aboard the 7,500-ton cargo ship, due here tomorrow at 8.00 am (New York time), although she carries 216 passengers of the British liner, torpedoed nine days ago. The ship normally has accommodation for only 12 passengers. Escorting her, a half mile away on each side, were the US Coast Guard cutters *Campbell* and *Bibb*, which removed seven injured survivors on Sunday.

'At first the *City of Flint* seemed like a dead ship', reported the pilot of the press plane. 'But the sound of our motors brought everyone on deck. Some were oddly dressed, others were wrapped in blankets. They shouted and waved to us almost hysterically each time we flew overhead. We noticed no mattresses or beds on the decks.'

'An American flag flew at half-mast from the stern, indicating that the freighter carried the body of a 10-year-old girl from Ontario, who died of a brain concussion after her rescue from a lifeboat. Full arrangements have been completed here for the care of the 106 Americans and 110 Canadians on their arrival. Piles of medical supplies, food and clothing lie ready at the docks.'

Sadly, the *Athenia* was the first of many tragic disasters during World War 2.

Gross tonnage: 13,465
Length overall: 538 feet
Width: 66 feet
Machinery: Steam turbines, twin screw
Speed: 15 knots
Capacity: 516 Cabin and 1,000 Third (1923); 314 Cabin, 310 Tourist and 925 Third (1933)
Built: Fairfield Shipbuilding & Engineering Co, Glasgow, Scotland, 1923
Demise: Torpedoed and sunk by a German U-boat off the Hebrides, September 3 1939

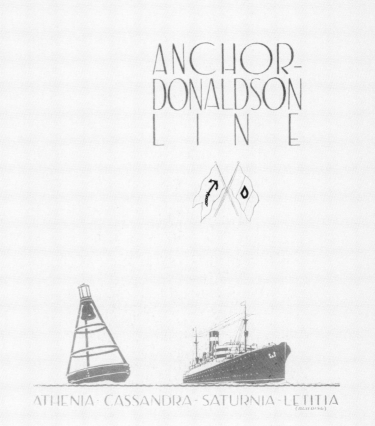

ATHENIA · CASSANDRA · SATURNIA · LETITIA
(BUILDING)

Columbus

The German merchant fleet was devastated following the First World War. The major shippers, such as the rival Hamburg American Line and North German Lloyd, were all but stripped completely. Their once glorious liner fleets, which included some of the largest and grandest ships of the pre-war age, had been lost or given away as reparations. For example, and perhaps most cruel for the Germans to accept, Albert Ballin's awesome trio of giants, the *Imperator*, the *Vaterland* and the incomplete *Bismarck*, were sailing under other flags by the early twenties—the *Imperator* as Cunard's *Berengaria*, the *Vaterland* as the American *Leviathan* and the *Bismarck* as White Star's *Majestic*. All but one of the famed German four-stackers were gone as well; the only survivor being the mechanically faulty former *Deutschland* of 1900, which was refitted as the demoted immigrant ship *Hansa*. Even German liners that were still on the stocks in that fateful summer of 1914 were eventually completed for reparation accounts. There were, however, a few exceptions.

In 1914, the North German Lloyd—in response to Hamburg America's incredibly ambitious plans with the statistically superlative *'Imperator'* class, three superliners that would begin at 52,000 tons and then increase to 56,000 tons—ordered twin 34,000 tonners. Ordered from the Schichau Shipyards at Danzig, they were to be named as the *Columbus* and *Hindenburg*, and were to have been delivered in 1915. Construction was, however, halted completely the year before as the hostilities erupted. Some years later, in 1919, under the Treaty of Versailles, the intended *Columbus* was ordered to be completed, but as reparations to the British. Afterward, she was assigned more specifically to the White Star Line and completed, in January 1922, as their *Homeric*. The projected *Hindenburg* was, in the kindness of the Allied victors, allowed to remain in German hands and was renamed *Columbus*. Construction resumed in 1920, and she was ready for launching by the summer of 1922. Unfortunately, the 775 foot long ship moved only a few yards during the launch ceremonies. With both her builders and owners embarrassed, a tug was called to assist, but even this attempt failed. The event was delayed for two

months, until August 12. She was delivered to the North German Lloyd in November 1923, but due to various other problems, including material shortages for the final fitting-out, she did not cross the North Atlantic for the first time until the following April.

The Lloyd managers and their publicists were rightfully proud of their new liner, the largest post-war German liner. Listed at 32,354 gross tons, her berthing arrangements were listed as 513 in first class, 574 in second class and 705 in third class. Her staff numbered 733. In an elaborate Lloyd brochure issued at the time of her maiden sailing, the descriptions were very enthusiastic. 'To the shores of America has come the crowning achievement of Germany's skill in shipbuilding: the new SS *Columbus*, the largest and fastest of German ships. It is over four hundred years since her namesake sailed in his caravels—mere cockleshells in comparison with this giant—into the danger of uncharted seas, heedless of obstacles that beset his voyage. Unfaltering and determined, he reached his goal. He was the first to bring news of the existence of a Western Hemisphere, which became the New World for later explorers.

'The *Columbus* is not the largest ship on the seas—but there is no other that can lay claim to being more beautiful; no other in which modern scientific

Fifty Famous Liners

A superb photo by Edwin Levick showing Columbus *with her original tall smokestacks partly hidden by steam from a Moran tug.*

attainment and artistic merit has dealt so lavish a hand in beautifying interiors and developing sea-going luxury. A glance through the *Columbus* will show that the architect selected, Professor Troost, to whom the North German Lloyd entrusted their artistic decorations, has in every way fulfilled his task most satisfactorily. With the practical collaboration of skilled German artists and artisans, he has created rooms which may well claim to be the most beautiful on any modern ship. Most imposing is the stately suite of social rooms, which, beginning with the Social Hall, leads through two side connecting Antechambers to the Library, Smoking Room and on to the Great Staircase. The Social Hall, the two side Antechambers and the Library form in architecture, decoration and colouring, one harmonious whole, in spite of their varied arrangement.

'The colour scheme is placed in charming opposition to the architectural form—where the intensity of the colouring relaxes, the architectural decoration becomes more ornate—for instance, in the hall with its natural undertone, raised to glowing life by single objects of more intense colour, with its mural decorations by E. R. Weiss, coloured, still-life studies, landscapes, etc, where at the evening dance the twelve candelabra enhance the beauty of the scene—there the colour scheme reaches its highest note. In the wainscoted Library with its massive double pillars, its built-in bookcases, its niches decorated with busts of classical poets—it is here the architectural note is accentuated. The more neutral tones of the two side antechambers between the hall and library promote the harmony of the colour scheme by bridging the contrasting colours of the two rooms, at the same time offering a change of design in upholstering and carpets.

'Particularly effective are the parallel lines of windows, mirrors, etc. The clever way in which the curve of the wall line is taken advantage of for the placing of writing tables and the harmony in the form of windows, arrangement of ceiling and wainscoting, are also noteworthy. Special attention should be given to the quaint, almost exotic hand-carved pictures in the hall, representing the continents and the "Four Seasons" by Joseph Wackerle, in the niches of the antechambers. The spacious dining halls, first and second class, are on the main deck. The architect's skill has made it possible for the first

Columbus

class dining hall to be particularly lofty, rising for the most part through two decks. This produces an effect of great space such as is found on no other large ship, and allows exceptionally good ventilation—an important requisite for a dining room.'

The initial success of the *Columbus* prompted the Lloyd directors to think of a new pair of 35,000-tonners, both near-sisters to the earlier ship. With designs in hand by 1925, the plans were changed shortly thereafter, especially as Germany recovered more fully, for twin 50,000-tonners. The size of their hulls was increased to over 935 feet and machinery would go aboard to produce record-breaking speeds. These ships were, of course, the Blue Riband champions *Bremen* of 1929 and *Europa* of 1930.

The *Columbus* endured some machinery changes as well. In August 1927, her starboard shaft broke in mid-Atlantic and consequently caused her engines to race and destroy themselves. Taken to the Vulkan shipyards at Bremen, she was repaired with substitute triple expansion engines that were transferred from the freighter *Schwaben*. Two years later, during an extended refit at the Blohm & Voss yards at Hamburg, she was given brand new steam geared turbines, so powerful that her service speed increased from 18 to 22 knots. At the same time, to conform with the appearance of the sleek *Bremen*, the *Columbus* was fitted with new squat funnels. These gave her a particularly racey appearance, one

much associated with the streamlined motorships of the 1930s.

The *Columbus* sailed in company, at least during the peak summer seasons, with the *Bremen* and *Europa* on the Lloyd's express route, between Bremerhaven, Southampton, Cherbourg and New York. At the other times, especially in the winter months, she went cruising, often on long, luxurious trips. One of these was her Round South America cruise, which departed from New York, on February 5 1938. In 47 days, she would call at Havana, Cristobal and the Panama Canal, Callao and Mollendo in Peru; Valparaiso in Chile; the Straits of Magellan; Mar del Plata for Buenos Aires in Argentina; Montevideo in Uruguay; Santos, Rio de Janeiro and Bahia in Brazil; Trinidad; and finally at Nassau, before returning to New York. Minimum passage fares began at $595 and all shore excursions could be purchased as a package for $162.50. Social life was especially geared to her cruising clientele and included such listings as:

Saturday

2.00 pm	Concert in the Social Hall
3.00 pm	Dancing class in the Social Hall
4.00 pm	Tea Dance, Social Hall
7.00 pm	Welcome Dinner
8.45 pm	Staff Presentation
9.30 pm	Welcome Dance
Midnight	Dancing in the Marine Grill

S.S. COLUMBUS CAPT. W. DÄHNE

Above right *All decked out in signal flags, the* Columbus *enters Havana.*

Right *A snapshot of two passengers and a very long, sleek looking* Columbus, *probably taken in the West Indies.*

Left *A postcard of* Columbus, *looking very much like* Bremen *and* Europa, *and her last master, Captain W. Dahne.*

Sunday

9.00 am	Holy Mass
11.00 am	Divine Services
2.00 pm	Tea Concert, Social Hall
3.00 pm	Horse Races, A Deck Aft
4.00 pm	Classical Concert, Social Hall
9.30 pm	Lecture on the Cruise
10.30 pm	Bavarian Beer Evening, Dining Room

On September 1 1939, an article appeared in the *New York Herald Tribune*, which read, 'All German liners on the high seas were heading at full speed for safe ports today under plans completed by the Nazi shipping combine only a few hours before the outbreak of hostilities with Poland. The major problem, disposition of the liner *Columbus*, which has been steaming towards New York from a Caribbean cruise, was solved last night when the North German Lloyd ordered the ship to put into Havana. It will discharge its 745 passengers, mostly Americans, and will return to Germany. Whether

FAHRPLÄNE

A beautiful poster style cover to a North German Lloyd brochure.

the line will make arrangements to get the passengers to New York was not determined. It is scheduled to dock today at 4 pm at the Cuban port.' Thereafter, the ship fled for the sanctuary of Vera Cruz in Mexico.

A month later, on October 5, another newspaper article read, 'The North German Lloyd liner *Columbus'* unheralded departure from Vera Cruz and her reappearance at Point Anton Lizardo, about 12 miles to the southeast, has given rise to the suspicion that she is about to abandon Mexican waters. It is suggested that the liner may be

intending to refuel the German cruiser *Admiral Scheer* or else go into commerce raiding on her own account. Mexican authorities, however, state that the ship was thoroughly searched, that no war materials of any sort were found aboard and that a close watch is still kept over her.'

The same newspaper article also debated the liner's immediate use. 'According to naval experts, the *Columbus* could be converted into a very formidable commerce raider, since her great speed will render her very hard to catch. She could easily outstrip anything but a very fast modern cruiser. With the help of a couple of seaplanes, which could be lifted onto her deck when not in use, she would not be in grave danger even by such cruisers. Her only difficulty would be refuelling, since a ship of her size uses a very great quantity of oil. At present, as far as is known, the *Columbus* has only about 100 tons of oil aboard, which would not last very long.'

Two months later, on December 20, the *Columbus* was in front page headlines in American newspapers. The story in the *Philadelphia Inquirer* read, 'The huge German luxury liner *Columbus*, scuttled to thwart a British man-of-war which was close on her wake, was aflame and sinking tonight in the Atlantic [December 19] while an American cruiser performed the dramatic rescue of 579 of her crew. The 32,381-ton liner, the third largest in the German merchant marine, 13th largest in the world and familiar to thousands of American tourists, had slipped out of Vera Cruz, Mexico, last Thursday in a desperate attempt to elude the British fleet and possibly reach Europe—but her gamble failed. First word of her grim end came from the United States cruiser *Tuscaloosa*, which flashed that the *Columbus* was being scuttled about 400 miles from the eastern coast, off the mouth of Delaware Bay.' It was a very sad ending for such a glorious liner.

Gross tonnage: 32,354 (1924); 32,565 (1929); 32,381 (1939)
Length overall: 775 feet
Width: 83 feet
Machinery: Steam triple expansion engines changed in 1929 to steam geared turbines
Speed: 18 knots (22 knots after 1929)
Capacity: 513 First, 574 Second, 705 Third
Built: Schichau Shipyards, Danzig, Germany, 1914-24
Demise: Scuttled off the American East Coast to avoid Allied capture, December 19 1939

De Grasse

The French Line, the Compagnie Generale Transatlantique, is perhaps best remembered for its large, superbly luxurious ocean liners—ships such as the *France* of 1912, the *Paris* of 1921, the *Ile de France* of 1927 and, most assuredly, the extraordinary *Normandie* of 1935. The French Line's level of decor, of service and of cuisine were bywords in ocean travel, particularly in the years between the two world wars. Also included, however, in the French fleet were a number of more intermediate passenger ships. One of the finest of this smaller class was the *De Grasse*, completed in 1924 and used for many years on the prestigious North Atlantic route.

Ordered from British builders, Cammell Laird & Company at Birkenhead, her first keel plates were in fact put into place in March 1920. Rumour then was that she would be named *Suffren*. Delays and work stoppages followed, such that the launching did not occur until February 1924. By then, there had been some changes as well, including the decision to call the vessel *De Grasse*. Soon afterward, however, there were still more complications. Following yet another British shipyard strike, the nearly complete liner was moved to St Nazaire in France for final fitting out. Later, in the summer of 1924, she set out on her maiden crossing to New York.

The New York Times recorded the event, in an article dated September 6 1924. 'The new French liner *De Grasse* arrived here on her maiden trip yesterday with 463 passengers, after having been forced to put back into Le Havre when two days out. The ship, a 17,700-ton, oil-burning cabin class steamer, left Le Havre on 21 August. Next day the shaft of one of the electric fans broke in the after boiler room. There was no spare part onboard and the break was mended. Then, during the night of the following day, the fan on the forward boiler room broke.

'Captain Jules Robert, who was formerly in command of *La Bourdonnais*, called a meeting of the officers and principals of the crew, and it was decided to turn back. There was no immediate danger, according to Captain Robert. The fans provide a draft for the combustion of the fuel oil. With a broken fan, the ship might have proceeded at reduced speed. The possibility to be considered was that a storm might beset the ship. So when the passengers came on deck that day, the sea was the same and they did not know they were heading for Le Havre until the stewards told them. They felt the Captain had acted wisely. The *De Grasse* returned to Le Havre on 24 August. The broken fan was repaired and she set forth again on the 27th.'

Designed with space for 399 cabin class and as many as 1,712 third class passengers, the *De Grasse* sailed mostly on the New York run and was occasionally sent, during the winter season, to the Caribbean, specifically to the French islands of Guadeloupe and Martinique. She was in the news again, on November 10 1929. 'The French liner *De Grasse*, veering away from a string of lighters as it steamed slowly down the Hudson yesterday morning, was caught by a strong ebb tide and swung against the freighter *Pequonnock* and Pier 14 at Fulton Street. The pier was damaged and the bow of freighter smashed, but no one was injured. The French ship was not damaged. This is the second harbor incident in which French Line ships have been involved in a month. The *Paris* rammed and sank the Norwegian freighter *Beseggen* off the Statue of Liberty on the night of 15 October.'

The *De Grasse* was refitted in 1932, and given altered accommodation for far fewer passengers—536 in cabin class and 410 in third class. Her tonnage was relisted as well, at 18,435. Used more

and more for cruising, the *De Grasse* was laid-up for a time following the appearance of the giant *Normandie* in the summer of 1935. A year or so later, in May 1936, it was rumoured that she 'and possibly another French Atlantic liner' would be moved to the Pacific, to sail to Tahiti with connections from Australia, New Zealand and even the North American West Coast. This scheme never materialised, however. On Christmas Day 1938, it was reported, 'The *De Grasse* has been almost completely reconditioned for her series of West Indies cruises this winter and spring. Among the improvements onboard are the installation of a swimming pool, a double-deck dining room and a new sun deck. Three of the cruises which the liner will make are under the auspices of Simmons Tours: one for nine days [with fares from $100], one for ten days and two of twelve days. Havana, Nassau, Miami, Haiti and Jamaica will be visited by the *De Grasse.*'

A little less than a year later, on October 16 1939, a report in *The New York Times* was far less joyous. 'With a gun turret erected on her foredeck and 75 millimeter guns mounted fore and aft and manned by French naval crews, the French liner *De Grasse* slipped into New York harbor unexpectedly today,

De Grasse *in 1924, probably on her maiden arrival at New York.*

the first French Line passenger ship to reach here since the arrival of the *Ile de France* more than a month ago. Like all ships of the belligerents, the *De Grasse* had crossed the Atlantic in complete secrecy, blacked out from stem to stern at night and not sending any messages by radio. No announcement had been made of her sailing from Le Havre on 7 October or of her expected arrival here today. According to some of 281 passengers, the ship's officers must have enforced the strictest blackouts experienced yet on transatlantic vessels. Portholes and windows were painted over, glass doors and sky-lights were taped and so few lights were left on that it was difficult to read.'

The *De Grasse* returned to home water later in 1939, and thereafter was laid-up at Bordeaux. Quickly, she fell into Nazi hands and was used by them as an accommodation ship, having never left her moorings throughout the remaining war years. In their retreat, on August 30 1944, the Germans sunk the liner. She was salvaged exactly a year to the day later, on August 30 1945, and immediately brought to St Nazaire for post-war refitting. Two

De Grasse *is painted battleship grey for war service.*

years later, *The New York Times* recorded her triumphant return to service, 'New York Harbor gave the French liner *De Grasse* a full dress reception when she arrived here yesterday [July 25 1947] from Le Havre and Southampton. She was the first vessel of the French Line to come here in peacetime style since almost eight years ago when her country went to war against Nazism. Dressed brightly from stem to stern with signal flags, she received a raucous welcome as she moved up the bay from Quarantine to her North River pier. As harbor craft whistled their greetings, two city fireboats sprayed their salutes. Officials of the city and the French Government boarded the ship in the Narrows to pay their respects. The *De Grasse* will balance the French Line's service for at least the rest of the year with the freighters *Oregon*, accommodating 75 passengers, and the *Wisconsin*, with 57 berths.

'With the tricolor of France billowing proudly from her aft mast, the *De Grasse* showed no signs of having been a battered war casualty for more than a year. She had been disabled by a depth charge from a German trawler in the Gironde estuary in August 1944. She lay partly submerged for twelve months before she was towed to port for reconversion. In a St Nazaire shipyard, she was reborn. Her two sober, vertical stacks yielded to a single one with a rakish slope. After the ravages of silt and water had been overcome, French artisans modernised her interior and made her hull and superstructure gleam with bright paint. It was a long and discouraging process. A shortage of essential materials was the principal handicap. The trials of renovation were forgotten yesterday, however, as champagne corks popped and photographers' flash bulbs flared aboard the 23-year-old liner.

'Beneath her decks was a significant prize of war—a black Mercedes automobile with reinforced body and bullet-proof glass. Once, it had been the property of Adolf Hitler. The 3½ ton vehicle, now owned by the French Government, was bound for an exhibition in Toronto. There was also a wistful note with the *De Grasse*'s gay arrival. Many of her crewmen had served aboard the *Normandie* when that ship was the unchallenged queen of the Atlantic. She lay in the harbor yesterday as the *De Grasse* was being welcomed. Now only a tragic metal hulk, the *Normandie* is undergoing the final stages of scrapping at her Port Newark pier.'

In her first two seasons, 1947 and 1948, the *De Grasse* was booked almost continuously to full capacity. She ran the French Line's luxury service singlehandedly. The arrival of the *Ile de France*, first thought to be during 1948, was delayed and finally rescheduled for the summer of 1949. The *Liberte*, the former *Europa*, seemed even more remote. She was to be commissioned in the summer of 1950.

In 1952, the *De Grasse* was moved permanently to the West Indies trade, sailing from Le Havre and Southampton, in company with another pre-war French liner, the *Colombie* of 1931. It was a short-lived change, however. A year later, she was placed on the sales lists and found a buyer immediately. Canadian Pacific Steamships were in rather desparate need, especially considering the Coronation year traffic to Britain, after losing their *Empress of Canada* to a pierside fire at Liverpool, in January 1953. The *De Grasse* was the perfect replacement, at least temporarily. In very quick

Left *After the war she was rebuilt with one large stack* (courtesy of Moran Towing).

Below *Renamed* Empress of Australia, *the old* De Grasse *now has the Canadian Pacific houseflag on her single buff stack* (J. McNamara).

Fifty Famous Liners

time, the French tricolour was lowered and the British colours hoisted; her name was changed to *Empress of Australia*.

In October 1955, after three seasons on the Liverpool-Montreal run, an advertisement appeared in numerous shipping publications. It read, 'For sale: the passenger liner *Empress of Australia* (British flag). About 19,379 tons gross, British built 1924, Bureau Veritas Special Survey March 1955 for 4 years. Twin screw turbine machinery: oil fired boilers. Speed about 16 knots. Accommodation for 220 first class and 444 Tourist class passengers. In service between UK and Canada. Any enquiries to C W Kellock & Co Ltd, St Mary Axe, London.'

Once again, in rather quick time, she found new buyers, this time under the Italian flag. She was transferred, in February 1956, to the Grimaldi-Siosa Lines, who were actively engaged in the Caribbean migrant trades. Renamed *Venezuela*, she was assigned to a mid-Atlantic service—outwards from Naples, Genoa, Cannes and Barcelona to Teneriffe in the Canaries then across to Guadeloupe, Martinique, La Guaira and Trinidad in the Caribbean. In 1960, she underwent an extensive rebuilding wherein a new flair bow was fitted that

increased her length from 574 feet to 614 feet and her capacity enlarged to 180 first class, 500 tourist class and 800 third class passengers.

Unfortunately, while she surely would have continued for some years, possibly even to her fiftieth, she was stranded on rocks near Cannes, on March 17 1962. Her passengers and crew were taken ashore and a month later, on April 16, she was refloated. The inspections were, however, less than promising. The economics of repairing the 40-year-old liner were impractical. That summer, in late August, she was handed over to the shipbreakers at La Spezia, Italy. It was the end for one of the most enduring French Line ships.

Gross tonnage: 17,707 (1924); 18,435 (1932); 19,379 (1953); 18,567 (1956); 18,769 (1960)
Length overall: 574 feet (1924); 614 feet (1960)
Width: 71 feet
Machinery: Steam turbines, twin screw
Service speed: 16 knots
Capacity: 399 Cabin, 1,712 Third (1924); 536 Cabin, 410 Third (1932); 500 Cabin, 470 Tourist (1947); 220 First, 444 Tourist (1953); 180 First, 500 Tourist, 800 Third (1960)
Built: Cammell Laird & Co, Birkenhead, England, 1924
Demise: Stranded at Cannes, March 17 1962; later scrapped at La Spezia

At La Spezia the grand old lady awaits the scrappers torch.

De Grasse

Berlin

The *Berlin* of 1925 was one of the smaller, more intermediate German passenger ships to be built immediately following the First World War. She represented the moderate pace at which her owners, the North German Lloyd, began to re-emerge as an important transatlantic shipper. Copied to some extent from the larger *Columbus*, the overall design would lead, in less than four years, to the creation of twin superliners, the speed queens *Bremen* and *Europa* of 1929-30. Her German owners and builders could not have suspected, however, that while most other pre-war German liners would have long since disappeared, the former *Berlin* would continue to sail in the mid-1980s, at the time of her sixtieth anniversary.

A. G. Horton-White in his *Ships of the North Atlantic* wrote, 'When the *Berlin* was completed [in September 1925, from the Bremer Vulkan yards], she was rather strangely fitted with reciprocating engines, which were already considered to be past their height of efficiency as motive power for the rapidly soaring requirements of the modern liner, which include stability, more power and greater speed. The *Berlin* is engaged, with other large ships running under the 'Key and Anchor' flag, in their North Atlantic service between Bremerhaven and New York, calling at Southampton and Le Havre en route. She is also occasionally engaged in cruising, mostly to the Northern Capitals.'

Mr Horton-White described the ship's passengers quarters as well. 'The Promenade Deck is enclosed for nearly half its length by glass screens, which extend round the superstructure front on this deck and also on A Deck. A Deck is open for its whole length on each side and extends beyond the Promenade Deck right to the stern; the only deck-house being right aft housing the dog kennels. B Deck is open from beyond the end of the central superstructure right to the stern, which is of the elliptical type.

'The accommodation is of excellent quality and the cabin class has very well fitted staterooms and large public rooms. On the Boat Deck is the Verandah in which large sliding doors can make it open to the deck. Also on this deck is the Florist's Shop and the Radio Station. Most of the rest of the public rooms of this class are on the Promenade Deck. Aft is the Smoking Room and two passages —in which are the Bar and Coffee Kitchen—lead forward to the Library. Forward again of this is the Reading and Writing Room, which is divided by the engine room casings. Next is the large Social Hall and the small Entrance Hall. On C Deck, there is the Dining Saloon, which has a large seating capacity. There is also a Children's Dining Saloon and a Private Saloon.'

The *Berlin* appeared in the news, on November 13 1928, when she rescued 23 survivors from the sinking British passenger ship *Vestris*. In October 1937, she again featured in the headlines when, under rather mysterious circumstances, she was loaded at New York with 6,000 tons of scrap iron and then sailed for

Right *A superb painting of* Berlin. *Note the shadow of the smoke on the superstructure, a lovely artistic touch.*

NORTH GERMAN LLOYD
S.S. "BERLIN"
THE LATEST DE LUXE STEAMER
WITH 1st, 2nd AND 3rd CLASS.

Below *This picture was used in the* New York Herald Tribune *when* Berlin *helped to rescue* Vestris *survivors in 1928.*

Berlin

home waters without passengers. Earlier, just two weeks before, another German liner, the *St Louis*, loaded 3,000 tons of scrap bound for Germany and also sailed eastbound without passengers. It was assumed that these scrap cargoes were bound for the armament factories of Germany and rumours hinted that the ships had also been loaded with consignments of TNT. The *St Louis* was said to have carried 13,000 cases of the explosive, each of them weighing 50 lb. Shortly thereafter, in the fall of 1938, the *Berlin* was laid-up at Bremerhaven and awaiting further assignment.

In July 1939, she was again in service and again in the news. While steaming to Swinemunde to pick up 1,000 Nazi labourers, she had a boiler explosion that killed 15 and injured 18. Travelling without passengers, actual damages to the ship were said to be limited. Soon afterward the *Berlin*, along with most other German passenger ships, was requisitioned by the Germany Navy. She was fitted out as a naval hospital ship, painted overall in white and given large 'red cross' markings, including some that could be illuminated at night. Her actual movements are clouded, but in 1944, she was reassigned to duties as an accommodation ship. A year or so later, on 1 February 1945, she sank after hitting a mine off Swinemunde. She would remain in an underwater, nearly forgotten state for four years.

The Soviets claimed the wreck of the *Berlin* as war reparations and completed their salvage of the vessel in 1949. Renamed *Admiral Nakhimov*, her restoration for further service was a long, often tedious affair, one which lasted eight years. There were complications with the refit, material shortages and

Right *Cruising as the* Admiral Nakhimov (Peter Allan and Gary Glading).

Below left *Captain H. von Truelen (in the centre with the moustache) poses with his officers after bringing in survivors from the* Vestris.

even set-backs such as at least one recorded fire onboard. She resumed sailing in 1957, with her homeport at Odessa, for the Soviet's Black Sea State Shipping Co.

Used mostly on the Black Sea 'express route', sailing between Odessa, Eupatoria, Yalta, Novorossisk, Tuapse, Sochi, Sukhumi, Poti and Batumi, she occasionally detoured on sailings to Africa, the Mediterranean and across the Atlantic to Cuba. In more recent years, however, she was kept close to her homeport.

While the Soviets have disposed of most of their pre-war German passenger tonnage, the *Berlin* might well have proved to be the last of her kind, possibly even preserved as a museum of some kind. Having reached the age of 61, she was an exceptional tribute to her German builders. Most unfortunately, her history ended in tragedy. According to *Time* magazine, on September 15 1986. 'At 10.30 pm, on a mellow summer evening last week [August 31], Captain Vadim Markov ordered his aged passenger liner unmoored in the Black Sea port of Novorossisk The *Admiral Nakhimov* steamed out of the harbor, bound for Sochi, 115 miles to the southeast, with 1,234 souls onboard: a crew of 350 and 884 tourists, all Soviet citizens, enjoying a late season coastal cruise. A band was playing on deck, and some of the passengers danced beneath brilliant lights that reflected off the dark waters.

'Just 45 minutes after it got under way, the pleasure trip turned to disaster. The 41,000-ton Soviet freighter *Pyotr Vasev* suddenly loomed out of the darkness. The *Admiral Nakhimov*'s deck officers warned it off by radio, but the big cargo ship bore down steadily and struck the starboard side of the passenger liner. The ships collided at 11.15 pm. Eight minutes later, the liner sank in 155 ft of water. Many passengers managed to make it into the sea, but hundreds were trapped in crushed or flooded staterooms. As the ship slipped under, nearly 400 people went to their death in one of the worst acknowledged shipping disasters in Soviet history.'

It was a very tragic ending to a long career of the former *Berlin*.

Gross tonnage: 15,286 (1925); 17,053 (1957)
Length overall: 572 feet
Width: 69 feet
Machinery: Steam triple expansion engines, twin screw
Speed: 16 knots
Capacity: 220 First, 284 Second, 618 Third (1925); 257 Cabin, 261 Tourist and 361 Third (1929); no information available on Soviet capacity
Built: Bremer Vulkan Shipyards, Bremen, Germany, 1925
Demise: Sank in the Black Sea, August 31 1986

Berlin

Conte Grande

In the 1920s, Italy's representation on the North Atlantic run to the United States was comprised of three firms: the NGI—the Navigazione Generale Italiana, the Cosulich Line and Lloyd Sabaudo. With increases in passenger traffic, particularly the westward migrant business, all of them began to add new ships. The NGI produced the biggest of all, the 32,500-ton sisters *Roma* and *Augustus*. The Cosulich Line added the 23,900-ton sisters *Saturnia* and *Vulcania*. Hardly to be outdone, Lloyd Sabaudo commissioned two near-sisters, the 24,400-ton *Conte Biancamano*, built by William Beardmore of Glasgow and completed in late 1925, and then the 25,600-ton *Conte Grande*, which was created in home waters, at the Stabilimento Tecnico yards of Trieste. She departed on her maiden trip from Genoa to New York, in April 1928. These were peak times for Italian passenger shipping and would be highlighted, in the early thirties, with the building of the superliners *Rex* for NGI and *Conte di Savoia* for Lloyd Sabaudo. Just prior to their completion, however, Italian transatlantic shipping companies would be merged, under Premier Mussolini's direction, as the co-ordinated and more effective Italian Line, or its more abbreviated name of 'Italia'.

Marine Engineering reported on the creation of the brand new *Conte Grande*, possibly the finest Italian liner of her time. 'In keeping with the progressive policy of the Italian steamship lines, the Lloyd Sabaudo has just placed in its New York-Mediterranean service the 21-knot, twin screw turbine steamship *Conte Grande*, just completed at Trieste. She is a vessel of some 25,600 tons with accommodations for 578 first class, 256 second class, 164 interchangeable passengers and 720 third class passengers, and a crew of 532. Together with the *Conte Biancamano*, these ships will maintain the Company's express service between Genoa, Naples, Gibraltar and New York.

'The *Conte Grande* was launched on June 29 1927, seven months after the laying of her keel. On her official trial, she developed an average speed of 21.83 knots with the propellers turning at 110 revolutions per minute. Her contract speed was 21 knots.

'Cargo is carried in three holds forward, which are served by three cargo hatches and in refrigerated spaces aft which are served by two cargo hatches. Further aft, there is another hatch for handling mails. The holds have a capacity for 3,000 tons of general cargo and mails. Cargo is handled by five 1½ ton, ten 3-ton, one 7-ton and two 10-ton derricks served by steam winches. The refrigerating machinery consists of two Hall machines installed between the propeller shafts aft of the engine room.

'The lifesaving equipment includes 39 lifeboats, two of which are motorboats. The lifeboats are handled under Welin davits while the motorboats are handled by Libani davits.

'The First class accommodations are located on four decks amidships. The second class and second class interchangeable are on five decks and the third

A postcard of Conte Grande *when she was owned by Lloyd Sabaudo.*

class passengers are on four decks forward. The first class accommodations include 23 deluxe cabins and 2 deluxe suites. Each of the deluxe cabins and also the special first class cabins have a private bath. The furnishings, decorations and appointments are on a lavish scale. The public rooms are of special interest as five different decorative themes have been adopted, each carried out by a different architect or artist. A good idea of the manner in which these decorative themes have been handled include the notations that the dining room and lounge are decorated in Etruscan Roman style, the dancing hall is of the Renaissance period, the writing room of the English Elizabethan period, the smoking in Dutch style and the indoor swimming pool, which is exceptionally large, in Japanese style.'

On April 13 1928, *The New York Times* reported, 'Despite adverse weather conditions which have been encountered since leaving Gibraltar 7 April, the new Lloyd Sabaudo liner *Conte Grande* is due to make her first appearance in New York harbor today on schedule and will complete the first half of its maiden voyage in the New York-Mediterranean trade. The general agents for Lloyd Sabaudo said yesterday that the *Conte Grande* will bring something entirely new in the way of sumptuous appointments and interior decorations, excelling anything the company has done in the past. Her swimming pool, for example, done in Japanese style, not only ranks as among the most gorgeous on any liner, but the longest on any liner.'

Well received, immediately popular and most profitable, the *Conte Grande* was affected by the delivery of the speedy *Rex* and *Conte de Savoia*, and just as the Italian Line was organised. Among other changes, her funnels were repainted in the new Italian Line colours of red, green and white, and within a year, by 1933, she began to make sailings to Rio de Janeiro, Santos, Montevideo and Buenos Aires as alternatives to the New York run. Later, there would be some sailings out of the Adriatic as well as a number of cruises. One advertisement, dated December 21 1932, read, '*Conte Grande* cruises to the Mediterranean, Holy Land and Egypt. If you've never seen the Mediterranean, here's the cruise to take! 13 calls in 7 countries... the WHOLE Mediterranean, east and west... on one of the speediest and most luxurious cruise liners, in a month's time, 32 days in all. Or stopover in Europe, returning on any Italian Line sailing at no extra cost. First class $510 up, tourist class $225 up. (On this cruise the entire second class section will be allotted to tourist class.) Optional shore excursions to all ports: Madeira, Gibraltar, Palma de Majorca, Cannes, Genoa, Naples, Piraeus (Athens), Rhodes, Haifa, Alexandria, Naples, Cannes, Gibraltar.'

On May 6 1935, an article in *The New York Times* read, 'The Italian liner *Conte Grande*, which operated in the Company's service between New York and Italy several years ago and more recently between Italian ports and South America, is scheduled to sail from Trieste on 17 May for New

Conte Grande

York by way of Patras, Naples, Palermo, Algiers and Gibraltar, to replace the Company's motorship *Saturnia*, it was learned yesterday in advices from abroad. The *Saturnia* has been requisitioned by the Italian Government for use, it is believed, as a troop transport.'

When Italy entered the Second World War, in the spring of 1940, the *Conte Grande* was at Santos on one of her regular South American sailings. With the declaration of hostilities, she was promptly laid-up at that Brazilian port, with the intention that she would sail eventually for Italian waters. Instead, within a year, in August 1941, she was seized by the Brazilian Government and then continued to remain at Santos. On March 11 1942, the *New York*

At New York with Tice Towing tugs alongside (Loran Graham).

Herald Tribune reported, 'The United States Government has completed a deal with Brazil for the 25,000-ton Italian liner *Conte Grande* and the 16,000-ton former German liner *Windhuk*. These Axis ships have been holed up in Brazilian ports since the war started and subsequently were taken over by the Brazilian Government.' The *Conte*

Another snapshot of Conte Grande, *but this time taken when she was on military service in Naples by one of her wartime crew.*

Grande was assigned to the US Navy and fitted out as the troopship USS *Monticello*; the German *Windhuk* became the trooper USS *Lejeune*.

The *Monticello* began troop service on November 2 1942, when she left New York for Casablanca, to take part in the Allied invasion of North Africa. Following a return to New York, she sailed on Christmas Day, via Norfolk and Panama, for Los Angeles. From the latter port, on January 20, she left for India, calling at Fremantle, Colombo and Bombay en route to Karachi, and at Melbourne and Wellington on return, via the Panama Canal, to New York, where she arrived on 24 April. Following a trip to Oran with a return to Boston, the ship underwent repairs at New York and then sailed on August 21 for Oran. From Africa, she headed for the Panama Canal, thence to San Francisco on October 2, from where she made a round trip to Sydney and another to Honolulu.

Voyages made by the *Monticello* during 1944 were: from San Francisco January 16 to Sydney, Milne Bay and Noumea; from San Francisco March 5 to Noumea, Espiritu Santo, Suva and Tutuila; from San Francisco April 28 to Noumea, Milne Bay, Suva and thence, via the Panama Canal, to New York; from New York July 2 to Liverpool; from Boston September 5 to Cherbourg and Plymouth; from New York October 6 to Marseilles and Oran; and from Newport News November 13 to Gibraltar and Naples.

In 1945, the *Monticello* made these voyages: from New York January 10, February 19 and March 31 to Le Havre and Southampton; from Boston May 10 to Le Havre and the UK; from New York June 8 and July 1 to Le Havre; a voyage to Naples, with a return to Hampton Roads November 27; from New York November 8 to Le Havre and return; from New York to Marseilles with a return on New Year's Day 1946. The *Monticello* subsequently underwent repairs and decommissioning in early 1946, being redelivered to the War Shipping Administration on May 27 at Norfolk.

Laid-up for a year, the *Conte Grande*—along with three under surviving Italian liners, the *Conte Biancamano, Saturnia* and *Vulcania*—were returned to their original owners by the Americans. *Fairplay* noted the *Conte Grande*'s return. 'The passenger liner *Conte Grande* arrived at Genoa from Newport News, on 23 July, after seven years' absence from her home waters. As a matter of fact, she had set out for the last time from Genoa for South America in 1940. The arrival of the liner, the largest vessel in the Italian merchant fleet, can be regarded as a godsend at a moment when a daily increasing amount of shipping is required in connection with the Government's long-range emigration program now under way. A

Conte Grande *restored to peacetime colours* (courtesy of Moran Towing).

Conte Grande

FROM THE MEDITERRANEAN TO NEW YORK
CONTE GRANDE
"ITALIA" FLOTTE RIUNITE · THE SECOND CLASS

great deal of heavy reconditioning and refitting, involving an estimated expenditure of two million Italian lire and requiring not less than three months' work, will have to be carried out before she can take the lead in providing the much-needed emigrant service that is expected of her. On her arrival at Genoa, the liner disembarked 70 passengers, including the wife of the Italian ambassador in Washington.'

Recommissioned in July 1949, the *Conte Grande* had been given new funnels, repainted with a white hull and restyled with far more contemporary accommodation (for 261 First class, 338 cabin class and 780 third class). The grandeur and the opulence that had belonged to this ship in the pre-war years was gone, most of it removed by the Americans when she was rebuilt as a troop transport. Hereafter, she steadily sailed in the South American trades, from Naples, Genoa, Cannes, Barcelona, Lisbon and Dakar to Rio de Janeiro, Santos, Montevideo and Buenos Aires. The only change seems to have

occurred in 1956, when she was temporarily swung on to the New York trade following the loss of the national flagship *Andrea Doria*.

In 1960, just before she was decommissioned, the *Conte Grande* made one migrant voyage out to Melbourne and Sydney under charter to another well-known Italian shipper, Lloyd Triestino. Laid-up for a time, she was handed over to the breakers at La Spezia, on September 7 1961. Her memory remains, surely one of the most glorious of all Italian liners.

Gross tonnage: 25,661 (1928); 23,861 (1942); 23,562 (1949)
Length overall: 665 feet (1928); 667 feet (1949)
Width: 78 feet
Machinery: Steam turbines, twin screw
Speed: 18.75 knots
Capacity: 578 First, 256 Second, 164 Interchangeable, 720 Third (1928); 261 First, 338 Cabin, 780 Third (1949)
Built: Stabilimento Tecnico, Trieste, Italy, 1928
Demise: Scrapped at La Spezia, Italy, 1961

California

In a drawing by artist Worden Wood, they were a trio of passenger liners—the largest yet to be built in the United States—with one tall funnel and all-white hulls. Evidently, during the early phases of construction, plans were changed and the ships modified as twin stackers (the second of which was a dummy) and painted with black hulls. Built by the Newport News Shipbuilding & Drydock Co at Newport News, Virginia, they were completed for the Panama Pacific Line as the *California* in January 1928, the *Virginia* in the following December and then the *Pennsylvania* in July 1929. Carrying two classes of passengers, 384 in first class and 363 in tourist class (onboard the *California*), they were placed on a more unusual service: the North American intercoastal trade between New York and San Francisco with calls en route at Havana, Cristobal, Balboa, Acapulco, San Diego and Los Angeles. In retrospect, they were always, at over 20,300 tons, somewhat too big for that service. Trading was also complicated by the Depression of the early thirties.

In the latter part of 1938, with the inauguaration of President Franklin D. Roosevelt's Good Neighbor Policy and the promotion of trade with South America, the United States Maritime Commission, the Government agency which controlled most American merchant ships, withdrew these three sisters and, after extensive alterations and modernisations (that included the installation of a wider, single funnel), renamed them as the *Uruguay, Brazil* and *Argentina* respectively. The ships were transferred to the American Republics Line, a division of the better-known Moore McCormack Lines, for service between New York, Trinidad, Rio de Janeiro, Santos, Montevideo and Buenos Aires.

In a booklet entitled *The Good Ship SS 'Uruguay'*, author Joseph C. Nunn described the maiden voyage of the former *California*. 'On the maiden voyage of the *Uruguay* to South America, an elaborate reception was held in Montevideo, the capital of the Republic for which the ship was named. On 8 November 1938, at this reception, the President of Uruguay, in the presence of high officials of the American and Uruguayan governments, presented the vessel with a plaque commemorating the first arrival in the country whose name it bore. This plaque was placed in the stairwell bulkhead in the main staircase between Promenade and A Decks. The outstanding citizenry of Montevideo and the Uruguayan Republic were entertained at a dinner onboard given by the United States Maritime Commission and the Moore McCormak Lines, operators of the American Republics Line.

'While in the South American trade, the *Uruguay* made 28 voyages for a total of approximately 350,000 miles. On one occasion [apart from her normal South American itinerary], the vessel made the "Carnival Cruise," putting into Fort Lauderdale, Florida, to pick up sun worshippers and transport them to Rio for the February fiesta of the Cariocas.'

Mr Nunn also described life onboard a liner such as the *Uruguay*. 'The world seemed to be turning toward an easier way of life. The days onboard ship were filled with sunshine and gaiety and laughter. The good things of life were in abundance. Nights were glamorous and one was occupied with dancing

California

in the moonlight and intriguing flirtations. Two luxurious swimming pools and the broad lido decks catered to the devotees of sun and water. The long Promenade decks with their sheltered chairs offered quiet reading for the sedentary. Pre-release moving pictures were shown, being replaced on alternate nights with floor shows presented by talented groups of artists carried solely to contribute to the enjoyment of the passengers. Foreign language instructors and Arthur Murray dancing teachers helped many to pass the hours intellectually and artistically. The cuisine was superb, not being surpassed by the finest shore establishments. Exotic fruits and delicacies from all over the world tempted the palate of the epicure. The entire table service was of silver, and the flash of crystal and the gleam of silver marked the dining room as one of the outstanding memories of the voyage.'

The *Uruguay* was called to war duties in January 1942 and fitted out as a troop transport. Her travels thereafter became quite diverse: out to Australia and New Zealand, transatlantic to such ports as

Left California's *hull takes shape at Newport News Shipbuilding and Dry Dock Company in Virginia.*

Below *Being undocked at Manhattan.*

Liverpool, Swansea, Gourock, Oran, Casablanca and Naples. Her last military sailing, after attaining a record of 263,600 miles steamed and 125,500 wartime passengers, was a transpacific round voyage, in November 1945, from Long Beach to Yokohama and then return to Seattle. One other, quite special occasion during the war took place in November 1944. The *Uruguay* was selected to transport the cadets of the US Military Academy at West Point, New York on their indoctrination cruise and which was to include a stopover at Baltimore for the Army-Navy football classic. In order for the 601 foot long liner to navigate the upper Hudson River, it was necessary to lower the top masts and to lighten the ballast. No other vessel of like tonnage ever accomplished this New York-West Point-Baltimore trip. The *Uruguay* was also the largest vessel at the time to have entered the port of Baltimore.

The *Uruguay*'s conversion was a divided task. At first, she was taken in hand for stripping, cleaning and initial restoration work, in November 1947, by the Todd Shipyards at Erie Basin, Brooklyn, in New York Harbor. That facility was later hit by a strike and consequently the *Uruguay* had to be shifted. Under the guidance of several tugs, she was taken through the narrow Kill van Kull, brought under the Bayonne Bridge and delivered to the Federal Shipyards at Kearny, New Jersey, where the task was completed. Simultaneously, the *Argentina* was converted by Bethlehem Steel, at their 56th Street yard in Brooklyn, and the *Brazil* at the Atlantic Basin Iron Works, also located in Brooklyn.

The *Uruguay* made news on 9 August 1952. In an article in *The New York Times*, the story read, 'Three hundred and twenty-two passengers who sailed Thursday night aboard the Moore-McCormack liner *Uruguay* for South America will have a day of sightseeing in Williamsburg, Virginia, today because the liner bent her propeller on a submerged object shortly after leaving New York. The steamship company announced yesterday that excessive vibration after the ship struck the object indicated that one of the vessel's two propellers was disabled. Rather than risk the comfort of the passengers who had sailed for a pleasure cruise, the liner was ordered to the Newport News Shipbuilding & Drydock Co yard in Newport News, Virginia, for drydocking and repairs.

'While the bent propeller is being replaced, a job

Her old black and white stacks are changed to red, white and blue in 1936.

that is expected to take about twelve hours, passengers will be accommodated in Newport News and Old Point Comfort hotels and treated to a tour of Williamsburg at the steamship company's expense. The *Uruguay* is expected to arrive at the shipyard at 5.00 am today and be off on her way again by midnight. She will be bound for Trinidad, Barbados, Bahia, Rio de Janeiro, Santos, Montevideo and Buenos Aires.'

Unfortunately, the *Uruguay* was soon to leave commercial service forever. On 23 March 1954, *The New York Times* reported, 'Moore McCormack Lines announced yesterday that it is withdrawing the liner *Uruguay* permanently from service and is replacing her with the liner *Brazil*. A side-along-side exchange of stores and ship's equipment will take place Monday in Baltimore.

Fifty Famous Liners

'The *Uruguay* was en route from East Coast ports in South America to Pier 32, Canal Street, New York, when she was diverted to Baltimore. The *Brazil*, now in Todd Shipyards in Brooklyn, will join her there. After discharging passengers and mail at Pennsylvania Railroad Pier 1, the *Uruguay* will load stores directly aboard her replacement, which will resume the regularly scheduled voyage on 1 April, at 5.00 pm.

'The executive vice president of the Moore McCormack Lines said a survey by the line's engineers showed that the *Uruguay* is the least efficient of its three liners. The *Argentina* has remained in service while the *Brazil* has been laid up in the fall and later reconditioned. Another study by the line revealed that passenger service between the United States and South America requires only two vessels to accommodate the traffic. Though the ships can carry 500 passengers, a booking of 385 is considered a good trip. The line said that the *Uruguay* would probably be returned to her US Government owners. Once discharged of passengers and mail, the *Uruguay* will proceed to an anchorage in the Chesapeake with her cargo onboard in anticipation of an end to the docker's strike in New York.'

The *Uruguay* spent nearly a decade in the James River National Reserve Fleet in Virginia and was joined, in 1958, by her sisters, the *Argentina* and *Brazil*. They were replaced by a brand new pair of Moore McCormack liners for the South American and cruise trades. On November 18 1963, *The New York Times* reported, 'Three old Moore McCormack Lines' passengers vessels that once plied the luxury cruise route between the United States and South America have been auctioned off for scrapping. The Maritime Administration has revealed that the apparent high bidders for the over-age sisters *Brazil, Argentina* and *Uruguay* were three scrap metal firms. The *Argentina* was sold to the Peck Transportation & Metal Co for $206,206; the *Brasil* to Portsmouth Salvage Inc for $133,333; and the *Uruguay* to the North American Smelting Co for $180,513.'

Ten months later, on September 6 1964, in *The Trenton Sunday Times*, a large article began with, 'The luxury cruise liner *Uruguay*, once a fashionable floating vacation land and which visited the glamor ports of South America, is now on its last journey—the scrap heap at Fieldsboro. The plush accommodations that once catered to the socially elite are giving way to the cutting torches of the North American Marine Salvage Co on the banks of the Delaware River. It would be hard to recognize the *Uruguay* from her heyday as one of the top names in the Moore McCormack fleet of liners. More than half of the superstructure has been removed and carried to the scrap piles. What is left is marked by peeling paint, falling plaster, debris-filled passageways and rusty decks and hull.

'The scrapyard supervisor explained that the *Uruguay* arrived at the facility on 18 May, and said that it would probably be January or February before the demolition can be completed. Even as he explained the operations, workers finished cutting loose a large section of bulkheads and a crane swung it down to the ground. Other men began cutting it into smaller pieces. The salvage yard was, however, getting more than scrap metal from the former liner, which was bought fully equipped from the US Maritime Commission. On display in the sales room last week were champagne buckets, china from the two dining rooms, furnishings from the Second class dining room, sofas from the lounges, exercise bicycles, reducing equipment, dumbbells and Indian clubs, a large bronze figure, 'The Spirit of the North Sea', which had dressed the First class dining room; the engine room telegraph, cribs, paintings which had hung in the staterooms and an assortment of electrical and plumbing fixtures.'

These were the final days of the former *California*.

Gross tonnage: 20,325 (1928); 20,183 (1938); 20,237 (1947)
Length overall: 601 feet
Width: 80 feet
Machinery: Turbo-electric, twin screw
Speed: 17 knots
Capacity: 384 First, 363 Tourist (1928); 500 First (1947)
Built: Newport News Shipbuilding & Drydock Co, Newport News, Virginia, 1928
Demise: Scrapped at Bordentown, New Jersey, 1964

Above left *Uruguay being prepared for her postwar refit.*

Left *On her way to a Kearny shipyard, the Uruguay passes under railway bridges in Newark Bay.*

California

Statendam

The Holland America Line, the foremost Dutch passenger firm, had established a superb reputation on the North Atlantic. Their ships were so well scrubbed and polished that they were known as 'the Spotless Fleet'. Company directors believed in comfort above all else. They were less concerned with great speed or enormous size or even opulent luxury. The design of their ships was traditional, often even throwbacks to the past. A Company brochure of the mid-thirties echoes this outlook. 'Long before Hollanders became identified with the New World, they were famous as skillful mariners and builders of beautiful, strong, seaworthy ships. For centuries, their vessels have carried explorers and settlers to the farthest corners of the world in order to open up new routes and establish new colonies. Between whatever ports their ships have plied, trade has increased and commerce flourished. The histories of Holland and America have been inseparably linked together ever since the first settlement, Nieuw Amsterdam, was founded on the island of Manhatten over 300 years ago. Slow, picturesque sailing craft have long since given way to swift steamships; but the sea-loving people of the Netherlands have always kept pace with and often led in maritime progress. Today, the ships of the Holland America Line are built and equipped to appeal to all travellers who desire the best that the Old and New Worlds have to offer. The *Statendam*, the *Volendam* and the *Veendam* enjoy an enviable patronage because of their classic design and interior decoration they exemplify a traditional type of beauty, charm and comfort, which cultured people consider indispensable to the fullest enjoyment of a sea voyage.'

The plans for the Company's new flagship, the *Statendam* of the twenties, seemed to be duplicates in fact of an earlier *Statendam*, a liner built at Belfast just as the First World War exploded. She was requisitioned by the British, converted to the trooper *Justica* and became a war loss before the hostilities ended. Hers was a tragically short career. Soon after the war ended, the Dutch turned, rather sensibly, to the same Harland & Wolff builders at Belfast for a replacement, a 'new' *Statendam*. She was laid down in 1921, but thereafter work continued at a sluggish, often interrupted pace.

As this new 29,500-tonner sat on the ways, her owners at Rotterdam were facing problems as well. The transatlantic trade, particularly following the US Government's immigration quotas, had cut deeply into passenger shipping. The era of very lucrative, almost overflowing third class migrant travel was over forever—or so it seemed. Most companies, especially by the mid-twenties, were far more cautious, hesitant almost. Certainly, the conservative Dutch were thinking twice. The *Statendam* was launched, already well off schedule, on September 11 1924, but then, once again, almost shunted aside. Nearly three years passed, with little happening, when it was decided to tow her to the Netherlands for completion. A unique decision in shipbuilding at the time, it almost represented the strides made by Dutch shipyards, who could now accommodate and complete such a vessel. She arrived at the Wilton-Fijenoord yards at Schiedam, on April 13 1927. Within two years, by the spring of 1929, she would be ready for commercial service.

The *New York Herald Tribune* recorded her maiden arrival at New York, on April 20 1929. 'The trim, spotless *Statendam*, pride of the Holland America Line, reached here yesterday afternoon on her first voyage across the Atlantic. Starting in service just in time to serve the summer tourist trade, which.

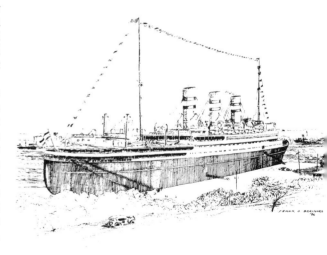

Built just before World War 1, the 35,000 ton Statendam *was renamed* Justica *and sunk during the conflict. This is an artist's impression of her. She is frequently confused with the* Statendam *completed in 1929, a slightly smaller vessel.*

promises to be larger this year, she holds forth in advertisement in the latest tricks to tempt the Europe-bound. Her 30,000 tons have been shaped primarily for comfort, the ship boasting of no exceptional speed, but promising the newest luxuries that have been devised for the Americans, who seek relaxation abroad. With the City authorities establishing a precedent by giving official welcome to new craft under any flag but that of the United States, Captain Piet van den Heuvel was turned into a second Henry Hudson. It was 320 years ago that the Englishman brought the *Half Moon* through the Narrows and the welcome committee of the Mayor insisted that the master of the *Statendam* pretend to be a descendant of the old explorer, who was in the service of the Dutch.

'With the harbor giving a bit of greeting to her, the *Statendam* pushed through to her Hoboken pier. There she will remain over the weekend, to be the scene of almost constant festivities as one party follows another to introduce the ship to New York. The ship's engines, despite their newness, were opened to 19 knots on one part of the trip. The seas were heavy most of the voyage, but the pasengers were unanimous in saying that there was a minimum of discomfort from the high waves.'

The new *Statendam* was a four-class liner: 510 in first class, 344 in second class, 374 in tourist class and 426 third class. Her first class quarters were, as to be expected, the most noteworthy. The main lounge resembled a state ballroom from a French chateau. Panelled, carved oak walls extended two decks high and were embellished with magnificent, hand-loomed Gobelin tapestries, subdued paintings, heavy maroon velvet draperies and richly wrought bronze lighting fixtures. In this opulent setting, gracefully designed walnut and cane Louis XIV chairs and settees, upholstered in handsomely patterned cut velvet, were grouped about mottled marble top tables. Dances and special concerts were given here daily for the pleasure of the passengers. The smoking room, adjoining the bar, was nothing short of baronial in its subdued splendour. The architecture was masculine, with elaborately panel-

led walls of carved and inlaid oak hung with superb tapestries, chairs and tables that corresponded, ebony pillars, polished brass fixtures, a dome and windows of old stained glass, and an imposing fireplace of veined black marble and coloured tile over which hung a fine marine painting. The dining room, which could seat over 400 passengers at one sitting, was classically decorated with ivory coloured mirrored walls relieved by gold leaf ornaments, pastel murals and an impressive hand-loomed tapestry, mahogany chairs upholstered in figured

rose velour and a regal carpet of red rose and pink. The indoor swimming pool was constructed almost entirely of Delft tile. Dozens of frosted glass chandeliers in the ceiling flooded a soft, soothing light over the pool and the surrounding terrace. A constant flow of preheated salt water kept the supply fresh and at a comfortable temperature. The sixteen deluxe cabins were decorated in brocaded silk walls complemented with mahogany wainscoting and furniture. Heavy velvet drapes could separate the sleeping area from the sitting room, trunk room and

124

Left An artist's impression of the post-war Statendam, *dated 1928.*

Right An advertisement for cruises on Statendam *published on March 20, 1938.*

Left Statendam *arriving at New York on April 19, 1929 at the end of her maiden voyage.*

IDEAL
SPRING CRUISES

For a perfect Spring tonic
cruise on the Palatial Spotless Fleet Liner

S.S. STATENDAM

New, Modern, Air-Conditioned Dining Salon

MAR. 30

12 DAYS
$157 UP

visiting **Port au Prince (Haiti), Kingston (Jamaica), Havana and Nassau**

EASTER CRUISE · BERMUDA-HAVANA
APRIL 15 · 8 DAYS · $107.50 UP

Famous cuisine and service, Gymnasium and Turkish Baths, two swimming pools, two dance orchestras.

●●●●●●●●●●●●●●●●●●●●●●●●

ALSO 4 SPECIAL CRUISES TO
BERMUDA
S.S. VOLENDAM
MARCH 26 · APRIL 2 · 9 · 16

2½ Days in Bermuda   Docks right at St. George's

●●●●●●●●●●●●●●●●●●●●●●●●

Ship your hotel throughout   **Consult Your Travel Agent, or**

Holland America Line   MAR 20 1938

29 Broadway, N.Y.   Phone: BOwling Green 9-5600

wardrobe/luggage area.

The *Statendam* ran Holland America's express service, between Rotterdam, Southampton, Boulogne and New York, and went cruising in the off-season. As examples, her 11-day Christmas-New Year's cruise of 1935 called at five Caribbean ports and was priced from $132, and her 28-day 'Springtime in Europe' cruise of 1939 (to North Africa, the French Riviera, Spain, Portugal and Northern Europe) had minimum fares that began at $410 First class and $290 Tourist class.

The *Statendam* made headline news on at least three occasions during the 1930s. On April 4 1931, *The New York Times* reported, 'With the higher tide this evening and the assistance of six tugs, the Holland America liner *Statendam*, which grounded Saturday on South Bramble Shoal, off Cowes, was refloated shortly after 7.30 this evening. The liner was undamaged and after shipping a few hundred tons of fresh water headed for New York early tonight. According to her usual practice, she anchored Saturday in Cowes Roads to embark passengers in Southampton, and 58 boarded her from a tender. The weather was foggy, and when the liner weighed anchor and began to swing around to continue her voyage, she grounded in the mud.'

On June 24 1935, *The Herald Tribune* recorded her delay at New York. 'Two ocean liners arrived here yesterday, slightly delayed by heavy fog. The Holland America liner *Statendam* had lost her way, cautiously picking her way through a fishing fleet. Meanwhile, the Cunard-White Star *Britannic* had slipped by within hailing distance of a Coast Guard patrol boat, which was in grim attendance of a suspected rum runner forty miles east of Nantucket. The *Statendam* arrived, a full day off schedule, off Quarantine during the night, started up the Bay before 7.00 am and then slowing up off the Statue of Liberty to take on the boarding officers of the Customs and Immigration Services. The ship landed her 165 passengers soon after 8.00 am. She will sail for Europe tomorrow with a capacity list of 1,300 passengers.'

Several months later, on November 3 1935, the Dutch flagship was again featured in a news story. 'Less than three weeks ago, shipping men in New York expressed anxiety over the outcome of Mediterranean cruises scheduled for the winter, and since that time five of the most important of these have been either cancelled outright or altered to suit the disturbed ports in the Mediterranean. As a result of war scares, the Holland America Line announced yesterday that the fifth of these, the *Statendam*'s cruise, would not go to the Mediterranean at all. The ship, which was to leave New York on 6th February, had 110 advance bookings two months ago. At the end of last week, the bookings had dropped to 31. The *Statendam* would be diverted instead to the West Indies, making 9 cruises ranging in length from 5 to 18 days.'

The same story continued, 'The first cruise to be cancelled was that of the *Columbus*. The North German Lloyd announced cancellation two weeks ago and said the *Columbus* would make a cruise to South America instead of the Mediterranean. Later, the Hamburg American Line changed the itinerary of the world cruise liner *Reliance*, routing her around Africa and to Bombay instead of through Suez. Canadian Pacific held out until the last week on two cruises of the *Empress of Australia* and the new *Empress of Britain*. The latter, scheduled to make a world cruise through the Mediterranean and Suez, will now call at South African ports and pick up her itinerary at Bombay. The *Australia* has dropped her Mediterranean-South Africa cruise altogether and will substitute a series of West Indies cruises instead.'

Most unfortunately, the *Statendam* was laid-up at Holland America's Wilhelminakade Terminal at Rotterdam, in December 1939, and caught by the invading Nazi armies in the following May. She was lost completely, the total destruction of a superb liner. Caught in a crossfire, she was hit with bombs, caught fire and then burned for as many as five days. That August her wreckage—the blackened corpse of the former national flagship—was taken to the Hendrik Ido Ambacht to be scrapped. Her remains found their way to Nazi munition factories.

Gross tonnage: 29,511
Length overall: 697 feet
Width: 81 feet
Machinery: Steam turbines, twin screw
Speed: 19 knots
Capacity: 510 First, 344 Second, 374 Tourist, 426 Third
Built: Harland & Wolff Ltd, Belfast, Northern Ireland, 1921-24; completed by Wilton-Fijenoord Shipyards, Schiedam, The Netherlands, 1927-29
Demise: Burnt out at Rotterdam, May 14 1940, then scrapped

Fifty Famous Liners

Hikawa Maru

'The Orient-Seattle service of the Nippon Yusen Kaisha is to be reinforced with three motorliners, the *Hikawa Maru, Hiye Maru* and *Heian Maru*. When they are all completed, the present vessels on this route will be transferred to other services and the *Siberia Maru* and *Korea Maru*, now engaged on the Orient-San Francisco route, will join the new motor vessels in order to improve the Orient-Seattle service. This route commences at Hong Kong and terminates at Seattle, with calls at Moji, Yokohama and Victoria', so reported *The Motor Ship* in May 1930.

'The first of these ships, the *Hikawa Maru*, has already run sea trials and will be put into service in early May. The vessel was laid down on 9 November 1928 and launched on 29 September 1929. The *Hiye Maru* will be completed in July and the *Heian Maru* in November.

'The special feature of this ship, the *Hikawa Maru*, is the passenger accommodation. In order to improve the service, the NYK Line decided to equip her as a cabin class passenger vessel, with the Tourist cabin class and Steerage accommodations combined [76 first class, 69 tourist class, 186 third class], which is a new arrangement for this company. Various public rooms and spacious promenades are provided for passengers, whilst the ship also carries a large amount of cargo, so that the conflicting requirements of a cargo ship and a luxurious passenger ship seem to have not been sacrificed in order to ensure that the vessel may be one of the most up-to-date and efficient cargo carriers.

'The public rooms for cabin class passengers are situated on the bridge deck and upper deck amidships. The dining salon has a lofty dome at the centre and is in the modern French style. The walls are wainscotted with grained wood, walnut pilasters with nickel-bronzed motifs and silvered shades, on which luminous appliances in silvered bronze are fitted. All the furniture is of walnut. A staircase abaft the dining saloon leads up to the entrance hall on the bridge deck. The walls are panelled in sycamore varnished in soft shades, the wing ceilings are of painted panels surrounded with gilt fillets, and a well lighted glass dome with decorated frames is in the centre. The reading and writing room on the port side of the main entrance is wainscotted in lemon tree. The smoking room is decorated in modern French style with palisander wood and walnut. A cosy nursery is situated near the dining saloon and is provided with two dining tables. The sides of the lounge and the smoking room are allotted for the cabin class passengers' promenade and dancing space, the front and forward sides being enclosed with Beclawat sliding windows. The public rooms for the tourist cabin class passengers comprise a dining room in the Louis XVI style, a lounge in the Adam style and a smoking room in the Spanish style. A large dining saloon, a lounge and a smoking room are provided for the steerage passengers, who are much more comfortably berthed than in former ships.

'The cabin class accommodation is arranged on the upper deck amidships and on the bridge deck. The en suite rooms, consisting of a bedroom, a sitting room and a toilet room, were designed by Messrs Kawashima, the well known decorators and upholsterers of Kyoto, in modern Japanese style with specially rich upholstery. Other staterooms comprise two single-berth cabins with private toilet rooms, one two-berth cabin with a private toilet room, six three-berth cabins with private toilet rooms, six single-berth, six two-berth and 12 three-berth cabins. All are spacious and are panelled with specially thick plywood in order to make each cabin soundproof. Cot bedsteads, wardrobes, washbasins

Left *An NYK postcard of* Hikawa Maru.

Right *The* Hikawa Maru *as a hotel and museum ship at Yokohama* (courtesy of Yoshitatsu Fukawa).

with hot and cold running water supply, folding tables and chairs and electric radiators are provided. The 69 cabin tourist class passengers are accommodated in eight two-berth, six three-berth and nine four-berth cabins, all washbasins having a cold fresh running water supply. The 186 steerage passengers are berthed in 20 four, six or eight berth cabins on the forward part of the upper deck and second deck.'

The *Hikawa Maru* and her sisters sailed in uninterrupted commercial service until the dark days of the Second World War. In 1941 she was requisitioned by the Imperial Japanese Navy and refitted as a wartime hospital ship. She managed, through the most incredible good fortune, to be the only deep-sea Japanese liner to survive the hostilities intact as well as being the largest member of the greatly reduced Japanese merchant marine. She was used, however, for two years beginning in 1945, as a US transport on transpacific service. She was returned to the Japanese in 1947, who, in their devastated state at the time, had little alternative but to restore the former liner as a freighter.

On October 1 1951, the *Herald Tribune* ran a story on this most special Japanese vessel. 'Although Japan has not resumed its deep-sea passenger service, she has a first-class passenger liner in operation today as a freighter. She is the *Hikawa Maru*, here [in New York] on her first visit. Of 11,622 gross tons, she is Japan's sole surviving liner of a large and modern pre-war fleet. She is owned by Nippon Yusen Kaisha, for whom she is operating on a monthly service between Japan and New York. The spick-and-span public rooms and the well-appointed A Deck passenger staterooms aboard the *Hikawa Maru* bely her humble role as a cargo vessel, a tour of inspection aboard the vessel yesterday, at Pier 17, Joralemon Street, Brooklyn, showed. She is due to sail at 8.00 am today for Boston.

'Captain Oamu Sakomoto is proud of his ship and believes she will soon be placed in regular passenger service between Japan and Seattle. He led the tour through the vessel's unused and locked-up public rooms. A grand piano, once the main feature of the ship's lounge, was thrown overboard by Japanese Navy officers when they took over the ship in the early days of the War. The Italian fireplace remains, quite fortunately.

'There are seventeen men in the purser's department aboard the *Hikawa Maru*, another factor which suggests that she will not remain a freighter for long. Her crew and officers number 99. The motorship's passenger cabins below A Deck have been stripped and are now used for carrying packages, but they could be restored quickly and inexpensively, Captain Sakomoto said. The *Hikawa Maru* will return to New York next week after ceremoniously delivering 1,000 paper carp. The carp, representing fortitude and the symbol of boyhood in Japan, were sent to Philadelphia by Japanese school children in return for a model of the Liberty Bell sent recently to Japan.'

In 1953, it was finally decided to reactivate the ship for Pacific passenger service. Her place on the

Fifty Famous Liners

New York run was then taken by several brand new 12-passenger freighters, some of the first large merchant vessels to be built in Japan since the early forties. On May 28, *The New York Times* wrote, 'The Japanese freighter *Hikawa Maru* is nearing her homeland for extensive reconditioning as a passenger ship and will be operated in the United States-Japan trade, it was learned yesterday. Scheduled to

A close up stern view of Hikawa Maru (courtesy of Yoshitatsu Fukawa).

re-enter service at the end of July, the 536 ft motorship will be the first large Japanese vessel to return to the passenger trade since the start of World War 2. She will run between Yokohama, Osaka and Kobe and the West Coast ports of Portland, Seattle and Vancouver. The vessel, which was employed on that run in the 1930s, will be fitted with passenger accommodations for 34 travellers in first class and 200 persons in third class. The reduction in passenger capacity [from her pre-war standard] will result in larger staterooms from those she had in pre-war days. First class rates will range from $350 to $450. Third

class rates will be divided into two categories: $290 for the equivalent of a pre-war second class berth and $280 the regular third class accommodations. The vessel's conversion for passenger use will not reduce her cargo capacity, according to the NYK Line. Present plans are to keep her on regularly-scheduled freight services. She is slated to make five round trips this year. The *Hikawa Maru* made several appearances in local waters (New York). The last one was in February 1952, when she was one of five cargo ships assigned to the Company's New York run.'

Once employed in transpacific passenger service, the *Hikawa Maru* made further news. The *Marine Digest* of January 12 1957 reported, 'NYK Line's *Hikawa Maru* ran a tight race with time to win the 8th Annual Golden Horseshoe, presented each year by the *Marine Digest* to the first vessel of the new year to enter and discharge foreign cargo at the Port of Seattle. The *Hikawa Maru* tied-up at Pier 50, at 8.00 am on 2 January. Fred Olsen's *Buffalo* arrived on New York's Eve, just 20 minutes too early to qualify, and General Steam's *Lagos Michigan*, which arrived on 1 January, unfortunately, came in empty. As well as inbound cargo, the *Hikawa Maru* brought 95 passengers to Seattle. Captain Sawada, who accepted the award for the NYK Line, made his first trip to Seattle, in 1932, as third officer of NYK's *Kaga Maru*.'

The *Hikawa Maru* was not a huge success as a post-war passenger ship. Her profits, at least from the passenger side, did little to arouse the directors and accountants at the NYK Line home office. While there were rumours of some new post-war Japanese liners for transpacific service, none of these plans ever left the drawing board. The Port of Seattle especially mourned the loss of the *Hikawa Maru*. On July 2 1960, in the *Seattle Post-Intelligencer*, a tribute to the ship was written. 'So in September, the *Hikawa Maru* will write its farewell in a long wake on Puget Sound. She will go with memories and there will be no goodbye whistle salute from another passenger liner coming in past Dungeness Spit; no waves from sourdoughs and tourists lining the rail of an Alaska Line ship slanting past Point Wilson toward a Seattle pierside welcome. For the *Hikawa Maru* will be the last of the luxury passenger vessels to sail out of Puget Sound on a regular basis. They are now all gone from Puget Sound—the ships that once spoke the *Hikawa*

along the lonely sea trails of the wide Pacific. Gone are the President liners, the P&O packets, the gleaming white Canadian Pacific *Empresses*. A China hand remembers the *Hikawa* lying off Customs Jetty in the filthy stream of the Whangpoo at Shanghai; the sampans scurrying about as the anchor comes up dripping mud into the yellow water. Soft warm nights on the decks of the *Hikawa* cruising through the Inland Sea of Japan are among the other memories of the China hand. In the ancient teaport of Shimdzu, tiny women loaded bales of tea from lighters. The China hand remembers wallowing through towering waves of a typhoon's fringe east out of Honshu; sake and sukiyaki and paper hats at the Captain's dinner at the entrance to San Juan Strait before docking at Vancouver. So in September, the *Hikawa* will go forever. The seagulls will wheel and cry along the keel foam and Seattle will say goodbye to the last of the deep-water passenger liners.'

In a letter sent to Frank Braynard, dated February 14 1961, the conversion of this historic ship was outlined. 'For the past week or so, the *Hikawa Maru* has been in Mitsubishi Drydock No 1, which is located directly outside my office windows. As I mentioned in my previous letter, she is being converted to a hotel ship. The local *Shipping & Trade News*, for 20 January, stated that NYK, Yokohama City and Kanagawa Prefecture (a governmental division similar to the English county) have formed a corporation which they have called Hikawa Maru Tourism Co Ltd, with a paid up capital stock amounting to 110 million yen. As the work is now underway in earnest, it may be assumed that this is something more than just a mere pipedream. The area around the dock is, in fact, beginning to resemble a shipbreaking yard or junk dealer's lot, what with all the furniture, bathroom fixtures and other similar items that have been strewn about. Such is, however, the job of converting a ship to a youth hostel.

'As to what they are doing to the ship, a few notes may be in order. They have removed the propellers, tail and line shafting, and the lower portion of the rudder, and are going to close up the shaft openings with plate. These alterations have been made for the obvious purpose of reducing maintenance expense and realizing some scrap value for materials. Furthermore, much of the miscellaneous engine

A brochure issued by NYK in 1931 featuring Hikawa Maru *and her sisters* Hiye Maru *and* Heian Maru.

room equipment is being removed. The fate of those marvellous old Burmeister & Wain main engines is not known to me at this time. They are nightmares of cam-shafts, push rods, lubricators, rocker arms and all the other pieces that one might find on thirty-year-old double-acting air-injection four-stroke deisel engines. The furniture has been removed from the second class staterooms and from many of the rooms of the officers and crew in preparation for conversion to youth dormitories. Some joiner bulk-heads have been removed for the same reason. Changes are undoubtedly forthcoming in her dining saloons and galley. Outwardly, she will apparently be little changed, although her hatches are being plated over in the cheapest possible way and several cargo winches have been removed. Her boot-topping line has been lowered about 2 ft, reflecting in part the amount of weight being removed, and her

bottom is being painted for only about 3 ft below this line, reflecting the air of austerity forthcoming as the conversion and the new career proceed. Probably the most noteworthy and, if you will, poignant thing about the ship was a sign, in English, on her engine room black-board—"October 1960—The End—*Hikawa Maru*—Port of Yokohama".'

Most forunately, at the time of writing, the *Hikawa Maru* remains in use as a hotel and museum at Yokohama.

Gross tonnage: 11,622
Length overall: 536 feet
Width: 66 feet
Machinery: Burmeister & Wain diesels, twin screw
Speed: 17 knots
Capacity: 76 First, 69 Tourist, 186 Third (1930); 34 First, 200 Third (1953)
Built: Yokohama Dock Co, Yokohama, Japan, 1930

Exochorda

This author (FOB) believes that the *Exochorda* and her three sisters were among the most beautiful little liners ever built. In a day when the cruiser stern was 'the thing', they had superb counter sterns of the old style. When companies were experimenting with all kinds of odd smokestacks or even no stacks, they were built with a perfect, beautifully-raked stack of large enough proportions, both lengthwise and athwartships, to fit to perfection their sleek hulls. Their superstructures were large enough, their masts just right and their bows strong and clean. Of the four, the *Exochorda* had the longest and most interesting history.

American Export Lines began after World War 1 as one of several dozen new companies using war-built ships. They were first known simply as the Export Steamship Corporation. While most of the others died, they established firm routes on the run between east coast ports in the United States and Mediterranean ports. They expanded into the passenger trade with several excellent conversions of Hog Island-type cargo ships. Then, in July 1928, they announced funds borrowed from the US Government under the new Jones-White Act. The four-ship proposal was the first new ship project for deep-sea liners under this new law. Accommodation for 100 passengers with ample public rooms and deck space would be provided, it was announced. The design work was done by Donald & Sharp. The Sharp of this firm was the same George Sharp in our chapter on the *Minnesota* of 1907 in *Fifty Famous Liners 2*. He will also be alluded to in the chapter on the first nuclear passenger cargo ship, the NS *Savannah* (see p 208).

In due course the bids were opened and early in 1929 the preliminary contract was awarded to the New York Shipbuilding Corporation, Camden, New Jersey. The propelling machinery was to be one set of three-unit, triple-expansion, condensing turbines, developing 6,300 shaft horsepower and operating a single propeller through reduction gearing. Steam was to be supplied at 325 lb per square inch working pressure at 150 degrees superheat by four oil-fired watertube boilers. In the summer of this same year a $6,675,000 loan from the US Shipping Board was approved and on August 31 1929, the contract was awarded.

It was traditional with American Export that their ship names all began with 'Ex'. First of the four new liners was called the *Excalibur*, and she was christened by Mrs Herbert Hoover, wife of the President, on August 5 1930. The *Exochorda* was next, followed by the *Exeter* and then *Excambion*. Part of the innovative Sharp design permitted a number of staterooms that would have been inside to be listed as outside cabins. There were four semi-private verandah decks each with five large windows. Five to six cabins faced on to these decks and therefore could all be called outside cabins. Shipyard talk called the scheme the 'saw-tooth plan'. It would be widely copied by other liners built at this period. Passenger capacity was 152, all first class. Each ship could carry 6,000 tons of cargo. Line publicity called them fast and their contract speed of 14 knots could be substantially bettered. There were four passenger decks. The sun deck offered space to walk beside the three lifeboats on either side. The promenade deck featured two one-and-a-half deck high public rooms—the lounge-library forward, and the

An accurate model was photographed over an ocean scene to get this builder's idea of what Exchorda *would look like at sea.*

smoking room aft, extraordinary rooms for a ship of this size. Each had attractive domed ceilings. A large foyer extending the width of the ship on A Deck had a well that looked down into the dining room, making the latter have the 'feel' of a two-deck room. All passengers could dine at one time. Many of the earliest brochures stated that all the staterooms were 'outside', but this was not so. There were a number of so-called Bibby-type rooms that could be called 'outside' because they had long corridors stretching to a porthole, but a few cabins were definitely inside rooms. Perhaps the fact that they opened on to a long athwartship hall with a port at either end led to the 'all outside' claim. They were all very comfortable cabins, however, and a large number of them had showers or tub baths.

The new 'Four Aces' as they were called made long cruises (42 to 45 days) from New York to the Mediterranean. With many of the luxuries of most great liners they were at the same time small, yacht-like steamers with a pleasant intimacy. Their stops at Mediterranean ports were longer than those made by the ordinary liners on luxury cruises, quite often overnight and even at times stretching to two or three days, a real plus for the serious traveller. All four of the ships were in service by late summer of 1931. Rates for a 43-day cruise began at $460. Much less

expensive cruises were also offered by American Export on their World War 1 type cargo ships, with a 60 day trip costing $265 and up.

Life on the 'Four Aces' was several notches above ordinary cargo ship travel, with huge menus like the finest liners offered. One from the *Exochorda* was published in a marine journal in April 1934. It listed 18 types of hors d'oeuvres. Then there were four types of soup and a choice of five kinds of fish. Entrees listed were: 'Tourne—Do Waldorf, Mock-Turtle Ragout, Legume, Broccoli, Sauce Holland-aise.' Then there were seven kinds of cold buffet offerings, followed by three choices in the way of roasts with various sauces and dressings. Five kinds of vegetables came next, followed by five types of potatoes. There were four salads available with a wide variety of dressings. Next California peaches, then seven types of desserts and six cheeses, plus nine more things like dates, figs, mints, raisins, nuts etc.

Advertisements in 1934 stressed the company as 'the great American fleet in the Mediterranean', and emphasised 'first class only, no second, no third'. Very elaborate brochures were done each year using heavy, coated stock and many colours. The deck plans were shown in a three-dimensional manner, far more elaborate than many regular transatlantic liners offered. A swimming pool was added on the forward end of the promenade deck, very large for the day. Aft on the same deck a large deck tennis court was set up. The opening double-page spread of the November 1934 folder featured a large, coloured painting of one of the 'Four Aces' by Worden Wood,

Exochorda

The launching of Exochorda *at Camden, New Jersey on October 20, 1930.*

noted Shipping Board artist who had been so well known for his *Leviathan* paintings.

The Spanish Civil War in 1936 forced the elimination of the stop at Malaga and a call at the Azores was substituted on the outbound voyage. On return trips the port of Piraeus was substituted for Palma. The *Exochorda* was the first ship to make these new stops.

Still another fine Worden Wood painting was featured in the 1937 'Yankee Cruises' brochure. It showed the *Excalibur* at anchor off Naples, with Vesuvius in the background. Each ship made five voyages a year. Those done by the *Exochorda* left New York on February 1, March 29, May 24, September 13 and November 8 in that year. Then World War 2 came and the Mediterranean became a battle ground. On December 20 1941, American Export suspended its steamship services with neutral Portugal and the era of the original 'Four Aces' ended. The *Excambion* picked up the staff of the company's Lisbon office and brought them home.

Well before this the *Exochorda* had been taken over by the US Navy. She completed her last voyage

as a merchant ship on October 26, 1940, bringing in 186 passengers and $3,000,000 in gold. American Export chartered the Ward Line's *Siboney* to replace her and her 128 officers and crew were transferred to this slightly-smaller vessel. It was made known that the *Exochorda* would be used as a submarine tender. She was well suited for this on account of her large and unusually fine machine shop and because she had two fuel tanks each with a capacity of 2,500 tons of oil. She was converted at the Todd Shipyards plant in Hoboken, New Jersey and on December 27 1940, was commissioned as the USS *Harry Lee* (APA 10). She was put into service as an armed combat transport carrying Marine Combat teams to Cuba and the Virgin Islands. After several engine breakdowns and a wide variety of assignments the all-grey troopships won her most notable awards in the invasion of Scoglitti, Sicily. Captain J. G. Pomeroy was given the Legion of Merit for having 'valiantly fought his ship through enemy bombings and

134

Renamed Harry Lee, Exochorda *enters service as a troopship.*

embarked troops and equipment to bring the ship through the engagement unscathed'. From then on the *Lee* served in the Pacific. She participated in the invasions of Tarawa, the Kwajalein Atoll, and Guadalcanal. She helped in the recapture of Guam. Then she served in the Philippine campaign, making landings of both troops and equipment in the Lingayen and Leyte Gulfs and surviving many attacks by both suicide planes and warships. She served as a hospital ship during the invasion of Iowa Jima. She earned six battle stars in the Asiatic-Pacific Theatre and one on the African-European-Middle Eastern Theatre. The *Harry Lee* was decommissioned on May 9 1946. Her 1928 construction subsidy had been well earned.

But her career was not over. She was bought by the Turkish Government, renamed *Tarsus* and operated for the next 15 years on Mediterranean routes, across the Atlantic, and even on Caribbean cruises out of New York. More lifeboats were added and her capacity tripled. She became the flagship of the Turkish Maritime Lines which included six other former American liners at the time. Folders issued were joyous in their praise of how fine things were aboard the now-ageing liner: 'One feels completely comfortable and delightful to travel in the first class cabin of SS *Tarsus*. This single bed cabin is beautifully furnished and modernized; having every means of heating and air conditioning systems.'

She was sent to New York with passengers early in 1950. Arriving again in the summer she made a special 'Holy Year Voyage' to Marseilles, Genoa, Piraeus and Istanbul, carrying pilgrims to Rome for as little as $140. She came over again in the autumn and special folders were put out for her return trip, with prices as low as $140 for dormitory space. First class cost $396 all the way to Istanbul. In 1953 she made a 30-day cruise of the Mediterranean as a trade fair ship, showing Turkish fashions and boosting tourism. Students from the Turkish Institute of Arts and Design sailed aboard to model up-to-date adaptations of ancient garments. In 1954 she brought this exhibition to New York, with 500 Turks

aboard as part of a goodwill mission. Some 8,000 New Yorkers visited the ship. In 1955 she again came to America bringing 280 tourists. Finally in 1960 she made her last arrival, this time on charter to Fiesta Cruise Lines. She offered a series of five-day cruises, pioneering in the short cruise field. Seven-day cruises could be had for $110. She ran into several problems with the Coast Guard over safety and was also stopped several times by creditors seeking to collect bills.

Back in Turkey in December 1960 her end came in a sad way, especially for a ship which had survived so many battles. She was at anchor in the Bosphorous, having just come out of a shipyard after a refit. There was a collision nearby between two tankers, a Yugoslavian ship named *Peter Zoranic* and the tanker *World Harmony*. Burning oil drifted down on her and set her afire, killing a number of those aboard. She lay listing for months and was eventually scrapped.

Gross tonnage: 8,700 as US ship, 9,359 as Turkish ship
Length overall: 475 feet
Width: 61 feet 7 inches
Machinery: Triple expansion turbine
Speed: 14 knots, increased to 17
Capacity: 152 as US ship; raised to 189 First, 66 Second, 210 Third
Built: New York Shipbuilding Corporation, Camden, New Jersey, 1930
Demise: Burned in Turkey 1960, scrapped

Fifty Famous Liners

L'Atlantique

She was called a 'first cousin' to the exceptional *Ile de France*. She was by far the largest and the grandest liner ever intended for the South American trade. If the French Line had extraordinary acclaim on the North Atlantic, she would give her owners, the Compagnie de Navigation Sud-Atlantique, the competitive edge in the South Atlantic. Ordered from the famed Penhoet shipyards at St Nazaire, the builders of the aforementioned *Ile de France* and other notable French liners, she was launched, quite appropriately, as the *L'Atlantique*, on April 15 1930. Her completion was scheduled for the following summer, with her maiden voyage beginning at Bordeaux, on 29 September, and sailing to Rio de Janeiro, Santos, Montevideo and Buenos Aires. It would appear that her only shortcomings were her external appearance and the onset of the economic Depression. As built, she looked top heavy, almost clumsy, and later, in an effort to enhance her appearance, her three funnels were heightened. As for the Depression, her passenger loads were assuredly affected by the bleak times, with the possible exception of westbound loads in Third class where migrants were seeking new lives in Latin America.

Tragically, her life was extremely brief. In less than two years, she was a loss. On January 5 1933, *The New York Times* reported in a major news story of the day that, 'The luxurious new 42,500-ton *L'Atlantique*, the twelfth largest ship afloat and the pride of France's South Atlantic fleet, was wrecked by fire in the English Channel, and it was feared that a score of the more than 200 men of the crew who were aboard drowned or perished in the flames which swept the ship from stem to stern. The others were rescued by four freighters [the *Achilles, Erato, Ford Castle* and *Ruhr*] which responded to the only call for help which the wireless operator was able to send out before he was overcome by smoke.

'The liner carried no passengers, as it was being sailed from Bordeaux to Le Havre for overhauling before resuming its run to South America, but the fire apparently started in a first class stateroom. Captain Rene Schoofs said it was discovered there at 3.30 am, and before the crew would organise effective measures against it, the fire had spread through a section of first class cabins, apparently making its way along the electric wire conduits. Just before six o'clock, it was obvious that the *L'Atlantique*, ablaze from end to end, was beyond saving, and the order was given to abandon ship. One of the first boats lowered met with disaster when the davit ropes broke, throwing seven or eight men into the sea, where they were drowned. Others, according to the Captain, particularly the boiler-room crew, stayed at their posts until too late to save themselves from asphyxiation, and still others were trapped by swift-spreading flames.

'Captain Schoofs, the last to leave the ship, jumped overboard half dressed, following seven or eight of his crew who had remained until the last minute working the lifeboat winches. In the half light provided by the glow of the burning vessel and the first rays of dawn, a lifeboat from the Dutch steamship *Achilles* made its way to the point where men were struggling in the water and rescued all of them. They were landed at Cherbourg, Captain

Schoofs coming ashore in a Dutch officer's uniform lent to him by the Captain of the *Achilles*.

'Late this afternoon, the *L'Atlantique* began to list to port and when last observed had a twenty degree list. The flames were no longer visible, but smoke was pouring out of the hulk. The ship still was too hot for tugs to approach it to attempt to tow the hulk, which was 25 miles west of the Island of Guernsey. The French Ministry of Marine announced tonight that the liner was a total loss.'

Another story, on the same day, referred to the loss of another French passenger ship. 'The loss of the *L'Atlantique* is the second among French liners that have been destroyed by fire within a year. The 17,000-ton *Georges Philippar* of the Compagnie des Messageries Maritimes burned in the Gulf of Aden last May while returning to France from her initial voyage to China. The *Georges Philippar* carried approximately 600 passengers and a crew of 250. Fifty persons were listed as missing after the fire. The loss of that liner was believed to be due to defective electrical wiring, which led to an accumulation of

Left *A striking poster of* L'Atlantique *which was also used on the cover of an advertising brochure* (Richard Morse collection).

Below *A starboard side view of* L'Atlantique — *one of the most impressive but ugly ships ever built!* (Michael Ralph collection).

high electrical charges in the ship's framework, causing fires to occur simultaneously all over the vessel.' Some French newspapers suspected similar reasoning for the fire aboard the *L'Atlantique* while others hinted at 'sabotage'.

Several days later, on January 7, the *Herald Tribune* reported, 'A story of gallantry and rivalry among seamen of three nationalities, all striving for the honour of being first to salvage the burning hulk of the 742 ft long *L'Atlantique*, has developed as the ill-fated ship was being towed slowly toward Cherbourg by nine tugs. Buffeted by waves, winds and currents, the great hulk towered above the puny tugs and listed heavily to starboard, raising doubts whether it could gain Cherbourg harbour before sinking. It was anchored in the outer harbor early this morning.

'From the stern, the French tricolor flew proudly. It was hoisted yesterday by two Frenchmen, the first to board the floating furnace, at the risk of their lives and for the sake of claiming the wreckage for France [the other claimants were the Dutch and the Germans]. The tricolor was blackened by thick clouds of smoke which engulfed it intermittently.'

On January 8, *The New York Times* continued this sad saga. 'The captains of the French, Dutch and German tugs which towed the burning liner *L'Atlantique* into Cherbourg tonight filed reports with the Chamber of Commerce there as a basis for settling the international controversy over claims for salvaging the French vessel. All are entitled to compensation. If it is determined *L'Atlantique* was abandoned, however, then the first tug to undertake salvage operations can claim a large percentage of the prize money. It also remains to be settled whether the salvaged hulk now belongs to the Compagnie de Navigation Sud-Atlantique or to the insurance companies which carried policies on her.

'Captain Schoofs contends his ship was never abandoned because when he went ashore, he invested the captain of the French tug *Minotaure* with authority to superintend the salvage operations. He charges that the Dutch and German tug captains later refused to obey, or at least ignored his orders. The French press generally deplores that the gallant work of saving the stricken liner should have given rise to a bitter fight among salvagers.

'The Cherbourg maritime fire brigade today finally extinguished the last fire aboard *L'Atlantique*. It will not be until considerable work has been done, pumping out the hull and clearing up the wreckage, that an accurate estimate can be made of the value of what remains. If the ship is only good for scrap iron, it will bring $80,000 to $120,000. If, as is more likely, she can be reconditioned, she will be worth from $2,500,000 to $3,000,000. It was also rumored tonight that several waiters and other workers had secretly boarded the ship at Bordeaux to

The tremendous length of the promenade deck is shown here (Michael Ralph collection).

obtain transportation to Le Havre and may have perished.

A year-long battle followed between the marine underwriters and the ship's owners. She, in her blackened state, remained at Cherbourg. Later, it was finally decided, with the insurance monies amounting to $6,800,000, in favour of the Compagnie Sud-Atlantique. In February 1936, with no further need for the ship as evidence and with no intention of rebuilding her for further service, she was sold to shipbreakers. She was towed, passing the brand new outbound *Queen Mary* on one occasion, to the Smith & Houston works at Port Glasgow and demolished. It was an extremely sad ending for one of France's most luxurious liners.

Gross tonnage: 42,512
Length overall: 742 feet
Width: 92 feet
Machinery: Steam turbines, quadruple screw
Speed: 21 knots
Capacity: 414 First, 158 Second, 584 Third
Built: Penhoet Shipyards, St Nazaire, France, 1931
Demise: Burnt out in the English Channel, January 4 1933; Scrapped at Port Glasgow, 1936

Left *An air view of the fire* (Michael Ralph collection).

Below L'Atlantique *after the fire — note her huge smokestacks* (Michael Ralph collection).

Fifty Famous Liners

Monterey

They are not only among the most splendid passenger ships of their type, they are also among the best built. Known affectionately as the 'Matson trio', they were named as the *Mariposa, Monterey* and *Lurline*. (The latter ship was covered in *Fifty Famous Liners 2* and, undoubtedly, the *Mariposa* will feature in the next volume.) The *Mariposa* survived for over forty years, until 1974; the *Monterey* and the *Lurline* remain afloat at the time of writing, in the summer of 1986, both well past their fiftieth anniversaries. More importantly, the former *Monterey* is still in very active service, cruising in North American and Caribbean waters as the Greek-owned cruiseship *Britanis*.

This Matson threesome was created as a follow-up to the enormous success of an earlier passenger ship, the 17,200-ton *Malolo* (see also *Fifty Famous Liners 2*), which was the first luxury liner ever commissioned for the California-Hawaii trade. She was completed in 1927. The three later and larger ships, identical sisters at 18,000 tons each, were planned in 1930. Their construction came under the terms of the so-called Jones-White Bill, which allowed the US Government to grant construction loans and mail-carrying contracts for ships, especially passenger ships, which may be converted (at a future date) to wartime naval auxiliaries.

On October 11 1931, *The New York Times* reported, 'Amid the cheers of more than 5,000 spectators, the $8,000,000 steamer *Monterey* slid down the ways at the Fore River yards of the Bethlehem Shipbuilding Corporation [this plant, later sold to General Dynamics Corp, was closed in 1986]. She is the second of three liners for the Matson Navigation Co. Her sistership, the *Mariposa*, was launched in July and the keel for the third vessel, the *Lurline*, was laid at the yard here last week. Mrs E. Faxton Bishop, wife of a Matson Line director, was the sponsor of the *Monterey*.'

Some months later, on May 9 1932, *The New York Times* again reported on the new *Monterey*. 'The new Matson liner *Monterey* will arrive here [New York] today from the Fore River yards of the Bethlehem Shipbuilding Company and will dock at Pier 58, North River, from where she will sail next Thursday in command of Captain Andrew

Townsend on her initial voyage to Los Angeles and San Francisco. The *Monterey* is the second vessel to be completed in the Matson Line's big $25 million shipbuilding program of three sisterships, which were designed for the San Francisco-South Seas-New Zealand-Australia service [the *Lurline* was, in fact, intended from the start for Hawaiian service only]. The *Monterey* sails from San Francisco on 3 June. On her recent trials off Rockland, Maine, she attained a speed of 23 knots.'

Together, the sisters *Mariposa* and *Monterey* sailed regularly from San Francisco to Honolulu, Samoa, Suva, Auckland and Wellington in New Zealand, then across to Sydney and Melbourne before reversing course and heading home. Accommodation was balanced between 472 in first class and 229 in cabin class. The Matson line was very pleased with the ships, both appraised from the start as superbly modern liners. In one Company brochure, a description read, '*Mariposa* and *Monterey* are new sovereigns of the Pacific vested with every attribute of ocean royalty! There is majesty in their poise, all white against the blue of sea and sky...a royal power in their swift conquest of distance...a queenly graciousness in the atmosphere which pervades throughout. They are nine decks in size...they

Launched on October 10, 1931, this ship and her two sisters would live through many careers. Monterey *was still sailing at the time of writing, one of the world's longest lived and most successful ships.*

accommodate over 700 passengers each...their speed is over 20 knots...they run the gamut of sumptuous living at sea. From a byway to a highway, they are transforming the route between California and the Antipodes. Ship life vibrant with the sorcery of the South Seas, yet keyed with perfect harmony to the luxury you always expect on liners like these. Patrician lounge...staterooms spaciously charming...outdoor swimming pools ...talkie theatres...night clubs...shops...daily newspapers...every modern facility...and so much more. Tropic sunshine splashing with you in that pool...peacock-colored seas no movie can ever screen...night club gaiety catching its glitter from the Southern Cross! No ocean can boast a finer crossing—in ships, in route, in service.'

Cutting the running time between Australia and California by nearly one-third, they radically altered the flow of Pacific passenger service. They diverted a substantial percentage of regular travel between England and the South Pacific commonwealth, New Zealand and Australia, to the Matson route and across the United States; in turn, a growing number of Americans were sailing in them to the glamorous South Seas when the war abruptly ended their regular service. With only two or three interruptions, the *Monterey* maintained regular service to the South Pacific until war called her to duty as a troopship, in December 1941. Among the notable

moments of her peacetime service was when she carried a special cargo of canned milk, phonograph records and sweets for Admiral Byrd's ship *Bear* during its famous voyage to the South Pole. They made contact at Wellington, New Zealand. Also, just before being called to war service, she received her first grim taste of hostilities when she was selected for a special voyage to evacuate refugees from Japan, China and Korea. Fitted with hundreds of cots and special supplies, she carried some 150 members of Navy families, missionaries and others out of the Orient. Her return home was by way of Yokohama, Shanghai, Manila, Sydney and Honolulu to San Francisco. Once converted, at the end of 1941, and with all of her elegant fittings and appointments removed so as to increase her troop-carrying capacity, she was shrouded in military greys. Instead of a regular passenger list of some 700, she could now accommodate over 3,000.

Travelling to ports throughout the world, one episode in the wartime history of the USS *Monterey* was especially documented in a Matson publication, *The Story of a Gallant Ship: the 'Monterey'*. 'In the Allied advance on Naples, in November 1943, the Matson luxury liner *Monterey* played an heroic part which will go down in the annals of sea history as one of the most dramatic rescue missions in the traditions of the American Merchant Marine. The convoy started from a United Kingdom port after the assault troops, which were destined to break the Allied-Nazi deadlock on the shin of the Italian boot, had boarded the ships. In the convoy were many well known American ships. One of these was the *Monterey*.

'From Gibraltar, the convoy struck out in somber columns for the Italian coast. The day of 6 November was of beauty possible only in the Mediterranean. At sunset, Captain Johanson of the *Monterey* remarked to his navigation officer the night was perfect for enemy attack. The enemy thought so, too. With no warning, waves of German torpedo bombers dived out of the skies as the sun was setting. Officers of the *Monterey* cleared the open decks of troops, as from low flying clouds, the planes singled out the troopships through the smoke screen laid by the escort vessels. Methodically and ferociously, they began to sow their torpedoes abreast of the midships and engine rooms of the convoy vessels. One bomber came at the *Monterey* so low, it had to raise to clear the ship's stack and, in these seconds, midships gunners, on what had once been the liner's tennis courts, fatally sprayed the plane's belly, causing it to crash on the starboard side. So close had the plane come to crashing on the vessel that it dragged the ship's radio antenna from between the masts and into the water.

'As night fell and a half moon played optical tricks with the dark water, the torpedoes struck two ships: one a Dutch vessel and the second, the United States troopship *Santa Elena*, a famed liner of the Grace Line [9,900 tons, built 1933]. The stricken *Santa Elena* gave up her 1,675 troops quickly as her stern lowered slowly into the black waters. The *Monterey* was ordered by the Commodore of the Convoy to pull out of convoy formation and remain behind to conduct the rescue. Two destroyers dropped back to circle the sinking ship and its rescuer.

'*Monterey* lifeboats were lowered from one side of the ship to pick-up persons in the water and side ports were opened on the other side to receive the survivors from the water. Stewards aboard the Matson ship received survivors with towels, fresh clothing, blankets and hot coffee as they came from the water. Taxed with an already capacity load of troops, the *Monterey* fed and provided emergency accommodations for the additional 1,675 servicemen from the stricken *Santa Elena*. But, the night's work was finished none too soon. As the last boatload was

Flag-bedecked, she enters San Diego, California on May 28, 1932 while on her delivery trip. At that time she was the largest vessel ever to have entered the port.

hoisted aboard, a protecting destroyer standing-by flashed the word that submarines were appearing. One torpedo crossed the bow of the destroyer. With all the power to her mighty turbines, the *Monterey* departed the scene of one of the greatest spectacles of the sea...a successful rescue by one troopship of another, at night, with loss of but four lives. The gallant *Monterey*, with two trooploads aboard, made the run to Naples alone, save for two escort vessels.'

Decommissioned from war duties in 1946, the initial reconversion of both the *Mariposa* and *Monterey* had started when it was realised that the sky-rocketing costs of the project was beyond Matson's means. The plans for both ships were shunted aside, supposedly only temporarily, and the ships moved to an unused shipyard berth across the Bay, in Oakland. One Matson executive commented at the time, 'We still have all the hotel accoutrements for the *Mariposa* and *Monterey* stored away since they began their five-year stint as transports in World War 2. It is now only a matter of time before they are restored.'

The *Mariposa* would, in fact, never sail again for Matson. She was sold to the Panamanian-flag Home Lines, in 1953, and then refitted as their *Homeric*. She was scrapped on Taiwan in 1974. The *Monterey* was, after nearly a decade, finally selected for a full refit. In the care of 25-staff 'riding crew' and two sea-going tugs, she was towed from San Francisco via Panama to the big Newport News Shipyard in Virgina, in the spring of 1956. Restored at a cost of $17,500,000, she was modernised, improved (and later described as 'Hawaii afloat) and renamed *Matsonia*. Once again, just as in 1932, she then went to New York for her maiden voyage, an 18-day cruise to Nassau, Port-au-Prince, Kingston, Cartagena, the Panama Canal, Balboa, Acapulco and Los Angeles. The *Herald Tribune* reported, 'The third Matson liner to be christened *Matsonia* will be welcomed at the Port of New York next Sunday [May 19 1957] and where she will be given a major role in the National Maritime Day celebration on 22 May. Maritime Administrator Clarence G Morse will be the principal speaker at the Maritime Day luncheon [for 500 guests] the Matson Line will give aboard the California-Hawaii passenger ship at Pier 86, West 46th Street.

For several years, the *Matsonia* was teamed with her pre-war sister, the *Lurline*, on the Honolulu run. In 1963, the latter ship became mechanically faulty, in the meantime trade requirements had changed on the Hawaiian service, such that only one liner was sufficient. As a result of these developments the *Lurline* was sold to the Chandris Lines and became their *Ellinis*, with 1,668 berths, for the Australian migrant trade. The *Matsonia*, which would now sail alone, adopted the other ship's more popular name. She was renamed *Lurline* by the end of that same year.

Seven years later, in May 1970, she too was sold to the Chandris Group of Companies (the Ajax Navigation Corporation) and was sent to Piraeus, where she was rebuilt (with 1,655 berths), also for the Australian migrant run. She was renamed *Britanis*,

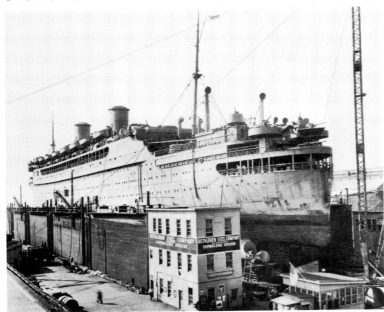

War came and here Monterey *is being converted for troopship use. Under heavy fire in the Mediterranean she rescued 1,675 of those aboard the sinking* Santa Elena. *A German plane attacked so close that it flew into her radio antennae and crashed!*

and for a time sailed once again in company with her former sister, the *Ellinis*. However, once the Australian trade began to wane by the mid-seventies, both ships were detoured more and more for cruising. In 1981, the former *Monterey* was transferred to the United States, cruising on one to ten day voyages under the dual banners of Fantasy Cruises and Chandris Cruises. She is still popular and still profitable.

At that launching ceremony in 1931, neither the builders nor the Matson Line could have envisioned that their ship would have given such exceptional service. She is now well into her sixth decade.

Gross tonnage: 18,017 (1932); 18,655 (1957); 18,254 (1970)
Length overall: 632 feet (1932); 642 feet (1957)
Width: 79 feet
Machinery: Steam turbines, twin screw
Speed: 20 knots
Capacity: 472 First, 229 Cabin (1932); 761 all First (1957); 1,655 all Tourist class (1970)
Built: Bethlehem Shipbuilding Corporation, Quincy, Massachusetts, 1931

Above *A hospital ward on* Monterey — *the beautifully decorated bulkhead.*

Below *Randolph Sevier (left), Matson president, and Robert Tate, vice president, look at a model of* Monterey, *now renamed* Matsonia, *as she has been redesigned for service with* Lurline *in 1957.*

Acadia

Between the two world wars, in those pre-aircraft years, America maintained a sizeable fleet of coastal passenger ships. These were not over-sized excursion or pleasure boats, but miniature ocean liners. If not the size, they had the decorative styles within their passenger accommodation that could rival some of the biggest and best of the trans-ocean liners. One of the finest of these 'little liners' was the *Acadia*. She was one of the 15 small passenger ships which, prior to America's entry into World War 2, in December 1941, were run by the Eastern Steamship Lines. After the hostilities, Eastern and its ships virtually faded away.

The *Acadia* was delivered in June 1932 by the Newport News Shipbuilding & Drydock Company. A large article was featured in the journal *Marine News* at the time. 'The palatial $3.5 million passenger and freight steamship *Acadia*, the second of two large, fast coastal liners, is splendidly equipped for service between the United States and Canada's Maritime Provinces [and also between New York and Boston]. The delivery of the *Acadia* marks another chapter in the record of efficiency in management and production for which the Newport News Shipbuilding & Drydock Company has long been noted, and once more brings to mind the motto of the founder of this shipyard, Collis Potter Huntington:

> We shall build good ships here
> At a profit if we can
> At a loss if we must
> But always good ships!

The confidence reposed in the Newport News Yards by her designer is attested by the fact that during the past seven years 16 of the passenger and cargo vessels designed by him [Theodore E Ferris] have been built at this shipyard and represent a total of approximately 101,000 gross tons. The yard has constructed some 350 vessels, representing a total of approximately 1,390,000 gross tons since the *Dorothy*, a small tug, was delivered in the spring of 1891.'

The addition of the *Acadia* and her twin sister-ship, the *Saint John*, brought Eastern Steamship's fleet to a total of 33 ships, with a gross tonnage of approximately 96,300. The *Saint John* and *Acadia* represented their owners' latest and, quite sadly, their last passenger ship creations. Their designs were based on their immediate predecessors, the sisters *Evangeline* and *Yarmouth*, which were built by the Cramp Shipyards at Philadelphia in 1927. The newer ships became the speediest in the Eastern fleet, being over 2 knots faster than the earlier pair of sisters.

The name *Acadia* is that which was given by the early French settlers to Nova Scotia, a land made famous by Longfellow's 'Evangeline'. The *Saint John* was named for the city of the same name in the province of New Brunswick, Canada. According to initial plans, during the summer vacation season, from May until November, the *Saint John* would operate between Boston and Saint John, covering 260 nautical miles in an easy overnight run. She would make three round trips a week during the so-called 'rush season'. The entire main deck freight space would be given over to auto storage, thereby providing excellent facilities for the transportation of

Fifty Famous Liners

tourist motor cars. During the remainder of the year, she would operate between New York and Boston by way of the Cape Cod Canal and alternating with the *Acadia*. The latter ship would sail during the summer months between New York and Yarmouth, Nova Scotia, accomplishing the voyage in about 22 hours.

The *Acadia* was designed to carry a maximum of 657 first class passengers. *Marine News* was high in its praise of her high standard accommodations. 'Old English, with a slight modern timbre, is the dominant note in design and furnishings of the principal public areas. From the standpoint of passenger comfort and provisions for the welfare of their personnel, both the *Acadia* and *Saint John* compare favorably with the most modern transatlantic liners. The first class passengers [an additional 87 passengers could be carried in so-called 'berth travel' space] are berthed in staterooms and deluxe suites on the main, upper, bridge, promenade and boat decks. There is a total of 266 staterooms and each of these is arranged to open on inside or protected passageways leading directly to the various stair lobbies.

'Of the fourteen deluxe suites, two are fitted up specially for the owners, one for the president and one for the director. All of these suites are splendidly furnished—some are finished in white mahogany, others in Oriental woods and the remainder in maple. There is a commodious wardrobe, a dressing table, chiffonier, night table, two easy lounge chairs

Above Acadia's *launching ceremony* (courtesy of Newport News Shipyard).

Below Acadia *when spanking new and on her trials* (courtesy of Newport News Shipyard).

Acadia *as a World War 2 troopship.*

and a side chair in each suite. The 'special staterooms, those which have private toilet and shower, are fitted with large wardrobes and large dressing tables, and comfortable side chairs in addition to the furnishings mentioned for the regular staterooms. The furniture in the staterooms and suites is finished in Santo Domingo mahogany.

'Numerous public baths, showers and toilets are provided on every deck for the convenience of passengers. These are entirely enclosed by light steel bulkheads with flat bar stiffeners to simulate panel work and finished in white enamel. Accommodations are provided on the lower deck aft for 'berth travel' passengers. The men are berthed on the starboard side in one large space, provision being made for 57, and the women berthed on the port side in a smaller manner with 30 berths in the space. White enameled pipe berths are fitted three-high. With the exception of the entrance lobbies and the main dining saloon, which are located on the upper deck, all the public spaces such as the lounge and music room, smoking room, ballroom and verandah terrace cafe, and library and writing rooms are located above on the Promenade Deck. At the forward end of the Promenade Deck, there is an observation deck for the passengers. Aft of the observation deck, there is a complete circuitous promenade, protected across the forward end and part way down the sides by large storm windows.'

The *Acadia* settled down to a happy and profitable life. She made news on at least two occasions. On July 9 1936, *Marine News* reported, 'The *Acadia*, bound for her Manhattan pier from Yarmouth, Nova Scotia, with about 600 passengers onboard, ran aground in the East River, near the foot of Grand Street, Brooklyn, while attempting to avoid a collision with the tug *Richard Peck*. Two other tugs later pulled her out of the mud and she proceeded to her pier.' Later in the following year, she was again part of a feature news story. The *Herald Tribune* wrote, on December 22 1937, 'Three vessels of the Eastern Steamship Lines at New York and one at Norfolk were unable to sail yesterday as a result of sit-down strikes by members of their crews, who acted on orders from the National Maritime Union, following the refusal of the Company to reinstate a union crewmember on the *Saint John*. Hardest hit by the tie-up was the big liner *Acadia*, which was to have left Pier 18, Hudson River at Warren Street, at 5.30 pm for Boston with 75 passengers, the majority of whom were bound for New England for the holidays. It is understood that a large number of the passengers made the trip by rail. Also affected by the strike at New York were the freighters *Sandwich* and *Wilton*. The former was to have left Pier 18 for Portland, Maine and the latter was to have sailed from Pier 25, Hudson River, for Richmond, Virginia. The vessel affected at Norfolk was the Company's Old Dominion Line freighter *Madison*, which is engaged in the trade to New York.'

148

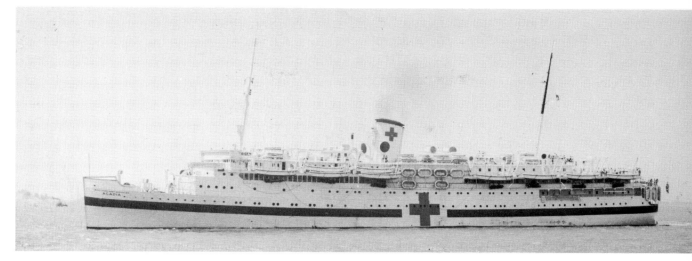

As World War 2 dragged on and more and more American soldiers were wounded a large fleet of US hospital ships were needed, so Acadia *underwent further conversion to serve in this role.*

While periodically used for some cruises to Bermuda, Nassau and in the Caribbean, the *Acadia* was called to wartime duties in the autumn of 1941. Her first such voyage was to West Africa, carrying American technicians who established a chain of African air bases to speed delivery of American-made planes to the British. Soon afterward, however, she was converted to a more specialised duty: as a hospital ship. Her transformation took seven months and cost $1.4 million. Her troop transport armament was removed, the hull painted white, a horizontal green band painted the whole length of the ship on each side, with a Red Cross painted on the middle of each side, on deck and on the funnel, and the entire vessel equipped to provide electrical illumination from sunset to sunrise. Her berthing arrangements were revised for 802 medical passengers—714 ward patients, 46 isolation cases and 42 mental patients. She carried an operational crew of 164 and an accompanying medical staff of 160, which included 10 doctors, 43 nurses and 93 physiotherapists. Just after the War in Europe ended, in the summer of 1945, the *Herald Tribune* reported on one of the *Acadia*'s more heroic returns to New York. 'The *Acadia*, the Army's largest hospital ship, arrived at Pier 15, in Stapleton, Staten Island, yesterday with 778 wounded soldiers from Europe, including 100 who came off in stretchers.'

Further news of the *Acadia* appeared in the *Herald Tribune*, on July 28 1947. 'The 6,185-ton liner *Acadia*, a notable member of the pre-war American coastal and cruise fleet, is likely to resume her peacetime operations after a varied wartime career. Berthed in the James River, Virginia National Reserve Fleet after finishing service as an Army hospital ship [in 1946], the vessel was turned back to her former owners, the Eastern Steamship Lines, by the Maritime Commission. She is one of the last modern passenger ships to revert to private hands after wartime requisition by the Government.'

Unfortunately, the *Acadia* would not see commercial service again. While Eastern wanted to return her to the Canadian trades and also for seasonal use as a cruiseship, a lengthy legal battle began with the US Government over her refurbishment. By the early fifties, Eastern was suing the Government for as much as $5 million to restore the *Acadia* to her passenger ship status. On November 30 1952, the *Herald Tribune* reported on the entanglement, one which would never be settled. 'A fast coastal passenger ship that has not visited its home port [Boston] since the early days of World War 2 is lying idle in the James River, where she is more securely tied by legal red tape than by her hawsers. This 'orphan ship' of the US merchant marine is the *Acadia* of the Eastern Steamship Lines,

Acadia

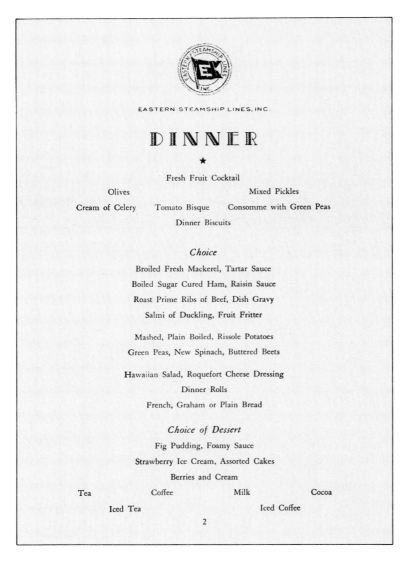

EASTERN STEAMSHIP LINES, INC.

DINNER

★

Fresh Fruit Cocktail

Olives   Mixed Pickles

Cream of Celery   Tomato Bisque   Consomme with Green Peas

Dinner Biscuits

Choice

Broiled Fresh Mackerel, Tartar Sauce

Boiled Sugar Cured Ham, Raisin Sauce

Roast Prime Ribs of Beef, Dish Gravy

Salmi of Duckling, Fruit Fritter

Mashed, Plain Boiled, Rissole Potatoes

Green Peas, New Spinach, Buttered Beets

Hawaiian Salad, Roquefort Cheese Dressing

Dinner Rolls

French, Graham or Plain Bread

Choice of Dessert

Fig Pudding, Foamy Sauce

Strawberry Ice Cream, Assorted Cakes

Berries and Cream

Tea   Coffee   Milk   Cocoa

Iced Tea   Iced Coffee

2

a 22 kt vessel that has not steamed a mile since the end of the War.'

The case was later settled in the Government's favour and while there were rumours that the *Acadia* might be sold to foreign interests, possibly even for rebuilding as a transatlantic low-fare Tourist class liner, nothing came to pass. With ever mounting costs within the American fleet, Eastern was no longer able to consider using the ship. In 1955, she went to the breakers.

Gross tonnage: 6,811 (1932); 6,185 (1945)
Length overall: 402 feet
Width: 61 feet
Machinery: Steam turbines, twin screw
Speed: 22 knots
Capacity: 744 passengers: 657 First, 87 berth travel
Built: Newport News Shipbuilding & Drydock Co, Newport News, Virginia, 1932
Demise: Scrapped at Bruges, Belgium, 1955

Stratheden

P&O—the Peninsular & Oriental Steam Navigation Co Ltd—is assuredly one of the most historic steamship firms of all time. Their creation, development and much of their success literally traced the development of Britain's Eastern Empire, from India and the Middle East, and then out to Australia, New Zealand and the colonies in the Far East. They ran the express mail service to Bombay, delivered hundreds of thousands of settlers to the likes of Fremantle, Melbourne and Sydney, and untold numbes of civil servants and their families to the ports such as Aden, Singapore and Hong Kong. Their passenger ships, with such appropriate sounding names as *Rawalpindi* and *Viceroy of India, Cathay* and *Bendigo*, were mostly conservative vessels, all reflections of quiet British taste and design. It was not until the early thirties when the Company, wanting to strengthen its competitive edge with such rivals as the Orient and Shaw Savill lines, embarked on a plan of new style passenger liners. These were to be the biggest, finest and fastest P&O liners yet.

The first of these new ships were the twin sisters *Strathnaver* and *Strathaird*, delivered by Vickers-Armstrongs in 1931-32. At over 22,500 tons, they were unique in being painted overall in heat-resistant white, had their three funnels in buff and offered a new level of comfort for the Australian run that included every passenger cabin having running water. Furthermore, in addition to their Australian passenger sailings, the design also included provision for cruising, mostly of a fortnight's duration, to the Atlantic Isles, the Mediterranean, the Northern Cities and the Norwegian Fjords, and at a later time, from Sydney to the South Pacific islands. As expected, these twins —known as 'the White Ships'—were a huge success. Despite a slight lapse in trading, P&O ordered an improved version, also from Vickers, which was delivered in September 1935, as the 23,400-ton *Strathmore*. Optimism obviously continued, for shortly thereafter the Company returned to Vickers with orders for not one but two identical sisters, the 23,700-ton *Stratheden*, commissioned in December 1937, and the *Strathallan*, delivered in the following March. This completed what can still be considered P&O's most successful team of ships, 'the Straths'. They became familiar, highly recognizable sights in the London Docks, passing through the Mediterranean and Suez, and along the waterfronts of Fremantle, Melbourne and Sydney.

The *Stratheden* was called to war duties, with less than two years of commercial service recorded, by the end of 1939. She was outfitted as a troop transport and continued in this role until 1946. Her return to civilian service was documented by *Fairplay*, on July 3 1947. 'The sailing of the P&O *Stratheden* for Australia at the end of last week, after a reconditioning that has lasted eleven months, marks the opening of a peacetime epoch which, for this Company, has been singularly long delayed. Not only were their wartime losses heavy, but their special suitability of their ships for trooping has meant that they have been retained on very necessary Government serviced longer than those of many other companies. On top of this, there has been the familiar and inevitable delays in building and reconversion, which were set out in *Fairplay* of 3rd April. It will be seen there that the *Stratheden* was originally due for completion in January last. During her war service, she steamed 468,094 miles and carried 149,697 troops and other passengers. The declaration of war came

while she was at sea, and that voyage is commemorated in a bronze plaque, which reads:

''This plaque is placed here by the Australian and New Zealand passengers as a token of appreciation of the courageous and successful navigation of the SS *Stratheden* by Captain F. E. French, his officers and engineering staff and crew, during her voyage from England to Australia, sailing 1st September 1939. The *Stratheden* was the first ship to pass through the submarine zone of the Atlantic and Mediterranean after war had been declared.''

'She took part in the invasion of North Africa, where her sister, the *Strathallan* was sunk, and her later trooping service included a transatlantic crossing to Quebec City. Her engines stood up exceptionally well to the severe demands of war service, during which the *Stratheden* never missed a sailing—a tribute to both her builders and engine room staff.

'Her post-war accommodation was nearly identical to its initial standard. The original panelling and glass murals in the public rooms were not stripped during the war, but boarded up. Excellent use is made of Australian walnut, elm burr, sycamore, betula and other Empire woods, and the lighting and furniture combine comfort with restraint. There is a particularly inviting outdoor swimming pool, especially useful on the long warm weather voyages to and from Australia. The appointments in the tourist class public rooms fall little, if at all, short of the first class. An innovation, which is to be extended to other P&O ships, is the presence of two lady stenographers, ranking as junior officers, in the purser's department, and four telephonists, mostly recruited from the WRNS.'

In 1950, the *Stratheden* made an unusual detour for a P&O liner in peacetime—she made four charter voyages for Cunard between Southampton and New York. On 16 June, *The New York Times* reported, 'A British luxury liner with a largely Oriental crew emerged from the fog-shrouded entrance to New York harbor early yesterday morning and steamed virtually unobserved to a North River pier. She is the 23,700-ton *Stratheden*, completing her maiden voyage to this port as a passenger liner. Inbound from Southampton and Le Havre with 450 passengers, the all-white vessel was finally warped into position alongside Pier 90, at West 50th Street, at 8 am. Though no welcome, official or otherwise,

awaited her, she was one of the most colorful ships to visit this port since the war. As longshoremen raised the gangway, Ebrahim Mohamed, chief serang—boatswain—of the liner, appeared in Indian costume, with red and silver turban and blew a sharp blast on a small silver whistle. The report brought immediate action. Several Lascar deckhands, in similar attire, scurried to secure the gangway and then stood at attention with arms crossed as passengers filed off the ship.

'There were 63 of these men aboard. All are Moslems recruited by Ebrahim Mohamed in Kathiawar, India. Despite the present discord between India and Pakistan, they share quarters with 50 Pakistanti Moslems employed in the engine department and 148 natives of Portuguese Goa. The Goanese are all Roman Catholics and served in the catering department.

'The 58-year-old serang said through an interpreter that he went to sea at the age of ten as a ''punkah boy'' for the P&O Lines, owners of the *Stratheden*. He added that he was following a career similar to that of his father and grandfather, who served as chief serangs in their day. ''I love the sea'', he said, ''and I am no stranger in New York''. He explained that he had come here several times on troopships and served for a time on the *Ile de France* during the war she was managed by P&O in the early forties].

'The 261 Asiatics make up nearly half of the *Stratheden*'s crew. According to Chief Steward Arthur Cookson, they get along ''famously'' with the British personnel. A tour of the crew' quarters, led by Mr Cookson, unfolded a picturesque scene. In the quarters of the Goanese was a large altar on which had been placed a picture of Pope Pius XII. One crewmember had just lit a candle and was kneeling in prayer. Fifty feet beyond, off a narrow passageway, was the Moslem prayer room. Originally intended as a mess hall, it was converted to a religious center by crewmen who resigned themselves to eating their own meals in their various bunks. The room was immaculately clean and contained a dozen or more prayer rugs. Hoossein Fackeer, leader of the Pakistanti Moslems, explained that the faithful come to the room five times each day to pray. Shoes are left in the corridor, he said. His flowing mustache and closely cropped hair apparently had been dyed red. Asked why, he replied, ''This is my privilege,

Above *The* Stratheden *was launched by the Duchess of Buccleuch and Queensberry on June 17, 1937. Note the drag chains proving their worth.*

Right *Six months and a day after the launching ceremony, December 18, 1937, workmen put the finishing touches to Stratheden's lifeboats before her maiden voyage.*

for I have been to Mecca''.'

The *Stratheden*, while returning to her Australian service, made further news, in March 1955. It was reported, 'The tiny Greek freighter *Iason* foundered in a storm off the toe of Italy and nineteen men perished during the rescue operations. Eleven members of the *Iason*'s crew and eight members of a small boat crew from 23,732-ton British liner *Stratheden* drowned when crashing seas capsized the

Stratheden

lifeboat. Four members of the *Iason*'s crew were saved, including the captain and first mate. The *Stratheden*, bound from Australia to Great Britain, went to the help of the *Iason*, a 449-ton converted corvette, after receiving distress calls from the Ionian Sea or Cape Stilo. The *Iason* was heading home from Sicily. She had disappeared when the *Stratheden* reached the scene and the crew was struggling in the water.'

As the P&O Lines built a large replacement fleet of liners and then merged with the Orient Line (to create the P&O-Orient Lines) in 1960 just in time for the delivery of their largest liners ever, the 41,900-ton *Oriana* and the 45,000-ton *Canberra*, completed in 1960-61, the older ships began to near retirement. The original *Strathaird* and *Strathnaver* were scrapped almost immediately. The *Strathmore* and *Stratheden* were soon to follow. On June 19 1963, *The Shipping World* carried a feature story on the ageing *Stratheden*. 'The P&O liner *Stratheden* is to be withdrawn from regular Australian mail service when she returns from her voyage terminating in London, on 23 October. Following this, the ship has been chartered to Mr Max Wilson as an additional cruiseship for his Travel Savings Association, for a series of four winter cruises in December 1963 and January 1964. The P&O Co will provide the ship and the ship's company and normal tourist one-class services. Berthing, booking, itineraries, short excursions and entertainments onboard are the responsibility of the charterers. The future of the *Stratheden* after the charter has not yet been decided.

'The success of the Travel Savings cruise program has been such that a change in plans has proved necessary. Three of the 20 cruises on the *Empress of Britain* from the UK are being replaced by the *Stratheden* cruises to allow the former ship to join the *Empress of England* in South Africa during December 1963 and January 1964. The cruises to be operated by the *Stratheden* are: December 2, London-Casablanca-Gibraltar-Lisbon-London; December 11, a similar cruise but from Southampton; the fares for TSA members on these two cruises are from £18 to £80, and for non-members £44-£124. The third cruise sails from Southampton on December 20, to Madeira, Teneriffe, Las Palmas, Ceuta and Lisbon. Prices are from £32 to £145 for TSA members and £63 to £168 for non-members. The last cruise sails from Southampton on January 4 and calls at Las Palmas, Trinidad, Curacao, Jamaica, Barbados and Madeira. Fares are from £72 to £296 for members and £159 to £376 for non-members.

'Travel Savings is reported to be interested in actually purchasing a ship and at present are attempting to obtain the Portuguese liner *Vera Cruz*, which is being sold by the Companhia Colonial de Navegacao. There are reported to be three parties interested in the ship, two Greek owners, John S. Latsis and A. J. Chandris, who is urgently requiring a replacement vessel for the *Brittany* recently lost by fire, and, of course, the TSA. Owing to the competition, the price is reported to have been considerably forced up to about £3 million.'

Once retired, the *Stratheden* and her near-sister, the *Strathmore*, found further commercial service with the Greeks. In the July 28 1966 edition of *Fairplay*, noted author Laurence Dunn wrote, 'Late in 1963, the *Strathmore* and *Stratheden* were sold to Mr John S. Latsis of Athens. The former was delivered at

Left *There is little disturbance on the water as* Stratheden *heads for the sea.*

Two views of Stratheden's *accommodation for first class passengers; the sports deck* (**above right**) *and the children's nursery* (**right**).

Piraeus that November, but the *Stratheden*, which still had to make a series of Travel Savings cruises, was not handed over until March 1964. Since then, these two—apparently little altered—have seen only a minimum of service, spending most of their time at their present anchorage [at Eleusis, Greece]. The *Strathmore*, initially referred to as the *Marianna II*, was soon renamed *Marianna Latsi* and as such was used during the early part of 1964 and 1965 to make a few pilgrim voyages between Libya and Jeddah. Handed over rather later, the *Stratheden*—renamed *Henrietta Latsi*—missed one season, and so it was not until the spring of 1965 that she carried her first pilgrim, from North and West Africa. This year both vessels again participated in the pilgrim trade, but only after their names had been switched, the *Marianni Latsi* becoming the *Henrietta Latsi* and vice versa. Their period of activity started in March and

ended in early May, when the pair returned to Eleusis. The question of names has become more confusing since the launch in Japan last February of a tanker of some 45,000 gross tons, which is also named *Henrietta Latsi'*.

Both the former 'Strath' liners finished their days in the spring of 1969, at the scrapyards of La Spezia.

Gross tonnage: 23,722 (1937); 23,732 (1947)
Length overall: 664 feet
Width: 82 feet
Machinery: Steam turbines, twin screw
Speed: 20 knots
Capacity: 448 First, 563 Tourist (1937); 527 First, 453 Tourist (1947); 1,200 all Tourist class (19617
Built: Vickers-Armstrong Ltd, Barrow-in-Furness, England, 1937
Demise: Scrapped at La Spezia, Italy, 1969

Stratheden

Seven Seas

In the late forties, just as the Second World War ended and the world began to return to some normality, there was—among other situations—a pressing demand for passenger ships to carry low-fare passengers on resettlement voyages. A number of ships, most of which had just emerged from war duties, were converted especially for this purpose. A most important member of this hardworking group was the little liner *Seven Seas*.

Launched on January 11 1940, at the Sun Shipbuilding & Drydock Co yards of Chester, Pennsylvania, she was intended to be a standardised C3-Class cargo vessel, the *Mormacmail* for the Moore McCormack Lines. A year later, just prior to completion, she was unexpectedly transferred to the US Navy for more urgent war duty. She was to be the first and highly experimental conversion of a cargo ship into an aircraft carrier, a 'baby flattop' if you will. The Newport News Shipyards of Virginia undertook this project in March 1941, and completed the transformation in an amazing 77 days. The *New York Journal American* reported, 'Major features performed during the conversion included the removal of a portion of the superstructure and all original cargo handling equipment, and the installation of a flight deck for airplane landing and a hangar deck for airplane stowage. Additional electric generators were added and practically all of the existing electric wiring was removed and complete new systems installed. Gasoline tanks and gasoline piping, airplane elevator from hangar deck to flight deck, airplane arresting gears and barriers were installed. The ship then had to be fitted out for a large complement of Navy personnel—a job which meant converting the ship's holds into living spaces, storerooms, galleys, pantries, cold storage places, workshops, toilets and hospital spaces. Furthermore, guns, ammunition and stowage for airplane bombs were installed. The peak conversion was going on about one month after the arrival and approximately 2,000 men were working on the job.'

So successful was this prototype when put to the test that the Navy immediately made a number of additional C3 ships and tankers available for similar conversions. Meanwhile, the USS *Long Island*—as the *Mormacmail* had been renamed—went on to win great acclaim. At Bermuda, on December 7 1941, she began the job of ferrying aircraft to outlying bases. This duty was interrupted only by periods when she was used as a training ship to teach young pilots techniques of carrier take-offs and landings. In May 1942, she moved from the Atlantic to the Pacific.

Encountering stiff opposition after their initial landings on Guadalcanal, the US Marines were in need of continuous air support, more than could be supplied by the few carriers available at the time. In this extremity, the *Long Island* was ordered to carry two squadrons of Marine Corps fliers in as close as possible and launch them. On 20 August 1942, when 200 miles distant, the ship catapulted her Grumman Wildcat fighters and Douglas Dauntless dive-bombers, and thereafter the two units became land-based. The ship spent the balance of the War in

Launched as the Mormacmail *on January 11, 1940 and intended as a cargo ship to link the USA and South America, this vessel would eventually become the immigrant ship* Seven Seas.

the Pacific, ferrying planes, training pilots and performing other useful tasks. As Escort Carrier No 1, she established the feasibility of a conversion that many 'doubting Thomases' had declared was impracticable. The *Long Island* was given a special plaque for distinguished service at the end of the War.

Decommissioned in March 1946, she was actually sold a year later for dismantling, but was instead then laid-up as a 'reserve ship'. A year later, in March 1948, in further re-thinking, she was sold to foreign buyers, the Caribbean Land & Shipping Co of Panama. In February 1949, she was renamed *Nelly* and, as a freighter, sailed from the US to Italy for further conversion. At La Spezia, she was rebuilt as an immigrant carrier, with 1,300 berths, and, in that June, set off from Italy to Australia with migrants. Subsequent voyages, under charter to the German and Dutch migration services, took her not only to Australian ports, but to Quebec City, Montreal and Halifax as well. Still later, while under special charter to the Dutch Government, she brought Dutch soldiers out to troubled Indonesia and then returned with evacuees and dependents.

In May 1953, she was renamed *Seven Seas* and considered an ideal candidate for North Atlantic tourist service. In December, she was sent to the North

German Lloyd shipyards at Bremerhaven and rebuilt thoroughly with far more comfortable space for 20 First class and 987 Tourist class passengers. Absolute maximum capacity was said to be as high as 1,250, of which 850 could be accommodated in two, four and six berth cabins, and the remainder in eight, ten and 12 berth staterooms. Wardrobes were fitted in every cabin, and the two, four and six berth rooms had hot and cold running water. The public facilities and amenities were listed as a Verandah Cafe, children's playroom, two lounges with a cocktail bar and dance floor, a separate bar, writing room, library, souvenir shop, beer hall, Ladies' Lounge, beauty shop, barber shop and information bureau. There was also a swimming pool and two dining rooms, in which all passengers were served in two sittings.

The *Seven Seas* was also upgraded for safety. Ninety-two fire doors were installed, together with automatic fire alarm systems and some 1,300 sprinklers. All the staircases were made fireproof and more than 7,000 square yards of fire wall insulation was renewed. Thirty-one miles of electric wiring was also replaced onboard the vessel.

Transferred from the Panamanian to the West German flag (and amidst a rumour that she would be renamed *Bremen*), her new owners were listed as the Europe-Canada Line, a partnership firm of the

The Seven Seas was taken over by the US Navy and converted as the first of a series of small aircraft carriers known as CVE class ships. She is pictured here immediately after delivery without an island or stack above the flight deck. She was to give excellent service in the Pacific.

Holland America Line and the Royal Rotterdam Lloyd. The ship was geared primarily for the West German market and the new Company stated their philosophy thus: 'The objective of the owners of the *Seven Seas* is to offer a vessel in which passengers can cross the Atlantic in comfort and safety, and at reasonable cost'. The ship was routed between Bremerhaven, Le Havre, Southampton, Quebec City and Montreal (and sailed to Halifax and / or New York during the winter season).

In the early summer of 1958, the *Seven Seas* took part in a record-breaking week for the Holland America Line and its affiliate ships. 'Eight thousand, eight hundred and six passengers were handled by the staff of the Holland America Line at its Hoboken, New Jersey and Montreal terminals during the week of Monday, 23 June to Monday, 30 June. It was one of the largest 7-day totals in the Line's history. The Hoboken figures incuded 1,616 passenger arrivals, comprised of 417 roundtrip tourists from abroad on 24 June on the Royal Rotterdam Lloyd liner *Willem Ruys*; 889 transatlantic passengers on the Holland America Line flagship *Nieuw Amsterdam* on 25 June; the Netherlands Government vessels *Zuider-kruis* and *Groote Beer* on the 26th and 28th, with 97 and 135 passengers respectively, and the *Westerdam*

on 30 June with 78 passengers. Passengers departing for Europe from Hoboken during the week's period totalled 4,693. There were 1,384 on the Netherlands Government vessel *Johan van Oldenbarnevelt* on 23 June; 417 on the *Willem Ruys* on 26 June; 1,288 on the *Nieuw Amsterdam* on 27 June; 806 on the *Zuiderkrius* on 28 June and 798 on the *Groote Beer* on 30 June. The grand total west and eastbound handled on the 5th and 6th Street piers at Hoboken was 6,309, of which approximately 20 per cent were American students sailing on the three Netherlands Government ships.

'The remaining passengers, 2,497 in all, is accountable to the Montreal office: 911 on the *Ryndam* eastbound on 24 June; 1,037 on the *Seven Seas* on 28 June, and 549 that same vessel brought in on 26 June.'

In the late spring of 1963, as the North Atlantic began its steady decline in face of the intruding jet-liners, the *Seven Seas* was shifted to longer periods in off-season service, namely on Australian voyages and then on something of a novelty to ocean shipping. Holland America in New York announced that, 'A fascinating new expansion on the idea of higher education has been instituted by the California-chartered "University of the Seven Seas", which is

Eventually, long after the war ended, she appeared as the passenger ship Seven Seas *linking Canada with Europe. She is seen here in New York Harbor while serving as the 'University of the Seven Seas' (courtesy of Moran Towing).*

offering two full semesters of college instruction on the high seas and to the historic ports of Europe, Asia, Africa and Latin America. Students who are qualified to enter college (or bona fide graduate students) are currently filing applications for one or both cruise-and-credit semesters—the first, a 110-day itinerary beginning on 22 October in New York, the second, a 120-day cruise beginning next 11 February in San Diego—and the response indicates some 500 students, with 35 highly qualified instructors from colleges and universities all over the world, will be enrolled for each of the study itineraries.

'The "University of the Seven Seas" in Whittier, California will offer a wide range of onboard courses: architecture, creative writing, music, painting, theatre, economics, political science, oceanography, anthropology, languages, literature and philosophy among them. The itinerary for the first semester is as follows: Lisbon, Barcelona, Cannes, Civitavecchia (for Rome), Naples, Piraeus, Beirut, Alexandria, Port Said, Suez, Bombay, Colombo, Port Swettenham, Singapore, Bangkok, Saigon, Hong Kong, Keelung, Kobe, Yokohama, Honolulu and San Diego. The second semester, which departs from San Diego, includes: Honolulu, Yokohama, Kobe, Keelung, Hong Kong, Manila, Djakarta, Singapore, Port Swettenham, Rangoon, Madras, Colombo, Tamatave (Madagascar), Durban, Capetown, Buenos Aires, Montevideo, Rio de Janeiro, Belem, La Guaira, Cartagena, Kingston and then to New York (on 9th June 1964). Tuition for each semester is

A painting of Seven Seas. *The white letter 'C' on her blue stack stands for Europe Canada Line.*

Seven Seas

A 1958 brochure for Seven Seas.

essential expenses except transportation in the US and Canada. Because of the slightly longer itinerary, rates for the second semester are somewhat higher.'

While she continued in summer season Atlantic service and in university cruising for the remainder, the ship's days began to be numbered when, on July 18 1965, she was disabled by an engine room fire while in mid-Atlantic. *The Herald Tribune* reported on July 21, 'The Dutch ocean tug *Ierse Zee* reached the disabled passenger liner *Seven Seas* at 5.00 pm yesterday and shortly later was headed toward St John's, Newfoundland, some 500 miles to the west with the stricken vessel under tow. The crippled liner is expected to reach St John's late this week, if yesterday's ideal towing conditions continue. After the *Seven Seas*' 610 passengers are debarked, the ship will be towed to Halifax for repairs. The extent of the engine room damage is not yet known and the future schedule of the ship has not been set, it was reported. The Coast Guard cutter *Absecon* reached the *Seven Seas* at 12.15 am yesterday. She is escorting the tow. Passengers are enjoying normal shipboard life despite the accident, which disabled the liner's engines. No one was injured.'

The *Seven Seas* returned to the North Atlantic for one further summer season, during 1966, but in that September, she was retired and sold off. Her future role was as a student's accommodation ship at Rotterdam, permanently moored in the shadows of that City's Euromast and adjacent to another accommodation ship, the *Jan Backx*, the former Anchor liner *Cilicia* of 1938. The *Seven Seas* remained in this role for over a decade, until May 4 1977, when she was towed to Ghent in Belgium for scrapping. She had had a very diverse 37 years; freighter, aircraft carrier, migrant carrier, transatlantic liner, floating university and accommodation ship.

$400 per student. Rates for the first voyage, according to the student's accommodation, range from $1,590 per student (in four and six berth dormitories) through $1,990 (in outside cabins with two and four berths), and the costs include all

Gross tonnage: 11,086 (1949); 12,575 (1954)
Length overall: 492 feet
Width: 69 feet
Machinery: Sulzer diesel, single screw
Speed: 16.5 knots
Capacity: 1,300 migrants (1949); 20 First, 987 Tourist (1954)
Built: Sun Shipbuilding & Drydock Co, Chester, Pennsylvania, 1940
Demise: Scrapped at Ghent, Belgium, 1977

Delbrasil

The first Board of Directors meeting of the Mississippi Shipping Co, better known as Delta Line, was held April 2, 1919. Like American Export Line it was one of the new firms formed to operate the 700 ships built in America for World War 1. Unlike most of these efforts the Delta Line survived. Before World War 2 it had embarked on a building programme of six new combination passenger-cargo ships. Plans for the first three were released in October, 1938. Cargo capacity would be 8,900 tons and passenger spaces would be done 'along modernistic lines'. There would be 24 outside staterooms, each with private bath and with hot and cold fresh water and shower. An open-air swimming pool would be aft of the single squat funnel. Turbine propulsion was called for with oil-fired boilers having a working pressure of 450 lb per square inch. The Bethlehem Shipbuilding Corporation, Sparrows Point, Maryland, was the winner when bids were opened. The first hull would be named *Delbrasil*.

The first brochure put out for *Delbrasil* and her two sisters, the *Delorleans* and *Deltargentino* were modest affairs. 'In the spirit of "lagniappe" no expense has been spared, with the end in view of offering an American flag service from the South equal to best Southern traditions. Sail the Southern Way from New Orleans.' The folder had an artist's conception of the *Delbrasil* by the noted painter Frank Vining Smith, showing her leaving Rio. A short, round smokestack was intended to make her appear streamlined. Like so many low stacks it would eventually have to be doubled in height. Round South America tours were given by offering an air link between Buenos Aires and Valparaiso via Pan American Airways and the northbound leg on the *Santa Lucia* or *Santa Clara* of Grace Line. Lengthy technical articles on the new liner appeared in many journals. One began with this happy comment: 'When the new passenger and cargo liner *Delbrasil* sails down the lower Mississippi on her way to sea on her maiden voyage with the green and orange house flag of the Delta Line proudly waving from her mast head, the vision and keen judgement of that small group of New Orleans business men, which brought about the organization of the Mississippi Shipping Co in 1919 will be fully vindicated.' Apparently the thought of a second world war was far from their minds at this moment.

The *Delbrasil* did much to introduce the use of aluminium as a basic material in the fabrication of liner equipment. One full page advertisement for the Warren McArthur Corporation showed the ship's main foyer, with chairs, a long table, light fixtures and grand staircase railings all made of aluminium. Countless other full page adverts featured other things used aboard the new ship. The Todd Shipyard's journal *Keel* for October-November 1940 had a cover painting of the *Deltar-*

gentino showing her Delta Line stack colours. The stack was yellow-buff with a thin black top and two thin green lines just below the black. She was the third of the new liners. Just when the *Delbrasil*'s stack was increased in height is uncertain, but it was before she was taken over by the Navy in the fall of 1943. The new ships so increased demand for passenger space on Delta steamers that in the autumn of 1941 the older ships *Delmundo* and *Delvalle*, whose capacity had been reduced to only 12 passengers with no doctor or stewardess, were returned to full passenger status, meaning they carried 35. The *Delbrasil* and her two sisters operated for three years as peacetime liners. Their three sisters built under the second order were taken over by the US Navy before completion. They were to have been named *Deluruguay*, *Delorleans* and *Delargentino* (a new variation of the name) and the company expected they would be replacements for the first three, thus the duplication of two of the names. These three became the troopships *Charles Carroll*, *Calvert* and *Monrovia*. The *Delbrasil*, requisitioned in September 1943, became the *George F. Elliott* (AP 105) and replaced an earlier transport of this same name which was sunk off Guadalcanal in 1942. The

Left *An artist's impression of* Delbrasil *(courtesy of General Electric).*

Below *For World War 2 transport use* Delbrasil *was renamed* George F. Elliot *and* Delargentino *named* J. W. McAndrew. *They are the two large vessels in this photograph showing them laid up in the James River, Virginia at the end of their war service. Note that their stacks have been substantially raised in height.*

Fifty Famous Liners

Delorleans became the *Crescent City* and the *Deltargentino* was renamed *J. W. McAndrew*.

The wartime career of the second *George F. Elliott* was spent in the Pacific. Rebuilt to carry 1,878 troops, she was based in San Francisco. Gun tubs and liferafts plus a coat of grey paint could not hide her attractive peacetime silhouette. She saw a great deal of action and earned four battle stars, but, apparently, not a life was lost aboard her due to enemy action in her four years of service. She was stricken from the Navy list on July 8 1946 and laid up in the James River, Virginia. Two years later the *George F. Elliott* and the *J. W. McAndrew* were bought by Farrell Lines for their service from New York to South Africa.

At first it was announced that the two doughty veterans would be rebuilt to carry 77 passengers, then this was increased to 80. As completed their capacity turned out to be 82. The reconstruction was done by the Gulf Shipbuilding Corporation, at Mobile, Alabama. 'They are being practically rebuilt, and when finished, will provide comfort and luxury hitherto unequalled in the South African trade', John J. Farrell, Chairman of the Line announced. The company will be remembered as having operated the only diesel-driven US passenger liner ever to serve under the American flag, the *City of New York* of 1929. It had built three elegant new passenger-cargo ships just before the war only to have all three requisitioned by the Navy.

Bought by Farrell Lines, they became African Endeavour *and* African Enterprise *respectively. This photo shows* African Endeavour *in New York (courtesy of Moran Towing).*

The *McAndrew* came out first and was renamed *African Enterprise*. The *Elliott*, ex *Delbrasil*, followed a month later being renamed *African Endeavor*. Described in an advertisement as 'two yacht-like luxury liners', they could reach Capetown in 17 days. The fare began at $650. The reconversion followed design work by Gibbs & Cox. The interiors were done by Dorothy Marckwald of Smyth, Urquhart & Marckwald Inc, who later would do similar work with the superliner *United States*. Captain John G. Waller, with Farrell since 1933, was master of the *African Endeavor* when she made her maiden arrivals at Savannah, Charleston, Baltimore and New York in August, 1949. The ship received 'enthusiastic ovations'. The only major change made in the layout was the fitting of seven more cabins on the promenade deck, accomplished by reducing the smoking room in size and sacrificing some open promenade areas.

The *African Endeavor* made her first sailing to Africa leaving New York on August 31 1949. She had 63 passengers. They were a cosmopolitan group, including people from Canada, Greece, England, Germany, Czechoslovakia, not to mention South Africa and the USA. The *African Enterprise* completed her maiden round trip in mid-September. She included among her passengers Mrs Gertrude Lintz, the woman who had raised Gargantua, the famous gorilla, then owned by Ringling Bros, Barnum and Bailey circus. The two ships settled down to their new careers under the red and blue houseflag of Farrell. Their stacks were decorated with this flag, whose design was a white cross separating two red triangles at top and bottom and two blue ones at either side. They sailed from the foot of 33rd

Delbrasil

A lovely shot of African Enterprise *off Capetown* (courtesy of Farrell Lines).

Street, Brooklyn, and berthed at the terminals of the South African Railways and Harbour Administration in Cape Town.

An elaborate menu for Christmas Day 1950 has been preserved from the *African Endeavor.* Its 44 items included Roast Vermont Turkey, Celery Dressing, Baked Virginia Ham, Pineapple Glace, and Roast Prime Ribs of Beef au Jus. The Chief Engineer was R. Estrada, P. F. Duffy was the Chief Officer, C. W. Maillard was Chief Purser and W. E. Scheitner was Chief Steward. Dr R. W. Finn was the Surgeon aboard. 'Passengers tell us it's almost like travelling on a private yacht', one Farrell folder opined. 'We're really proud of our food. Farrell Lines' chefs rank with those on the largest ships afloat.' Another company brochure listed comments by a dozen passengers. Here is what a Mr and Mrs W. H., of Rockland, Massachusetts, wrote: 'It is hard to say what impressed us most on this trip from our arrival in our comfortable and tastefully-decorated stateroom with the flowers—to the ''shellback initiation'' which was carried through with immense good taste and humor...'

Both liners were refurbished in 1952. Murals depicting South African subjects were commissioned from artist Robert Bushnell. New decorating schemes for the smoking room were created, with better lighting.

'For 17 glorious days we'll coddle you and make you comfortable', a full-colour advertisement in the *New York Times* magazine section boasted about the Farrell Lines trip to Africa.

The two ships began to suffer from competition of cargo liners of other nations on the New York to Cape Town run. An appeal for government help in the autumn of 1952 brought out the fact that the percentage of income derived from the passenger side of the operation as opposed to freight revenue declined from 28.77 per cent to 17.72 per cent in their first three years of service. Additional help was secured and the company announced plans to build two new passenger-cargo ships, plans that were never to be fulfilled.

The *African Endeavor* won the Ship Safety Achievement Award in 1954 for rescuing 24 men from the sinking Brazilian freighter *Loide-Panama.* The rescue was made in difficult weather conditions off the New Jersey coast. The two ships continued without incident until 1959 when they were laid up for economic reasons and eventually scrapped.

Gross tonnage: 7,977
Length overall: 492 feet
Width: 65 feet 7 inches
Machinery: Steam turbines, single screw
Speed: 16.5 knots
Capacity: 65 increased to 82
Built: Bethlehem Shipbuilding Corporation, Sparrows Point, Maryland, 1940
Demise: Scrapped at Baltimore, Maryland, 1969

Fifty Famous Liners

Stockholm

In October 1944, even before the Second World War had ended, the Swedish American Line placed an order with the Gotaverken shipyard at Gothenburg for what was to be the biggest passenger liner yet built in Sweden. The order was also noted as the first post-war transatlantic passenger ship (Cunard's 250-passenger *Media*, delivered in the summer of 1947, would actually arrive before this Swedish vessel). On September 9 1946, sparkling wine splashed across her bow as the name *Stockholm* was spoken. Two previous liners of the same name, of 28,000 and 29,000 gross tons and ordered from Italian yards in the late thirties, were lost, the first in a shipyard fire and the other, her immediate replacement, to Allied bombs. The launching of the new ship was described by her owners as, 'The proud, towering steel hull ran swiftly down the ways, entered the water, bowed graciously, and floated with the sure, yet delicate poise of a thoroughbred ship.' Then followed a year at the fitting-out quay; the preliminary trials, and the breaking-in process prior to delivery. And so, she was ready, and eager to commence her seafaring career—a fleet and slender yet staunch and seaworthy passenger liner.

'The MS *Stockholm* does not belong to the so-called 'giant liners'. She expresses quality rather than quantity. From the extreme point of her boldy raking stem to her elegant stern, she measures only 525 feet. On the regular run between Gothenburg and New York [via Copenhagen, occasionally Bremerhaven and/or Aahrus in Denmark and westbound at Halifax], she can accommodate 395 passengers in big, light, all-outside staterooms—113 in first class, 282 in tourist. With a service speed of 19 knots, she has ample reserves of power to ensure comfortable crossing in 9 days. Extensive use of electric welding and light metals relieves the graceful ship of much superstructural weight. She has the long, sweeping lines of a man-o'-war; the harmonious perfection of a super yacht—the ship of today and tomorrow.'

She entered service in the early part of 1948, and her arrival was reported by the *Journal of Commerce*, at New York on March 1. 'The new Swedish American liner *Stockholm* will be fêted in this port this morning as she arrives with a large group of Swedish shipping executives aboard her maiden voyage in the New York-Gothenburg service. The liner arrived at Quarantine last night and will proceed early this morning to Pier 97, North River. She made the direct crossing in eight days. Built along yacht-like lines, the *Stockholm* is a small ship by comparison with the *Gripsholm* [19,100 tons, 1925], with which she will be paired, or the *Drottningholm* [10,200 tons, 1905], which she replaces in this service. Among the 271 passengers making the first crossing in the *Stockholm* are several officials of the Swedish American Line and representatives and technicians of shipbuilding, industrial and business communities in Scandinavian countries. The former Prince Oluf of Denmark, and now the Count of Rosenborg, is also aboard on his wedding trip.'

Light and air were appraised as the dominant fea-

»Stockholms Ström med jakt till segels och barkskepp till ankars.» Oljemålning av amiral J. Hägg. ● "Stockholm Harbour. Sloop under sail and barque at anchor." From an oil painting by J. Hägg. (Swedish Admiral, † 1931.)

Above *An aerial view of* Stockholm *arriving at New York.*

Left *The cover of a menu from the* Stockholm *featuring an oil painting of Stockholm harbour.*

tures of the *Stockholm*'s passenger quarters. One report read, 'Many passenger liners strike a note of ornate luxury, which is rather unpractical and often gaudy. All that was done away with in designing the public rooms and staterooms of the *Stockholm*. Here, the all important thing was to provide pleasant and restful comfort in tasteful and artistic surroundings. Among the art items, Professor Sven Erixon, popularly known as "X:et", designed a gobelin tapestry. Its motif was the famous Gotaverken shipyard, where the *Stockholm* was built. Kurt Jungstedt did the paintings in the first class bar and depicted scenes of the wine-growing and wine-loving regions in France, Spain, Italy and Cuba. Gustaf Carlstrom did another entitled "Life in a Swedish West Coast Fishing Village", which told a fairy tale, highlighted by humor and wit, and which featured many notables including actress Greta Garbo, the Salvation Army and King Neptune. "Triumph of the Ocean Venus" was the name chosen by Einar Forseth for a mosaic that adorned the wall in the swimming

Fifty Famous Liners

pool and which unmistakably expressed the artist's intentions—an apotheosis of youthful joy and health. Gunnar Erik Strom depicted the first Swedish emigrants, which left Gothenburg in 1637 in two ships for the Delaware River, on their arrival after the Atlantic crossing. The technical procedure used represented an interesting application of an old and intricate Chinese method—painting on the back of a mirror.'

The *Stockholm* made news during a winter crossing in 1954. On February 25, *The New York Times* reported, 'Two Scandinavian passenger liners docked here yesterday one day and two days behind schedule after rough Atlantic crossings. Ice also slowed the vessels. The Norwegian America liner *Stavangerfjord* [included in the first volume of *Fifty Famous Liners*] was one day late. Her master reported encountering ice packs when leaving the Baltic Sea and strong westerly gales through most of the transatlantic trip. At one time, he had to go 80 miles off his course to avoid icebergs. The vessel docked at 10.00 am at Morton Street with 460 passengers from Oslo and Copenhagen. The Swedish American liner *Stockholm* arrived here at 12.55 pm, two days late. Among her 422 passengers debarking at West 57th Street was the newly appointed Danish Minister to Mexico. The vessel was unable to travel through the ice-choked Kiel Canal from Copenhagen to Bremerhaven and was forced to round Jutland on her way to the German port. The ocean trip was described by the ship's crew as marred by ''bad weather''. It was marred further by a slight brush with the British freighter *Starcrest*. This occurred late Monday night as the *Stockholm* was leaving Halifax. The ship suffered negligible damage. Her stern on A Deck was crushed inward over an area 24 ft wide and 6 ft deep. A flagpole was dislocated. The forward part of the white hull on the port side also was scraped. A company official said there was no structural damage. Repairs will not be made until the ship returns to her homeport of Gothenburg.

'The *Stockholm*'s silhouette was changed through extension of the Promenade Deck forward and aft, and lengthening of the Sun Deck toward the stern. In the process, the liner's gross tonnage was raised from 11,600 to 12,644. Passenger capacity was increased from 395 to 670. The vessel can now carry 24 First class travellers and 584 in Tourist class.'

Stockholm

However, considerable alterations and repairs were ahead for this little Swedish liner when, on the night of July 25 1956, she rammed the Italian flagship *Andrea Doria* in fog-shrouded waters off Nantucket. The *Stockholm* was outbound for Europe, the *Doria* headed for New York. The Italian ship later sank and the tragedy took 52 lives. Inquiries as to the cause and blame for the disaster began almost immediately. On August 9, the *Herald Tribune* reported, 'The Italian Line charged yesterday that the ''fault of the *Stockholm* was flagrant'' in the collision which sank the liner *Andrea Doria* on July 25. This was in direct dispute with the Swedish American Line's version of the tragedy, which placed the entire blame upon the *Andrea Doria* and charged carelessness, faulty equipment and other shortcomings. ''The facts are

This photo shows the damaged bow of the Stockholm after she hit and sank the Andrea Doria *(courtesy of Moran Towing).*

that the *Stockholm* was travelling about 20 miles to the north of its proper route, directly in the path of westbound ships'', Giuseppe Ali, Italian Line manager for North America, said in a statement. Then, while there is dispute over a number of matters—fog or no fog, quality of radar, competence of crews and whether sound signals were used and speed was excessive—Mr Ali went on to take up the heart of the matter, the position of the ships with respect to each other just before the collision 45 miles south of Nantucket.

'On this point, the versions of the Swedish American and Italian lines differ by 100 per cent. The Swedish version is that the ships were aimed to pass each other along parallel courses, port to port. The Swedes say that their ship turned to the right, as provided by maritime rules, to give the *Andrea Doria* wider berth. But, say the Swedes, the Italian ship then swung left, running right across the *Stockholm*'s course and causing the crash. Mr Ali added, "Although the *Stockholm* denies it, she had

been travelling in the fog for a substantial time also. The *Doria* spotted a vessel in its path at a considerable distance, but on a track that passed starboard to starboard, not port to port as claimed by the Swedish American Line. Captain Piero Calamai, who had been on the bridge of the *Doria* since the ship entered the fog area, changed his course to port to ensure even more room for passing, and his maneuver should have let the two ships pass in safety. However, instead of remaining on its course, or it too veering to port, the *Stockholm*, as is now admitted by the Swedish American Line, veered to starboard and toward the *Doria*, without reducing its speed to 18 kts.''

'An Italian Line official said that although rules call for right turns for approaching ships, sometimes left turns are imperative. He likened the recent collision to this situation with automobiles. Car A, the *Andrea Doria*, is proceeding along a two-lane road in the proper right hand lane. Car B, the *Stockholm*, is approaching. Car B suddenly begins to a persistent veering to its left into the lane of Car A. Although, it should normally keep out of the left hand lane, Car A veers to avoid collision. Considering Car B's course, a turn to the right would make collision quite certain. However, just as Car A turns left, Car B turns right back into its own lane and crash is inevitable.

'In his statement, Mr Ali said that it was 'significant' that although the Swedish American Line blames the Italian Line for the tragedy, the Swedes have not begun any suit for damages. He added, ''Our attorneys advise me that the full responsibility of the *Stockholm* will be established. We are confident that the conduct of the officers and crew [who were accused in some reports of leaving the stricken liner even before all of the passengers] will be fully vindicated.''

'Early reports from Rome said yesterday that the Italian Line might seek to attach the *Stockholm*, pending determination of the blame and damage suits. Line officials here said that no such action was necessary inasmuch as the Swedish American Line posted a bond for the value of their ship. The *Cristoforo Colombo*, sistership to the *Andrea Doria*, arrived here yesterday from Mediterranean ports with 1,228 passengers. Captain Filipino Randi reported that when he sailed over the grave of the *Doria* on Tuesday evening, the last night's ball was

Left Alice M. Moran *helping to dock* Stockholm *after her reconstruction. Note the larger enclosed area under this lifeboat in front of the bridge* (courtesy of Moran Towing).

The new motorliner "STOCKHOLM" will make her maiden voyage from Gothenburg, February 21, arriving in New York nine days later, on March 1. The return trip from New York is scheduled for:

SATURDAY, MARCH 6, 1948 (11 A.M.)

Here is a brand new ship, our first passenger liner built in a Swedish yard, introducing a novel silhouette in the New York harbor scene with its one mast, raking stem and long after-body with cruiser stern; Swedish in construction from the engines to the furniture, textiles and decoration; a comfortable ship with well-equipped cabins, ample deck space and public rooms for seagoing holidays and restful ocean travel.

The new "STOCKHOLM" is 524 feet in length, has a beam of 69 feet, and a draft, when fully loaded, close to 25 feet. Her gross tonnage is 11,000 tons, while her displacement is about 13,000 tons. She will carry 113 passengers in First Class and 282 passengers in Tourist Class, all in outside staterooms.

Here is an excellent opportunity for those of your clients who take pride and satisfaction in being "first". Operated in the Swedish American Line tradition of competent seamanship and unobtrusive attendance, she will offer her passengers the same standards of service, courtesy, and comfort which has made the White Viking Fleet famous.

WRITE, WIRE OR TELEPHONE US FOR RESERVATIONS
ON THE MAIDEN TRIP

Space also available in all classes on Feb. 27, and in First Class on March 26 and April 3, eastbound sailings.

SWEDISH AMERICAN LINE

Right *Swedish American issued this flyer to mark the maiden voyage of the new* Stockholm.

cancelled, a wreath was thrown into the sea and prayers were said.'

The *Stockholm*, minus much of her bow, limped back to New York following the tragic collision and was later sent to the Bethlehem Steel Shipyards in Brooklyn for repairs and replacement. She resumed sailing five months later, in December. The court inquiries, while always conducted under the tightest secrecy, never established the blame. Settlements amounted to some $48 million.

Running with the larger *Kungsholm* of 1953 and then with the brand new *Gripsholm* of 1957, the *Stockholm* soon became redundant to Swedish American's needs, both in transatlantic service and on occasional 'economy cruises'. She ran her last crossing out of New York, in December 1959, and very quickly thereafter was handed over to her new owners, the East German-flag Deutsche Seereederi. Renamed *Volkerfreundschaft*— meaning 'International Friendship'—she became the world's first trade-union cruiseship, carrying workers and their families on special voyages into the Baltic, Scandinavia, the Mediterranean, West Africa and even across to the Caribbean. She remained in this service for 26 years, until early 1986, when she was retired and replaced by the South African cruiseship *Astor* (18,500 tons, built 1981), which was renamed *Arkona*. First sent to an anchorage in the Oslofjord, she was later moved to Southampton, renamed *Volker* and awaited her fate. One rumour, at the time of writing, indicated that she would be sent to Stockholm for use as a floating museum and hotel. What a perfect idea!

Gross tonnage: 11,700 tons (1948); 12, 644 (1952); 12,387 (1960); 12,068 (1972)
Length overall: 525 feet
Width: 69 feet
Machinery: Gotaverken diesels, twin screw
Speed: 19 knots
Capacity: 113 First and 282 Tourist (1948); 86 First and 584 Tourist (1952); 568 one-class (1960)
Built: Gotaverken Shipyard, Gothenburg, Sweden, 1948

Stockholm

President Cleveland

California's Bethlehem Alameda Shipyards had good reason to feel proud of their latest product, the SS *President Cleveland*. In construction, machinery, outfitting, furnishings and interior decoration, she was a first class vessel, built to the highest standards, and capable of maintaining the most exact schedule in the long run to the Orient. And Bethlehem Alameda *was* proud. Say to any employee at the Alameda yard, from the office boy to the general manager, "This is a good ship", and the answer snaps back, "The only kind of ship that Bethlehem knows how to build!" The *President Cleveland* is the largest passenger vessel ever built in a Pacific Coast yard, and the largest built in an American yard since the *America* of 1939.

The *President Cleveland* and her twin sister, the *President Wilson*, were, however, intended to be wartime troop transports. The Government had ordered ten of the P2-SE2-R1 class, ships of over 17,000 tons and capacities as high as 5,000 each. However, as the orders for the last pair were placed in 1944, the end of the hostilities changed demands. Consequently, the keel plates for what was to have become the *Admiral D. W. Taylor* and *Admiral F. B. Upham* respectively were offered for sale to commercial buyers. Being able to redesign the ships to suit their needs, the American President Lines saw enormous possibilities in them for revival of their transpacific luxury passenger service from San Francisco.

Soon after taking over the construction of the ships—the *President Cleveland* was completed in December 1947, the *President Wilson* in April 1948—the president of that San Francisco-based company enthusiastically announced, 'American President Lines visualizes a fleet of four identical liners in their Oriental service: the *President Cleveland*, the *President Wilson* and two further twin sisters [the projected conversion of the wartime troopships *General M. C. Meigs* and *General W. H. Gordon* were, in fact, never realized]. The Company is also at present planning [in late 1947] to build five specially designed passenger vessels for their round-the-world service. They hope to have these vessels in operation some time in 1949 [three were actually built, in 1951, but then handed over to the

Government and completed as troop transports for use in the Korean War].'

The president continued, 'With revised and faster schedules, luxury passenger accommodations and most modern cargo handling facilities, this fleet, now in the process of organization, will raise new and higher standards in transpacific and round-the-world transportation. A passenger liner must be a first class hotel afloat and self contained. All her services must be maintained with a very high degree of reliability through her own machinery. In addition, she must be able to move herself on definite schedules from one port to another, almost regardless of weather. She is therefore one of the most complicated structures devised by the mind of man and her functioning is dependent on a great number and great variety of mechanisms. These together with the furnishings and equipment give work to a

President Cleveland *(left) and her sister* President Wilson *(right) undergoing completion at the Bethlehem Shipyard in Alameda, California* (courtesy of American President Lines).

great many artisans who are scattered all over the Nation and who in many cases may never have seen a shipyard or even seen salt water. The cost of a vessel is distributed over the whole country for labor and materials, to a greater degree than is true in any other industry. A partial list of the vendors supplying the *President Cleveland* indicates that it comes from 15 states, five of which are Middle Western states.'

Five-hundred passengers were aboard the maiden voyage of the gleaming new *President Cleveland*, as she steamed under the Golden Gate Bridge, in December 1947. The itinerary for this and many subsequent trips was:

San Francisco	December 27	Noon
Honolulu	January 1	6.00 am
Manila	January 13	6.00 am
Hong Kong	January 18	6.00 am
Shanghai	January 22	Tide
Yokohama	January 27	Tide
Honolulu	February 4	8.00 am
San Francisco	February 9	8.00 am

Fitted out as the finest Pacific luxury ships of their time, with their accommodation divided between three classes, cabin class, tourist class and third class, the passenger quarters were decorated in what was best described as 'American moderne', which was very deftly accentuated by the occasional introduction of Chinese motifs, thus saluting both America and the Orient. In a written appraisal of the *President Cleveland*, the descriptions read as, 'The first impression upon entering the Promenade Deck is of spaciousness. Much of the inboard bulkheads separating the promenade space from the public rooms is in large fixed glass windows and this combination produces the illusion of great wide-open spaces. The promenade itself is wide so that with six-footers stretched out on steamer chairs against the bulkhead, there is still a wide promenade free for pedestrians. Twelve times around this deck equals one mile, says the sign. The deck of the promenade is covered with dark green vinyl plastic molded into a diamond-shaped pattern with semi-abrasive surface and with small gutters outlining the

President Cleveland fresh from the yard. American President Lines discarded the old 'S' that had been used on smoke stacks by Dollar Line (from which APL evolved) and substituted a streamlined American eagle in white on the red band of the blue stacks.

pattern. On laboratory tests, this comparatively new material proves to have: many times the wearing quality of rubber or linoleum; a much harder surface than any other comparable deck covering; a great degree of fire resistance; and possibilities in color schemes that are only limited by the imagination of the designer.

'Interiors of the public rooms produce the same illusion of great wide open space that prevails on the Promenade Deck and for the same reason the lavish use of plate glass doors between the rooms. The Main Lounge, a large room with abundant fenestration, is decorated and furnished in restrained good taste. Focal point is the large fireplace with mirror above, central on the aft bulkhead. Into a niche in the mirror is set a specially-designed Chinese-style clock and flanking the fireplace on each side are green lacquered cabinets trimmed with golden bronze and supporting porcelain figurine lamps in modern Chinese motif. A beautiful pair of davenports with end tables form an inglenook. Occasional chairs and

tables in excellent taste and design for luxurious comfort are supplied in adequate quantity. Notably and thankfully missed is that great confusion of large, overstuffed atrocities that usually fills the main lounges on a passenger liner.

'Forward foyer and stairwell features a large mural on the after bulkhead of the well. This mural depicts the hills on each side of the entrance to San Francisco Bay, the Golden Gate Bridge and the outer portion of the Bay. The Smoking Room, a somewhat larger room than the Main Lounge, is panelled beautifully in mahogany. The predominant note in decor and furniture is a restrained moderne American and the Chinese motif is touched only in a modern Chinese chest with jade handles, and in the decorative treatment on the base of the table lamps. Next in order aft is the Main Entrance Hall and Stairwell with its flower and gift shops starboard, and service bar port, and an interesting brass stair rail design. Central in decor motif here are the elevator doors done in Chinese-style gold on black background. Short passages port and starboard contacting service rooms lead to the Cocktail Lounge where we pass immediately into modern China. The wall of this room is painted in a deep Chinese red and is decorated with Chinese line designs in gold wire. The Marine Veranda follows and, as its name suggests, there is a feeling of the outdoors and of a night club at the same time. The Cabin Class Dining Room cannot help but be an appetizing treat in decor as well as in food. Imagine a sumptuous Hawaiian foliage mural blended into a soft grey-blue and beige color scheme, edge-lighted glass panels and gold leather chairs at regular tables beneath a long range of lighted windows. Try Tourist Class—more carved glass—more mirrors, some bleached oak fluted columns—red chairs contrasting with French grey walls, all done with the light hand of restraint for long durability.'

The *President Cleveland* and *President Wilson* remained popular and very profitable ships for nearly two decades. By the late sixties, however, and as jet aircraft began to overtake most conventional liner trades, both ships were sent on periodic cruises: to Alaska, the Mexican Riviera and even farther afield, to the Mediterranean and to Northern Europe.

Operational costs continued, however, to increase and, by the early seventies, the American President Lines decided to phase-out its luxury passenger services. Both liners were placed on the sales lists and, primarily because of their superior construction and excellent maintenance, they attracted a buyer almost immediately, shipping tycoon C. Y. Tung, based at Hong Kong. He saw a bright future not only in transpacific passenger shipping, but in a round-the-world service as well. The *President Cleveland* was withdrawn from American President service in January 1973, and soon thereafter hoisted the Panamanian flag as the *Oriental President* for the Oceanic Cruises Development Corporation, a Tung

Twelve circuits of this deck equalled a mile — Cleveland's *rubber-tiled glass-enclosed promenade deck.*

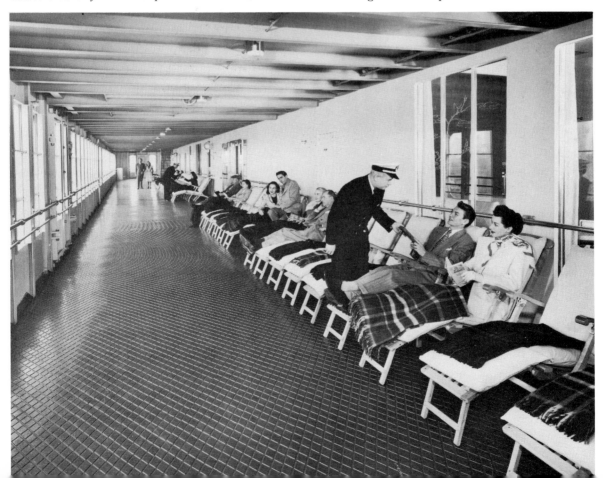

Gay departures marked President Cleveland*'s voyages from America's West Coast to the Orient* (courtesy of Palmer Pictures).

subsidiary and link to his Orient Overseas Line passenger division. The *President Wilson* , finishing her American President schedule that April, was handed over to the same owners and became the *Oriental Empress*.

The *Oriental President* was intended to run a Pacific service, sailing once more from San Francisco, and the *Oriental Empress* on the around-the-world trade. However, just as they were delivered to their owners, international fuel oil costs began to rise rapidly, from $35 to as much as $100 per ton. Almost all future plans had been revised or, more often, shelved—even for the thrifty Chinese. The former *President Cleveland* went directly to lay-up at Hong Kong and a year later, with little hope in sight, was handed over to shipbreakers at Kaohsiung. The

former *Wilson* saw some brief commerical service before she was permanently laid-up in September 1975. She was sold to Taiwanese scrappers a decade later, in 1985.

Gross tonnage: 15,359
Length overall: 609 feet
Width: 75 feet
Machinery: Turbo-electric, twin screw
Speed: 19 knots
Capacity: Approx 700 in three classes (1947); later changed to 324 in First, 454 Tourist; then to 304 First, 380 Economy class; and finally to 511 cruise passengers
Built: Bethlehem Alameda Shipyard, Alameda, California, 1948
Demise: Scrapped at Kaohsiung, Taiwan, 1974

174

La Marseillaise

A headline in the *Evening Telegraph*, dated August 18 1949, highlighted the long overdue completion of France's newest luxury liner. 'Maiden voyage of the liner *La Marseillaise* is scheduled to begin today from Marseilles to the Far East. During her voyage, the ship will call at Port Said, Suez, Djibouti (French Somaliland), Colombo, Singapore, Saigon, Hong Kong, Manila, Shanghai and finally Kobe and Yokohama. With a speed of 21 knots, *La Marseillaise* is expected to make the round voyage in 53 days.

'Designed for the Marseilles-Saigon (Indo-China) service of the Messageries Maritimes, *La Marseillaise* is the first big liner completed in France since 1939. She was originally laid down on 25 June 1939 [with completion planned for 1943], at the shipyard of Chantiers Navals de La Ciotat. Her construction went on slowly during the first months of the war, and was stopped after the armistice of June 1940. By that time, only 200 tons of steel had been assembled. Construction was restarted on 2 December 1940, as La Ciotat was then in the unoccupied area of France, and the Vichy Government wanted the various industries of this zone to have as much work as possible for French interests. At that time, the vessel, which had not been given a name and which hitherto has been known as Hull Number 161, was christened *Marechal Petain*, and she was launched as such on 10 June 1944.

'After the liberation of France, the Chantiers de La Ciotat had more urgent work to perform than to complete a deluxe liner so that her completion was much delayed, and it was only in August 1946, that the liner, then renamed *La Marseillaise*, was towed back to La Ciotat from the Jong de Berre, west of Marseilles, where she had been laid up since the end of June 1944. Her maiden festivities included a short cruise to Naples, with Mme Vincent Auriol, wife of the President of the French Republic, as one of the invited guests. Afterward, there was an inaugural cruise to Naples, Piraeus and Palermo.'

In a special commemorative brochure, Messageries Maritimes wrote of their new flagship, 'The decoration of *La Marseillaise*—with its choice of bright themes and use of fine materials, carefully selected and meticulously applied—make this vessel a sumptuous palace. The Main Lounge, with its white decor, picked out in tones of red, gold and grey, and enhanced by a richly embroidered tapestry by Jean Lurcat, communicates with the Card Room, walled with lacquer panels designed by Pierre Dunand, and the Writing Room with dilophane walls, enlivened with monochromes by Kaskoff. The first class Smoking Room, with its spacious window terrace brightened with ceramics by Colette Gueden, is decorated with three vivid lacquer panels by Pierre Bobot, setting off the green fabrics and leather upholstery. The first class Dining Room, in which the predominant shades of the carpets, curtains and chair covers are green and biege, is in the central portion a glass-roofed hall, two decks high; tapestries by Jean Picard Le Doux add to the rich and intimate atmosphere of this room, where film sessions are held regularly. Tourist class passengers have an elegantly furnished air-conditioned Dining Saloon, and a Smoke Room and Cocktail Lounge, which opens on to a splendid promenade deck. *La Marseillaise* provides a swimming pool and solarium, in addition to a gymnasium complete with a little bar. The children have a bright playroom of their own, decorated with vivid colored motifs as well as an open-air playground. The suites called Provence and Cote d'Azur comprise of a bedroom with twin beds, a small drawing room, bathroom and balcony. The partitions are of white maple to match the furniture draped with silk, navy blue for one, wine colored for the other. Priority cabins with shower rooms or bathrooms open on to private terraces, which look out to sea. Other facilities including a library,

hairdressing saloons and a laundry with ironing room are also available to passengers of *La Marseillaise*.'

La Marseillaise was, in her first years, a popular and successful member of the Messageries Maritimes express run out to the Far East. With sailings run every two to three weeks from Marseilles, she sailed in company with a series of pre-war liners, the *Andre Lebon, Marechal Joffre, Felix Roussel, Champollion* and *Athos II*, and then later with three brand new combination passenger-cargo liners, the *Cambodge, Laos* and *Viet Nam* of 1952-53. However, as France's political status in Southeast Asia changed and therefore the freight and passenger demands, ships such as *La Marseillaise* soon became superfluous. Used briefly as a hospital ship in Mediterranean waters, she was placed on the sales list in 1957, then barely eight years since her delivery.

Purchased by the Arosa Line, a Swiss-owned shipping company, her new purpose was to offer 'inexpensive, but comfortable' transatlantic crossings as well as winter cruises. Extensively refitted and given a greatly increased capacity, she was renamed *Arosa Sky* and entered service in the spring of 1957. On May 27, *The New York Times* reported, 'New York welcomed a new liner to port yesterday—the 17,321-ton *Arosa Sky*. As the trim, single-stacked Swiss-owned vessel moved up the Bay with an official welcoming party onboard, she was greeted by the traditional whistle salutes and fireboat sprays. She was also escorted by helicopters, tugboats and police

launches. The black-hulled, triple-screw liner passed the Battery at 9.12 am and tied up at Pier 88, at West 48th Street at 10.20 am. Her master expressed complete satisfaction with her sea-keeping qualities. Gale force winds in the Atlantic caused the 594 ft motorship to be a day late in arriving from German and Channel ports. The captain said that at the height of the storm, he was forced to slow to 8 kts. Large white patches where rough seas had torn away black hull paint on the liner's stem bore witness to the storm. Among the ship's 85 passengers was the Mayor of Arosa, Switzerland, for which the Arosa Line is named. He was delighted with the warmth of his welcome from the world's largest city and to a ship that is named after the smallest town in Switzerland (population 3,000). The *Arosa Sky* debarked 755 passengers at Halifax, her last port of call prior to New York.'

During her first season for the Arosa Co, the *Arosa Sky* sailed in the peak season months, between April and November, on the North Atlantic—trading between Bremerhaven, Le Havre, Southampton, Halifax and New York. Her accommoation had been enlarged considerably just for these sailings, to 64 in first class and 834 in tourist class. Beginning in December 1957, she cruised in the winter, off-season—on voyages ranging from seven days to Bermuda, with fares from $150, to an 18-day Grand Caribbean cruise, with prices from $395. Unfortunately, on that last named voyage, while sailing off

Suite 131, a de luxe cabin on La Marseillaise.

Wilmington, North Carolina (where she was to pick up extra passengers), a fire broke out in some of her passenger cabins. This caused some unpleasant publicity for the Arosa Line, a company formed as recently as 1952. Furthermore, there were other reports of unclean conditions on Arosa passenger ships, unhappy crewmembers who felt that they were inadequately paid and generally unsafe conditions. The Company suffered and advance reservations on many sailings were lower than anticipated. Matters did not improve and, by October 1958, the *Arosa Sky*, the latest addition and the Company flagship, went on the sales lists. On August 24 1958, *The New York Times* reported, 'Even an enlarged passenger capacity proved insufficient to make the *Arosa Sky* a money-maker in the highly competitive North Atlantic passenger field. Her earning capacity, it is believed, had been miscalculated to the extent that she just about broke even. The *Arosa Sky* was then considered unsuitable for anything but a cruise liner. Arosa, which bought the ship for $6.5 million from the French, spent another $3 million on improvements and extensions to her accommodation. The Costa Line of Italy is to take delivery of her at Genoa, on 8 November, and, following a purchase price of between $8,000,000 and $9,000,000 is reported planning to spend between $2,000,000 and $3,000,000 in refurbishing the vessel.'

While the Arosa Line itself soon collapsed fin-ancially and their remaining three passenger ships, the *Arosa Sun, Arosa Star* and *Arosa Kulm*, were auctioned-off for debts, the former *Arosa Sky* was reactivated as the Italian *Bianca C.* and placed in the Italy-Caribbean service. With her tonnage increased to 18,427, her accommodation was enlarged yet again, this time to 202 in first class and 1,030 tourist class. Her public rooms and cabins were finished in superb Italian contemporary styling. In his first edition of *Passenger Liners*, published in 1961, author Laurence Dunn wrote that the *Bianca C.* was 'given a major overhaul in which 75 per cent of the public rooms and cabins were renewed. Of the first class cabins, one-half have private shower and toilet. Has long sweep of public rooms on Lounge (Bridge) deck, with pool and lido above. Cabins are on Promenade, Veranda, A and B decks. First named has first class dining saloon right forward on port side. A special feature of the next deck are 20 deluxe cabins and two suites, each with private veranda. Tourist cabins include many two berth, several with own facilities.'

While the *Bianca C* sailed across the mid-Atlantic to Caribbean ports and on winter cruises to the same ports, but from New York and later Port Everglades, she did, in fact, become a victim to a malady well known to French and French-built liners—fire. On October 23 1961, the *Long Island Press* recorded her demise. 'Fire burned out an Italian liner within sight of St George's, Grenada today after all but one of the

La Marseillaise

Above *Bought by the short-lived Arosa Line,* La Marseillaise *was renamed* Arosa Sky. *She is shown here on her maiden arrival in New York* (courtesy of Moran Towing).

Below *A bit of company publicity on the top deck of* Arosa Sky — *her master poses with the young ladies designated as Miss* Arosa Star, *Miss* Arosa Kulm, *Miss* Arosa Sky *and Miss* Arosa Sun *on June 18, 1957.*

750 persons aboard escaped. All hopes were abandoned for salvaging the *Bianca C*, which burst into flames last night shortly after anchoring in the harbour about a mile off shore. Maritime officials were investigating reports of an explosion before the fire, but these could not be confirmed. The rescue was carried out smoothly in Caribbean waters, and another Italian liner, the *Surriento* of the Lauro Line, was ordered to Grenada to pick up passengers and crew if necessary. Bound for La Guaira, most of the passengers onboard the *Bianca C* were immigrants.'

Burnt out and most likely ruined beyond repair, the *Bianca C*—after a very variable career— quietly heeled over and sank on October 24.

Gross tonnage: 17,321 (1949); 17,408 (1957); 18,427 (1959)
Length overall: 594 feet
Width: 75 feet
Machinery: Sulzer diesels, triple screw
Speed: 21 knots
Capacity: 344 First, 74 Second, 318 Third (1949); 64 First, 834 Tourist (1957); 202 First, 1,030 Tourist (1959)
Built: Chantiers Navals de La Ciotat, La Ciotat, France, 1939-49
Demise: Burnt out and then sank off St George's Grenada, October 22-24 1961

Fifty Famous Liners

Ocean Monarch

She was called 'the largest liner yet built primarily for cruising' by at least one British shipping journal, but—more realistically—she was a specialised, yacht-like liner of some 13,600 tons. Thirty-five years later, the news media were heralding 'the largest cruiseship ever built', the 48,200-ton *Jubilee* of the Carnival Cruise Lines. Since the era of Furness Bermuda Line's *Ocean Monarch*, completed in the spring of 1951, the cruise industry throughout the world has changed and increased enormously.

Furness-Bermuda had hoped to restore both of its celebrated pre-war liners, the three-stackers *Monarch of Bermuda* and *Queen of Bermuda*, for revived weekly cruises between New York and Bermuda. Most unfortunately, the former was swept by fire while undergoing her post-war refit in 1947, and then was sold off (presumably for scrapping, but was, in fact, rebuilt by the British Government as the migrant carrier *New Australia*). The *Queen of Bermuda* was successfully refitted and resumed her Bermuda sailings in 1949, but was, in a rather lonely state, without a proper fleetmate. While Furness might have ordered a larger liner, similar to the 22,500 tons of the *Queen*, they opted instead for something of a 'cruising yacht', a smaller vessel that could travel deeper into the Caribbean and at the same time offer her passengers considerable intimacy.

Built by the Vickers Armstrong yard at Newcastle, the *Ocean Monarch* commenced her trials in March 1951, and then departed from London on April 18, for her transatlantic delivery and positioning at New York. The *Herald Tribune* recorded her first arrival, in their April 28 edition. 'The new vacation liner *Ocean Monarch* arrived yesterday with 19 passengers from London. Built specifically for luxury cruises out of New York to Bermuda and to nearby southern and northern waters, the liner completed a ten-day crossing from her British home port. Heading the list of passengers was the chairman of Furness, Withy & Co, the parent of the Furness Bermuda Line. The trim vessel swung up the Bay from Quarantine during the noon hour, answering every salute from other ships in port with three blasts from her deep-throated horn on her one funnel. Two city fireboats poured tons of water into the air as the *Ocean*

Monarch glided past the Statue of Liberty and several airplanes, including the Police Department helicopter, which performed aerial stunts as a welcoming gesture. Father Knickerbocker, impersonated by a mayoral aide, came down the bay in the tugboat *C. Hayward Meseck* to greet the vessel. The *Ocean Monarch* tied-up at 2.00 pm at Pier 95, West 55th Street and the Hudson River, and just across from the larger *Queen of Bermuda*, which will continue as the flagship of Furness Bermuda's cruise fleet. The *Ocean Monarch* is slated to sail on Thursday [3 May] on her maiden voyage, an eight-day cruise to Bermuda and Nassau. The new ship has a full schedule of cruises to these islands as well as a series of four 12-day trips from New York to the Saguenay and St Lawrence Rivers. Built at a cost of $10,000,000, the *Ocean Monarch* was designed and constructed based upon a series of specifications and rough drawings furnished by the Furness passenger staff in New York.'

Her accommodation for 440 all-first class passengers was apprized as, 'The ship's six passenger decks have been laid out according to the best standards of modern naval architecture. The Sun Deck will feature a lounge forward, the grand entrance foyer, a

smoking room and a large cafe-dance club. Fourteen staterooms occupy the central portion of this deck. The public rooms and cabins will be surrounded on the sides and aft by a promenade, enclosed forward. The aft end of the promenade extend in two wings to overlook the open swimming pool on the promenade deck below. Passenger cabins and the pool will occupy the entire promenade deck, with only one bank of staterooms on either side. The central portions of A Deck will be devoted to domes over the dining saloon and movie theatre, to be located on B Deck. The dining saloon will occupy the entire width of the vessel and will be air-conditioned. Additional passenger cabins are to be forward of the saloon and on the port side of C Deck. All staterooms will have private bathroom facilities and all cabins are to be connected to the ship's telephone exchange.

During her inaugural season, the *Ocean Monarch*, which was quickly acclaimed as a very comfortable and pleasant ship, ran a rather diverse series of cruises in addition to the normal six-day round trips to and from Bermuda. There was one six-day cruise to

Bermuda and Halifax; several nine-day sailings to Nassau and Havana; several voyages out of Boston; the 12-day Canadian cruises to the Saguenay River, Quebec City, Halifax or Montreal and Bermuda; a 12-day Christmas cruise to Port au Prince, Cartagena and Kingston; and, shortest of all, several four-day cruises to Bermuda (with fares beginning at $125 and including one over the New Year's holiday).

After some fifteen or so years of service, the *Ocean Monarch* and the aged *Queen of Bermuda* were hard hit by flashier, new cruiseships, rising costs for British-flag ships and, perhaps most important of all, new, very strict safety standards that were to be enforced by the US Coast Guard. While the *Queen* could not be expected to pass, even the newer *Ocean Monarch* would require a substantial refit to succeed. Furness evaluated the decision and, during 1966,

decided to terminate completely their North American cruise operations. In August of that year, the fifteen-year-old *Ocean Monarch* ran her final cruise from New York and then sailed empty across the Atlantic to await the inspection of potential buyers at a Falmouth mooring.

She went to rather unknown buyers, the Balkanturist Co of Bulgaria, who wanted her as a national cruiseship. Renamed *Varna*, little else was changed except that some Bulgarian art and commemoratives were placed in the public lounges. Used initially in the Black and Mediterranean Seas, she was chartered, in the early seventies, for cruising on the St Lawrence River out of Montreal. Her operators were a shortlived firm known as the Gala Navigation Co. However, by 1974, soon after the dramatic increases in fuel oil charges, she was without further

Although she proved too small, Ocean Monarch *was always a popular and fine looking liner.*

Ocean Monarch

She was one of the very rare ships which boasted a modern style figurehead decoration. It portrayed Father Neptune, the ocean monarch.

work and consequently laid-up. With little hope in sight for reactivation, she was sold to Greek interests several years later, but with little further change except that she was moved to an anchorage at Perama, near Piraeus. In 1979, she was to have been refitted for Mediterranean cruising out of Venice as the *Riviera*. This scheme never materialised and was followed by another shortlived plan, for the so-called World Cruise Lines, that was to see her return to the New York-Bermuda trade, possibly renamed as the *Venus*. In 1981, printed materials were issued for her as the *Reina del Mar*, cruising not only in the Mediterranean, but to Scandinavia and the North Cape as well. Unfortunately, while refitting at Perama, on May 28 1981, she was destroyed by fire and then later capsized. She became a total loss, a pathetic ending for such a fine little liner.

Gross tonnage: 13,654 (1951); 13,581 (1961)
Length overall: 516 feet
Width: 72 feet
Machinery: Steam turbines, twin screw
Speed: 18 knots
Capacity: 440 First class passengers, later revised to 414
Built: Vickers-Armstrong Shipbuilders Ltd, Newcastle, England, 1951
Demise: Burnt out and sunk at Perama, Greece, May 28 1981

Fifty Famous Liners

Flandre

Her builders, Ateliers et Chantiers de France of Dunkirk, were reported to have said, 'Well...you wanted a cheap ship and now you've got it!' As France's first brand new post-war transatlantic liner, the maiden voyage to New York of the 20,500-ton motorliner *Flandre* was a dismal, mortifying flop. With breakdowns in the mid-Atlantic, she had to be towed into New York harbor for her welcoming reception. Unsympathetic, dockers thereafter referred to her as 'the Flounder'.

On July 31 1952, *The New York Times* featured a lengthy story on the ship's first call. 'A modern marine precedent was established here yesterday as the new French luxury liner *Flandre* made her debut, but under tow. Anchored, and almost helpless after a power failure, the gallant ship was forced to remain off Staten Island for six hours before sufficient power could be restored to raise her big anchor chain. Then, operating on a single screw and towed by four high-powered tugboats, she slowly proceeded to her pier. She was nearly 23 hrs late. It was a bitter pill for the French Line to have to swallow, for the new ship was the largest and fastest vessel to emerge from a French shipyard in more than a decade.

'The vessel, with 634 passengers and 650 crew-members onboard, had been plagued by a series of mishaps almost from the start of her maiden voyage. She left Le Havre on 23 July, stopped briefly at Southampton and then headed west into the Atlantic. Within 24 hrs, she was temporarily disabled. Her fuel line filters, according to Company officials, had become clogged by impurities in her oil supply. It took 4 hrs to clean out the filters and restore the boilers to normal operation. The next night the incident was repeated with the loss of several additional hours. Taking no further chances, the skipper of the *Flandre* ordered her speed reduced for the remainder of the voyage. Shortly before daybreak yesterday, she passed Ambrose Channel Lightship at the entrance to New York Harbor and proceeded gracefully up to the Quarantine Station at Rosebank, Staten Island. At no time did the ship give any indication that she was about to suffer a severe power failure that was destined to dampen her harbor reception and humiliate her owners.

'It was just 6.30 am when the sleek black and white ship lowered her anchor with a resounding splash into the choppy waters of the Upper Bay and began dressing for her harbor reception. Within a matter of seconds, a short circuit in the main switchboard cut off nearly all the electric power aboard the ship. Technicians worked at a feverish pace to restore the current. This was partly accomplished by 9.15 am, but there was still not sufficient power to raise the anchor. For three more hours, the unusually attractive ''Mademoiselle'' drifted to and fro, tugging, as if in desperation, at the seemingly obstinate chain that hung taut from the starboard bow. At 12.55 pm, a mighty cheer reverberated through the ship as the anchor was finally drawn in. Ten minutes later, one and all were shocked to see four tugs of the Moran Towing & Transportation Co pull alongside to set the ship on her course and give her auxiliary power. Holding her bow high with true French gallantry, she moved slowly through the Upper Bay and to her pier at West 48th Street.

'Her single red and black funnel seemed to strain as it belched thick, black clouds of smoke in answer to the welcoming whistles of harbor craft. When her limited power caused her whistle to grow faint, the ship's siren was sounded. As she entered the North River, hundreds of persons filled Battery Park and lined the sea wall to wave and cheer the beautiful vessel that had suffered such misfortune. Meanwhile, the ship's passengers as well as representatives of the press, radio and television, and City and French Line

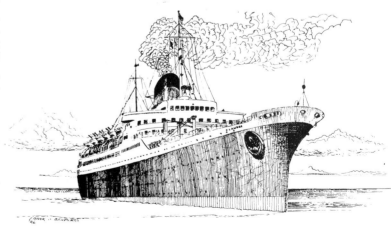

officials, who had boarded the ship off Tompkins-ville, Staten Island, took it all good-naturedly. The Fire Department band had also boarded the liner at anchor and spent the next six hours entertaining all onboard. Julie Wilson, a nightclub singer and passenger, donned a swimsuit and entertained with diving and other antics in the ship's pool. Sandwiches were served to the passengers in their staterooms and liquor flowed freely with the bars wide open and all drinks "on the house". Off Pier 25, at the foot of Franklin Street, the gallant ship exchanged greetings with the outbound Cunard liner *Queen Mary*. It was 2.45 pm when the liner was finally warped into her berth and the gangways were lashed to the starboard deck. Company officials warned last night, however, that the *Flandre*'s departure from New York, originally scheduled for noon tomorrow, might be delayed as local engineers would be asked to go over the ship's engines and correct any defects. What these may amount to is not known.'

This obviously was a bitter tonic to the French Line. She returned to Le Havre and then went immediately to her builder's yard at Dunkirk. Repairs would take some six months. All of her 1952 transatlantic sailings had to be cancelled and her passengers reassigned either to the already well-booked *Liberte* and *Ile de France* or to passenger ships of other companies. The *Flandre* would not reappear on the Atlantic until the spring of 1953. It was a very sad, very embarrassing beginning. She would be known as 'the Flounder' for some time afterward.

While her passenger configurations were changed on several occasions, she finally settled down to a balance of services: transatlantic to New York for about nine months of the year and then, together with her near-sister *Antilles* and the pre-war *Colombie*, on the Le Havre-West Indies for the remainder. In the early sixties, as the celebrated *Ile de France* and *Liberte* were both sent to the scrappers, the *Flandre* was briefly teamed with the mighty *France*, which was first introduced in 1962. It was, at best, an ill-matched arrangement and one further complicated by the diminishing Atlantic trade. In the fall of 1962, the *Flandre* was taken off the New York run permanently, repainted in all-white and sent year-round to the Caribbean. Her

A sad maiden arrival. With all electrical power lost the Flandre *had to be towed into her pier from Quarantine off New York.*

Fifty Famous Liners

OUTSIDE CABIN   S.S. FLANDRE   FIRST CLASS

These two interior shots of Flandre *show off her typical French charm and style.*

SMOKING ROOM   S.S. FLANDRE   FIRST CLASS

Sold to Costa, she was used by Princess Cruises and known as the Princess Carla *although her name was actually* Carla C.

only return to the Northern run came in 1967 when she made two crossings to Montreal in conjunction with Expo '67. Shortly thereafter, as the traditional two-class Caribbean trade slumped, the *Flandre* was withdrawn completely.

She joined Italy's Costa Line in February 1968 and, after extensive refitting that included the creation of 754 all-first class berths only, she was recommissioned as the *Carla C*. Her first assignment was, however, a charter to the Los Angeles-based Princess Cruises, who, in fact, marketed her as the *Princess Carla* (she was never officially renamed) on West Coast cruises to the Mexican Riviera and later through the Panama Canal to the Caribbean. She was said to be the inspiration for 'Love Boat', first a book and then a popular television series, which concentrated primarily on a subsequent Princess liner, the *Pacific Princess*.

The *Carla C* was returned to Costa in 1970, and assigned to the seven-day run out of San Juan, Puerto Rico, wherein she calls at Curacao, La Guaira, Grenada, Martinique and St Thomas. This has remained her operation ever since, with the exception of several 'drydock crossings' to Italy and several cruises out of La Guaira, which included revisits to New York in the early 1980s. One important change occurred in 1974-75, when she was converted at Amsterdam to a motorliner. Her original turbines were replaced by Stork-Werkspor diesels.

Gross tonnage: 20,477 (1952); 19,975 (1968)
Length overall: 600 feet
Width: 80 feet
Machinery: Steam turbines, twin screw (changed in 1974-75 to Stork-Werkspor diesels)
Speed: 22 knots
Capacity: 402 First, 389 Cabin, 97 Tourist (1952); 339 First, 285 Tourist, 100 interchangeable (1954); 232 First, 511 Tourist (1955); 754 First (1968)
Built: Ateliers et Chantiers de France, Dunkirk, France, 1952

186

Olympia

When launched, on April 16 1953, from the yards of Alexander Stephen & Sons Ltd of Glasgow, she was without a name and instead was simply referred to as 'Number 636'. She was to have been called *Frederica*, after the reigning Queen of Greece, but just before the christening ceremonies, a dispute over mortgages and other matters arose between her owners, the Goulandris Group, and the Greek Government in Athens. Intended to be new flagship of the Greek Merchant Marine, the argument was not settled and instead the ship was placed under the Liberian colours, with her home port listed as Monrovia (instead of Piraeus as planned). Her operators, the Greek Line, would have to be content with the distinction of 'the largest liner to be owned by Greek interests'. Just prior to her completion, in October of the same year, she was christened as the *Olympia*.

She was also the largest liner and flagship of the Greek Line and, at first, it was decided to use her on the booming North Atlantic run, sailing between Bremerhaven, Southampton, Cherbourg, Cobh, Halifax and New York. Her maiden voyage was, in fact, begun at Glasgow and sailed via Belfast, Liverpool, Southamtpon, Cherbourg and Cobh and then across to Halifax and New York. She would also be used, for about three months each winter, for Caribbean cruising.

The *Shipbuilding & Shipping Record* evaluated the brand new *Olympia* in their October 29 1953 issue. 'The keynote throughout [the accommodation] is simplicity. No money has been spent on elaborate cornices, very little on carpets and on the whole extremely effective results have been obtained by the use of simple materials. Although the ships are for absolutely different services, the *Olympia* corresponds in many respects to the Bergen Line passenger ship *Leda*. Both are generally of gay, contemporary decoration, with maximum use made of new plastic materials. Neither, while modern, is garish and both provide a stimulating holiday atmosphere. On both ships it is obvious that an intimate, cozy atmosphere has been a prime design requirement, and in each case the methods of achieving it have been somewhat similar. While the tourist saloon of the *Olympia* is claimed to be the largest

afloat, it has been broken up by pillars, flower boxes and other means to make the passengers feel at ease in their own little dining areas. This breaking up of sizeable spaces is perhaps even better demonstrated in the tourist Derby Room, where a metal grille gives the impression of completely dividing the space.'

On the other hand, another British publication, *The Shipping World*, was not as impressed with the new flagship. 'The interiors of the *Olympia* drove another nail into the coffin of the conventional, uninspired schemes for ship decoration to which we have been accustomed for so long' they also made preliminary arrangements for their own funeral. As a ship built to carry her tourist passengers in comparative luxury, the purpose of the *Olympia* is clear enough. But the way in which she was designed to do this leaves the senses confused. The lasting impression made of her 21 public rooms, created by a series of designers and decorators, and each of them working in a different way and at different times, were uncertain of the best way to set about their tasks. Their work taken collectively lacks the theme and unity that could have been achieved if one co-ordinating architect had controlled the project from the onset.'

Two months after her introduction into Atlantic service, the *Olympia* made headline news. In the December 15 1953 issue of *The New York Times*, the headline read 'Crippled *Olympia* To Enter Drydock'. 'The new Greek Line flagship *Olympia* will go into drydock early tomorrow after having run aground on a mud bank last night at Southampton. The liner damaged her rudder in the accident shortly after leaving here for the United States and Canada

An artist's impression of the Olympia, *to be built in Glasgow.*

with 1,000 passengers onboard, including many German immigrants. She has been refloated and today was lying at anchor about ten miles out. The accident reportedly was the result of a failure in the ship's electrical system. She was plunged into darkness and the steering motor affected. The *Olympia*, due here in New York on December 21, was to have

Hull No 636 under construction early in 1953.

picked up more passengers at Cherbourg and at Cobh. Onboard are 5,000 bags of Christmas mail for the United States and Canada. Passengers will live onboard the *Olympia* while repairs, expected to take from two to four days, are carried out. It will be decided tomorrow whether they will be allowed to go ashore.'

Like the early years of many new passenger liners, mechanical problems continued for the *Olympia* and during a winter cruise, in the following March, she had once again problems with her engines. The General Electric Co made the necessary repairs once she returned to New York.

In March 1955, the *Olympia* changed places with the pre-war *Nea Hellas*. The older ship, after a thorough refit and renaming as *New York*, would be moved to the Bremerhaven route; the *Olympia* would begin sailing from the Mediterranean. The latter ship was routed from Piraeus and sailed westbound to Halifax and New York via Messina, Naples, Lisbon and the Azores. On the outbound trips, the call at Halifax was eliminated and often replaced by Boston. In later years, this itinerary was extended to include Haifa In Israel and Limassol on Cyprus. During the winter, off-season months, she continued to cruise in the Caribbean and also began to make an annual eight-week luxury trip to the

Fifty Famous Liners

Launched on April 16, 1953, she featured an unusual 'knuckle' forward which prevented these cabins having sharply slanting outer bulkheads. Note the figurehead design on her stem.

Mediterranean and Black Seas.

It was not until September 1968, while moored at New York's Pier 97, that the earlier dispute with the Greek Government was finally resolved. Finally, she hoisted the Greek colours. However, she was no longer the national flagship, a distinction that had passed to the former *Empress of Britain*, which had become the Greek Line's *Queen Anna Maria* in 1965.

As the Atlantic trade declined, the *Olympia* was used more and more for cruising, mostly one-week trips to Bermuda and Nassau from New York as well as three-day cruises out to sea, 'voyages to nowhere'. In 1970, during a major refit, she was converted, in fact, to a full time cruiseship. Her lido deck was extended, plumbing put in all of her passenger cabins and restyled with 1,037 all-first class berths. She returned to New York cruising for a time, but, beginning in the spring of 1974, she was to run weekly Aegean cruises out of Piraeus, a new venture for the Greek Line. The Company wanted to capitalise on the rush of American tourists in particular to the Eastern Mediterranean. Simultaneously, however, the dramatic increase in fuel oil costs cut into

her projected passenger loads (because of the rising costs in airfares from the US) and also into her own operational expenses. Reluctantly, on March 24, she was laid up in Perama Bay, supposedly to await better times. Within less than a year, the Greek Line was bankrupt and its holdings seized by the Greek Government.

The *Olympia*—nearly forgotten, rusting and mostly neglected—sat in Perama Bay. Most commentators on the passenger ship industry felt that her next voyage would be to the scrapyard. The Lauro Line, Carnival Cruise Lines and even the Sheraton Hotel Co had a look over her, but nothing materialized. She was purchased, however, in 1981, by the Sally Line of Finland, who wanted to use her as a floating hotel that moved possibly once or twice a year, say between Europe and the Caribbean. The same company had also just purchased another Greek liner, the *Navarino*, formerly the *Gripsholm* of 1957, which they planned to use in the ever-increasing Miami cruise trades to the Caribbean. These plans went astray when, in November 1981, the *Navarino* capsized while in a floating dock and was declared a constructive total loss. (The decision

Olympia

This aerial view of liners in New York shows, from left to right; Britannic *(her low motorship stacks barely visible),* Queen Elizabeth, Mauretania, Liberté, Olympia *and* United States (courtesy of Transatlantic Passenger Conference).

was later re-evaluated and this ship has since been repaired and now sails as the *Regent Sea*.) The plan to convert the *Olympia* into a hotelship was abandoned and she was refitted for Caribbean service. Her refit, done in two stages, at Piraeus and then at Hamburg, produced a different looking ship—minus her original mast, funnel and kingposts. She resumed sailing, in Caribbean waters, as the *Caribe I* in the later summer of 1983. Life for the former *Olympia* continues.

Gross tonnage: 22,979 (1953); 17,434 (1968)
Length overall: 611 feet
Width: 79 feet
Machinery: Steam turbines, twin screw (changed to diesel in 1982)
Speed: 22 knots
Capacity: 138 First, 1,169 Tourist (1953); 1,037 First (1970); 1,154 (1982)
Built: Alexander Stephen & Sons Ltd Glasgow, Scotland, 1953.

Rebuilt by Commodore Cruise Line, Olympia *is renamed* Caribe I *and her classic profile modernized drastically. Only the bow knuckle remains to identify her as the 1953 Greek Line flagship.*

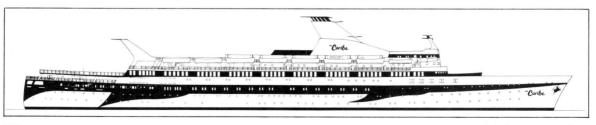

Saxonia

'As the *Queen Elizabeth* completed her first Atlantic crossing as a luxury liner, Frederic Alan Bates, new chairman of the Cunard-White Star Co, said in a report today [October 21 1946] that the Company had no desire to build bigger or better ships and that as long as an Atlantic service could be maintained like a railway timetable, he would be satisfied. ''The two giant liners we have are sufficient to do the job of maintaining a service in each direction from Great Britain and America weekly'', the new chairman declared. He succeeded his brother, the late Sir Percy Bates, who died on the eve of the *Queen Elizabeth*'s departure from Southampton.'

Consequently, from those immediate post-war years, the mighty Cunard Co had little interest in building new superliners. They would be, or so it seemed, content with more moderately sized tonnage. Their New York run was handled by the giant 'Queens', the *Mauretania*, the *Britannic*, the combination liners *Media* and *Parthia*, and on occasion by the big cruiseship *Caronia*. The separate Canadian service was run with four pre-war passenger ships, the *Ascania, Franconia, Samaria* and *Scythia*. All of them were, however, ageing and growing increasingly troublesome. Therefore, plans were made for some new tonnage on this route. The first announcement was made just before Christmas of 1951, 'Two of the largest Cunarders ever built specifically for the steamship line's Canadian service

are to be constructed by John Brown of Clydeside, the Cunard Steamship Co announced'. More realistically, the two ships—and in an order that was later extended two more sisters—were placed at some 22,000 gross tons, which was quite an average size for earlier Cunarders and those of the rival Canadian Pacific Co. They would appear at almost yearly intervals, between 1954 and 1957, as the *Saxonia, Ivernia, Carinthia* and *Sylvania*.

The launching of the first of this series was well recorded by, among others, *Shipbuilding & Shipping Record* magazine, dated February 25 1954. 'Before a large gathering in the shipyard of John Brown & Co (Clydebank) on 17 February, Lady Churchill named the *Saxonia*, the first of a quartet of new liners for the Canadian service of the Cunard Steamship Co Ltd. The new vessel and her sisters are the largest Cunarders built for service to Quebec and Montreal. Speaking at a ceremony after the launch, in acknowledging the gift of an 18th century diamond brooch presented by the director of the John Brown Co, Lady Churchill said as she had walked alongside the *Saxonia* on the launching berth that morning and saw her lofty and graceful lines, she had been thrilled. She hoped that the new vessel would have many happy and successful voyages. In company with Lady Churchill was the High Commissioner of Canada. Before she travelled north, she asked her husband [then Prime Minister]

Jack Gray, a noted Canadian maritime artist, painted this view of Saxonia *entering the Hudson.*

if he would give a little message for the occasion. His message was— ''Canada, as well as being a glorious member of the British Commonwealth of Nations, is also a link across the Atlantic Ocean of the English-speaking world. Here we are creating physical arrangements which helped to turn into actual important facts those aims for an even closer unity to which we all aspire.''

'The chairman of John Brown & Co, who expressed regret that Lady Churchill had been unsuccessful in her efforts to persuade Sir Winston to accompany her to Clydebank— although he was sure that she had done her best— said he would like to recall the occasion when the Premier was last in the shipyard. On 28 February 1940, when he was First Lord of the Admiralty, he was in attendance upon his late Majesty, King George VI, at the launching of the battleship HMS *Duke of York*. Two days before that event, the *Queen Elizabeth* had left the yard, gone down the river, paused at the Tail of the Bank for 24 hrs to take on oil, and then sailed without any previous trials and without escort across the Atlantic

at full speed to New York. During the whole of that voyage, the chairman continued, there was no mechanical difficulty with the ship at all, and no adjustment of any sort required to be made, and he knew of no greater tribute than that to the workmanship of the men on the Clyde.

'The *Saxonia* had been launched from the same berth and had been built by the same men, or their sons, who built that great ship and her earlier sister, the *Queen Mary*. She was the first of four ships which they were privileged to build for the Canadian service of the Cunard Co and would replace vessels more than 30 yrs old. He trusted that she would enjoy as long an innings. Had the *Saxonia* been of 26,000 tons instead of 22,000, she would have brought the total Cunarders built at Clydebank up to a figure of some 500,000 gross tons. He also read congratulatory telegrams from six Cunard captains, five of them

192

Saxonia passes the Statue of Liberty.

from Clydebank-built ships—the *Franconia, Queen Mary, Queen Elizabeth, Media* and *Caronia*. The sixth had come from the master of a retired ship, the Clydebank-built *Aquitania*.

The *Saxonia*—with her single domed funnel, somewhat reminiscent of the *Caronia* of 1949—entered service on September 2 1954, between Liverpool and the St Lawrence. Later teamed with the new *Ivernia*, she was transferred to her intended service: Southampton and Le Havre to Quebec City and Montreal, and then in winter, to New York and Halifax. On December 6, the *Herald Tribune* reported her first arrival at New York. 'The new Cunard liner *Saxonia* received the traditional welcome yesterday as she steamed to her berth on her first visit here—36 hrs behind schedule. Fireboats cascaded streams of water, other ships tooted their horns and city officials and spectators on shore did their bit to welcome the new ship. The *Saxonia* bucked headwinds of gale and hurricane force in the

Atlantic and docked at 9.20 am at Pier 92, West 52nd Street and the Hudson River, with 716 passengers from Liverpool. Her skipper said he encountered unrelenting headwinds after passing the Island of Cobh, off Ireland. ''There were very few passengers who were happy'', said the Glasgow-born captain. He said the rough weather, with headwinds sometimes reaching 100 mph, stayed with the vessel all the way to Halifax. After that, he said, the passengers were ''compensated'' with pleasant, calm weather.'

Shipbuilding & Shipping Record reported at that time, 'The wooing of the tourist classes is continued in the new Cunarder *Saxonia*. Not only do tourist class passengers outnumber first class by six to one, but their present importance has been adequately recognized by the appointment, for the first time in a Cunard ship, of a head waiter in the tourist restaurant. The appointment is symbolic of the Company's attitude throughout to tourist passengers. The head waiter's sole function, as always in the past in first class dining saloons, is to see that the passenger is contented with his food. Similarly, in

Above *Moran tugs assist her into her slip.* **Below** *Eight years later she was rebuilt and renamed, becoming the* Carmania. *This artist's idea of what was to be done with her pool area aft was sent to many newspapers.*

other public rooms and cabins, the tourist passengers will find the Company have gone out of their way to see that he is well catered for. Indeed, there are even some advantages over first class in travelling tourist in the *Saxonia*. As they serve so many more people, the tourist public rooms are much more numerous and spacious, whereas the first class public apartments, while more extravagantly furnished, are naturally somewhat small by comparison.'

The *Saxonia* and her three sisters were only mildly successful in their intended transatlantic purpose, primarily due to the appearance of the jet by the late fifties. In 1962-63, she and the *Ivernia* were returned to their builder's yard and refitted as green-hulled cruiseships that would only ply the North Atlantic in prime summer season. Virtually new ships, they were even given fresh names: the *Saxonia* became the *Carmania*, the *Ivernia* changed to *Franconia*. In winters, the former was based at Port Everglades, Florida for 'sunshine' cruising to the Caribbean. She went aground during one of these cruises, on January 12 1969, on San Salvador Island in the Bahamas. She was reportedly grounded not far from the spot where Christopher Columbus was said to have landed nearly 500 years before. Four months later, on May 14, she was in collision with the Soviet tanker *Frunze* off Gibraltar during a Mediterranean cruise from Southampton.

Used in her final Cunard years as a full time cruiseship, she was finally retired at the end of 1971, a classic victim of increasing competition within the cruise trades, rising operational costs and declining passenger loads. Thought to be sold to the Greek Chandris Group for the Australian migrant trade and to the Japanese, who wanted to create a deep-sea Pacific Ocean cruise service, she was transferred eventually to the Soviets, to their Black Sea Steamship Co of Odessa. Renamed *Leonid Sobinov* (and the *Franconia*, ex-*Ivernia* as the *Feodor Shalyapin*), she was used periodically on the CTC Lines' service out to Australia and New Zealand, on cruises and for Soviet Government purposes (including some troop transporting). She remains in service at the time of writing, well past her prime, which was predicted by her original builders on the Clyde.

Gross tonnage: 21,367 (1954); 22,592 (1963); 21,370 (1969)
Length overall: 608 feet
Width: 80 feet
Machinery: Steam turbines, twin screw
Speed: 19½ knots
Capacity: 125 First, 800 Tourist (1954); 117 First, 764 Tourist (1963)
Built: John Brown & Co Ltd, Clydebank, Scotland, 1954

An aerial view of the rebuilt liner. Her sister, Ivernia, *was also rebuilt and became* Franconia.

Southern Cross

She was the most revolutionary liner of her time: the first big passenger ship to mount engines and therefore funnel aft, the first to carry only all-tourist class passengers in comfortable quarters, the first to carry no cargo whatsoever and the first to run year-round circumnavigations. She was Shaw Savill's *Southern Cross*, completed in 1955, a ship that has somehow managed to escape the dreaded scrapper's torch and continue in successful cruise service to date.

In Shaw Savill's *The Log*, published in October 1954, the launch of this new ship was the subject of much attention. 'At 1.15 pm, on 17th August 1954, Her Majesty the Queen launched the new Shaw Savill passenger liner, the *Southern Cross*, at the Harland & Wolff yards at Belfast. Her Majesty broke her Highland holiday at Balmoral and, despite the inclement weather, flew to Belfast especially for the occasion. The thousands who were present at the shipyard heard the Queen's clear voice say: "I name this ship the *Southern Cross*. May God protect her and all who sail in her". As the vessel slid down the slipway and took the water, the cheering rose to a crescendo to mark the conclusion of a simple but impressive ceremony.

'Her Majesty, responding to the toast of her health, said that, "Our great shipbuilding industry might well take pride in the *Southern Cross*, for she was of an entirely new and original design." She congratulated all those who had planned and built the ship as well as the Company who had ordered her to replace some of the losses suffered in the war and to keep pace with the changing conditions of service.

'The Queen continued, 'I have recently travelled many thousands of miles in the *Gothic* [used as a royal yacht in 1953-54 for an around-the-world Coronation tour], one of the ships of this Company, and in her I have been through many of the ports to which the *Southern Cross* will sail. This new ship, I understand, will encircle the world four times a year. What nobler cause could she serve than to bring the countries of the Commonwealth and Empire and other places closer together?"'

The *Southern Cross*, fully booked for the occasion, set off on her first 76-day round voyage, on March 29 1955. Her ports of call, travelling westabout, included Trinidad, Curacao, the Panama Canal, Tahiti, Fiji, Wellington, Sydney, Melbourne. Fremantle, Durban, Capetown, Las Palmas and then return to Southampton. Soon afterward, *The Syren and Shipping* praised the new liner. 'The departure of the *Southern Cross* on her maiden voyage from Southampton was an auspicious event in the history

Above Southern Cross *on her trials in 1955.*

Right *A postcard of the new liner at her pier. She was the first to carry her stack right aft.*

Southern Cross

197

Renamed Calypso, *she became a cruise ship.*

of British shipping for she represents an entirely new conception in the design of large vessels of this class. Her unusual layout and profile have already aroused worldwide interest and admiration, and her owners and builders are justly proud of this remarkable ship. Their confidence has been backed in a most convincing way by the travelling public for she has been fully booked for the remainder of 1955 and a large part of the accommodation has already been reserved for 1956.'

The Syren and Shipping also examined her decoration and appointments. 'In addition to the luxury which the present-day travelling public is accustomed to expect in large passenger vessels, the interior designer concerned with a ship destined to spend much of her life in tropical waters is confronted with special problems. An atmosphere of heavy opulence, no matter how magnificent at first sight, rapidly becomes oppressive in hot weather. The designer's aim, therefore, must be to combine solid comfort with lightness, to employ rich materials with a delicate touch and to produce an effect of pervading airiness. This aim has been strikingly achieved throughout the public rooms of the *Southern Cross*.

'The main forward lounge is a good example. The room extends the full width of the ship with windows extending almost continuously along both sides and the forward end, fitted with Venetian blinds in pastel blue and draped with full length curtains in a contemporary print. A series of slender pillars in satin-finished stainless steel, arranged in an ellipse, provide a separate area at the centre of the room, like a pavilion within the lounge itself. At night the ceiling of this central area is illuminated from two floodlight bowls on bases of Nigerian walnut, in which the brilliant stars of the Southern Cross, carved from transparent plastic, are set like jewels. Inside the ring of pillars the deck is covered with large oval handmade carpet of deep pile in colors of wine and white. Deeply upholstered chairs and settees of contemporary design specially developed for this ship to provide the greatest possible comfort and having crisp, easily laundered loose covers of gay printed fabrics in colors of smoke-blue, daphne-pink and white, comprise the principal furnishings.'

The *Southern Cross* was an overwhelming success

198

Another name for a still-beautiful liner — Azure Seas.

and led, within seven years to the creation of a larger, near sistership, the *Northern Star*. She too had a royal launching, on June 27 1961, with Her Majesty Queen Elizabeth the Queen Mother as sponsor. She was commissioned in the following summer and then joined the *Southern Cross* in continuous around-the-world sailings.

The trade began to change by the late sixties. There was competition from aircraft, a decline in the number of migrants bound for Australia and New Zealand, less costly foreign-flag rivals and the mounting costs of running British-flag liners. Both the *Southern Cross* and the *Northern Star* began to cruise—from Southampton, then Sydney and even from Liverpool. However, operations and accounting were such that the *Southern Cross*, just sixteen years old, was withdrawn at the end of 1971. Laid-up at Southampton and then in the River Fal in Cornwall, she might well have gone to the breakers, especially as fuel oil costs rapidly escalated, but instead she was bought, in 1973, by the Ulysses Line of Greece. Taken to Piraeus, she was recommissioned

two years later, in June 1975, as the *Calypso*. Her patterns seemed to change continuously, however—from Tilbury to Scandinavia, the Mediterranean and West Africa, New York to Bermuda, the Caribbean from Miami and even to Alaska from Vancouver.

Successful as she was as a Greek liner, she was, in fact, sold to the newly formed Western Cruise Lines, in September 1980. Renamed *Azure Seas*, she was placed on three and four day cruises to Mexico from Los Angeles. Once again, success has come her way. In 1986, the thirty-one-year-old former *Southern Cross*, now a member of an international cruise fleet where more than two-thirds of the ships have their engines and funnels placed aft, was reportedly carrying record-breaking numbers of passengers.

Gross tonnage: 20,204 (1955)
Length overall: 604 feet
Width: 78 feet
Machinery: Steam turbines, twin screw
Speed: 20 knots
Capacity: 1,100 Tourist (1955)
Built: Harland & Wolff Ltd, Belfast, Northern Ireland, 1955

Southern Cross

Empress of Britain

The fifties were, as might easily be expected, the final great era of building new passenger ships for the Atlantic trade. The decade that followed, which while it produced a fair share of fine new vessels, seemed to be more moderate in approach and output, especially as the airlines had shown their might. In fact, in as early as 1957, the steamship lines were fighting a losing battle.

The Canadian Pacific Co had waited, for whatever reasons, for a full decade following the end of the Second World War to add new liner tonnage. They were quite cautious and prompted in large part by the quartet that their arch rivals on the St Lawrence trade, the Cunard Co, had ordered. Soon after the first of these, the previously mentioned *Saxonia* (see page 191) was delivered, Canadian Pacific ordered the first of a pair of sisterships that would be somewhat larger and better fitted. The order went to the Fairfield Shipbuilding & Engineering Co of Glasgow. This new ship and her identical sister (which was ordered from Vickers Armstrongs at Newcastle) were to be some 3,000 tons larger than the Cunarders and would rank as Britain's first fully air-conditioned liners. While they were intended mostly for the North Atlantic, sailing between Liverpool, Greenock, Quebec City and Montreal (and to Saint John, NB on some winter crossings), they would also be suitable for winter tropic cruising, namely from New York to the Caribbean. On the Atlantic, they were planned as two-class ships— 160 in first class and 894 in tourist class. This was a

sensible balance, especially as the bulk of their profits would come from the westbound migrant trade to Canada and, in both directions, the low-fare tourist business.

Since these ships represented a 'new generation' for Canadian Pacific, they were given extremely nationalistic names. The first was selected as *Empress of Britain* and was given added dignity when Her Majesty the Queen consented to launch her, on June 22 1955, at the Fairfield yards. The second ship was named *Empress of England* by Lady Eden, on May 9 1956. They were delivered to their owners in April 1956 and April 1957 respectively.

The Syren and Shipping were praiseworthy of the new *Empress of Britain*. 'In appearance, this ship differs substantially from any other vessel of a similar class now sailing, particular attention in the designing stages having been given to both the internal arrangements and the outside appearance of the ship. Every effort has been made to subordinate many of the functional fixtures, traditional in ship design and which cannot be removed, to harmonize with modern trends, while at the same time preserving a well-balanced ship appearance. The streamlined gracefulness of her lines from raked stem to the cruiser stern tells of her speed and hints of the care taken in her design to provide everything possible for passengers' comfort in the best traditions of ocean travel. The gleaming white hull has a green riband from stem to stern; the red-and-white chequered houseflag is painted on either side of the large buff funnel; boot topping is green. The arrangements of after decks in echelon emphasizes the streamlining and provides unusually generous open and covered deck space. The enclosed promenade decks have rubber floor-covering and there is very little camber apparent. Interior paintwork is in pastel shades.

'The modern tendency is to produce a vessel with piled-up superstructure, but in the case of the *Empress of Britain*, this has been avoided and it can be said that the silhouette is the lowest of any liner of comparable size. The structural design is stated to be more advanced than that of any previous large passenger liner built in Britain for North Atlantic trade.'

Right *An impression of what* Empress of Britain *would look like by Norman Wilkinson.*

Below *And the real thing...* Empress of Britain *passes under the famous Jacques Cartier bridge at Montreal.*

Empress of Britain

But North Atlantic business declined and she was sold to the Greek Line and renamed Queen Anna Maria. *The fuller stern and Greek Line stack markings completely transform her.*

The low, long look of the new 'Empress' liners gave them a racey appearance and certainly one of highly modern style. Pleased with their two new ships, the Company asked its designers to produce a slightly larger version, which developed as the *Empress of Canada*, commissioned in 1961 by Vickers-Armstrongs. This gave the Company three new liners on the otherwise rapidly dwindling North Atlantic. The two slightly older ships were chartered in the winter season (while the *Empress of Canada* handled the New York-Caribbean cruise trade) and often to the Travel Savings Association, which had them sailing not only from Liverpool but from Southampton as well, to the Atlantic Isles, the Mediterranean, West Africa and the Caribbean. There were also some sailings from Capetown, to the Seychelles and Mauritius, and across the South Atlantic to Latin America. However, without these lucrative charters, at least one of these ships would become superfluous. Regrettably, once the charters ceased, the *Empress of Britain* was selected for disposal.

Because of her age, her proper upkeep and even her conversion potential, she found new buyers almost immediately, in February 1964. She was sold to a subsidiary of the giant Goulandris Group, the Transoceanic Navigation Co, and would be used on the Greek Line service between the Mediterranean and North America. She was transferred in the following November and then raised the Greek colours for the first time.

Sent to Genoa for a full refit, her accommodation was enlarged—to 109 in first class and 1,145 in tourist class, a total of 1,254 against her Canadian Pacific maximum of 1,054. Her tonnage was revised, however, according to Greek standards and decreased from 25,516 to 21,716. Her stern area, in particular, was changed drastically and rebuilt as a full lido area with no less than five swimming pools. Made fully air-conditioned, she was also fitted with private bathrooms in all of her cabins, an essential, it was felt by her Greek Line operators, in the ever-increasing, ever competitive North American cruise trades. She was renamed *Queen Anna Maria*, in a royal ceremony by Her Majesty Queen Anna Maria of Greece at Piraeus, in March 1965. This event gave the liner a rather special distinction—the only passenger ship to be named by two reigning queens. She was sent on her first voyage to New York, on March 24.

Her Mediterranean itinerary, being teamed with the *Olympia* (see page 187), was from Haifa, Limassol, Piraeus, Messina, Naples, Lisbon and the

Azores to Halifax (westbound only) and then New York. Outbound to the Mediterranean, she often called at Boston the day after New York. In winter, she cruised to the Caribbean and on long, luxurious trips of some eight weeks to the Mediterranean and Black Seas. Her schedules were interrupted slightly when, on February 19 1967, she went aground off Kingston, Jamaica. She was refloated a week later.

With almost all of her transatlantic trade gone within five years, by 1970, she was, like the *Olympia*, restyled as a full time cruiseship thereafter. Sailing mostly from New York and occasionally other US East Coast ports, she ran very popular one-week trips to Bermuda and Nassau as well as three-day cruises 'to nowhere'. When, in 1974, the *Olympia* was recalled for Aegean cruising out of Piraeus, the *Queen Anna Maria* was the last Greek Line passenger ship left in American waters. At the time, few were aware that the Company was falling deeper and deeper into financial trouble and that, by early 1975, the Company flagship would be chased by New York bankers for debt. The *Queen Anna Maria* fled from New York, without passengers, on January 11 and reached Piraeus on the 22nd. She would never sail again as a Greek ship, her owners suddenly and dramatically were out of business.

Neglected and rusting, she was laid-up at Perama, quite near to the *Olympia* and other out-of-work passenger liners, until the following December. The Greek Government, who had taken over responsibility for the ship, auctioned the vessel to the highest bidder, the Carnival Cruise Lines of Miami. Their previous and only other cruiseship at the time was the former *Empress of Canada*, by then renamed *Mardi Gras* and highly successful in weekly Caribbean service. After a refit and overhaul at the Newport News Shipyards in Virginia, she entered Caribbean cruising as the *Carnivale*, in February 1976. Carnival Cruise, now called 'the busiest cruise company in the world', continued to add fresh tonnage; the converted *Festivale* (the former Safmarine-Union Castle liner *S. A. Vaal*) and then increasingly larger brand new ships, the *Tropicale, Holiday, Jubilee* and *Celebration*. The latter pair are the largest liners ever built purposely for cruising, at over 48,000 tons each.

Carnival reportedly will keep the *Carnivale* in service for some years to come. It has been a good life for that Glasgow-built ship.

Empress of Britain

Gross tonnage: 25,516 gross tons (1956); 21,716 (1965)
Length overall: 640 feet
Width: 85 feet
Machinery: Steam turbines, twin screw
Speed: 20 knots
Capacity: 160 First, 894 Tourist (1956); 109 First, 1,145 Tourist (1965)
Built: Fairfield Shipbuilding & Engineering Co, Glasgow, Scotland, 1956

This aerial view shows the new lido deck area far aft.

Brasil

They were the prime ships in a $400,000,000 rebuilding programme proposed by New York's Moore McCormack Lines in the mid-fifties. Previously, in the luxury passenger division, three ships—the original *Brazil, Argentina* and *Uruguay* (for the latter ship, see page 117)—were used on the East Coast of South America run. Then, as passenger numbers declined slightly, only two liners remained. But, as these remaining ships neared their thirtieth years, plans were drawn for their replacements. The new *Brasil* and *Argentina* were 'to usher in a new age in ocean travel'. The were commissioned in 1958, already too late for the South American liner trades.

Advertised as the largest liners ever built in 'the Deep South' of the United States, they were ordered from the Ingalls Shipbuilding Corporation at Pascagoula in Mississippi rather than other yards, such as Newport News or Bethlehem Steel, that were more accustomed to large passenger ship construction. The *Brasil*, which was now spelled in the Portuguese fashion on the request of the Brazilian Government, slid down the ways on December 16 1957. Months later, at the time of her maiden arrival at New York, on September 9 1958, the *Herald Tribune* added, 'The new $26,000,000 *Brasil* arrived here yesterday at noon on her delivery voyage from Pascagoula and received a gala

welcome. However, aboard the liner as passengers were scores of workers from the shipyard who were busy putting the finishing touches to the interior during the three-day trip from the Ingalls Shipbuilding Corp yard in Mississippi. The *Brasil*, which was originally scheduled to be delivered on 5 February, has been delayed by a variety of circumstances including a steel shortage during the early stages of her construction.' Soon afterward, she set off on her first 31-day round trip cruise to South America—to Trinidad, Rio de Janeiro, Santos, Montevideo and Buenor Aires. The *Argentina* joined this service that December.

Already aware of aircraft competition, Moore McCormack set about to win the upper-end of the cruise market as well as the Latin American business set. The *Herald Tribune* added, 'Among the many features incorporated into the *Brasil* to help compete against air travel, the most discussed is the solarium on top of her dummy funnel [the exhausts were through twin uptakes placed farther aft] where passengers are able to sunbathe in the nude under tropic skies. One Company executive mentioned, ''These vessels will be the only passenger ships in the world on which the discriminating passenger may get an all-over tan in a solarium atop the dummy stack, 100 ft above the water.'' The *Brasil* is also equipped with two outdoor pools, a junior pavilion with snack bar and juke box for teenagers, a nightclub, a theatre, a deck area for dancing under the Southern Cross and a suitable number of bars for mature passengers.'

Both the *Brasil* and *Argentina* were also sent on other cruises—five weeks in summer to Scandinavia and the Northern Cities, and nine weeks around Africa and through the Mediterranean. In later years, they would also make a number of short-distance voyages, to Bermuda, Nassau, Florida and the Caribbean. Just after she was retired, the *Argentina* was to have made a three-month cruise around-the-world.

Both ships were refitted in 1963, at Baltimore, when the superstructures were heightened, their capacities extended and the smokestack-solariums removed. However, the ships became increasingly serious money-losers, caused in great part by foreign-

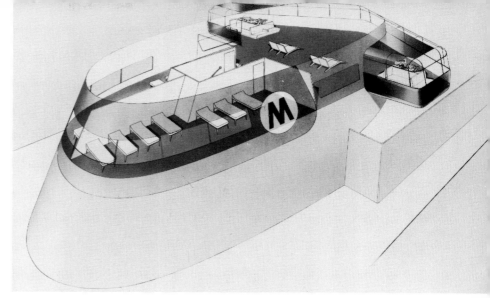

Nude sunbathing inside the dummy smokestack was the big publicity story when Brasil was first announced. This artist's impression shows how the funnel could be divided for men and women.

Brasil *is poised and ready for launching into the Gulf of Mexico.*

Brasil

MOORE-McCORMACK LINES, Inc

cordially invites you

to a

LUNCHEON and INSPECTION

of the

New Passenger Accommodations

Aboard the

S. S. BRASIL

at

Pier 97, North River, New York City

(Foot of 57th Street)

on

Wednesday, June 26, 1963, 12 Noon to 2:30 P.M.

R.S.V.P.

flag competition and the ever-increasing operational costs for American-flag liners. Furthermore, their schedules were often disrupted by frequent US maritime strikes, interruptions that would cause these sisters to miss scheduled sailings and cruises, and instead sit for months in the quiet, darkened loneliness of backwater shipyard berths. Within a decade, by 1968, as Moore McCormack Lines joined with the Grace Lines in a dual marketing effort, they seemed to regret more and more having built the two sisters. A year later, in September, in a flash decision, they were laid-up permanently. For nearly three years, the pair sat nested together at Baltimore.

While the US Government might have retained them in reserve status for future use as troop transports or hospital ships (they were, in fact, placed 'on call' during the Cuban Missile Crisis in the fall of 1961), they were cleared for sale, even to foreign buyers. In the summer of 1972, they both crossed to a Bremerhaven shipyard for their new owners, the Holland America Line. The *Brasil* was to be rebuilt as the *Volendam*, the *Argentina* as the *Veendam*.

Intended for long, luxurious cruising—the Mediterranean, South America, around-the-world etc, they were used instead mostly on short-distance trips, to the Caribbean, Bermuda and Alaska. Soon after resuming service in 1973, however, their

operations were clouded by the rapidly increasing cost of fuel oil. In 1974, both ships had to be laid-up for a time at Hampton Roads in Virginia. Holland America was unable to use them for some time and, in the summer of 1975, the *Volendam*, ex-*Brasil* secured a charter with the newly formed Monarch Cruise Lines of Miami. Owned and managed by Greeks and with a multinational staff, she was placed under the Panamanian flag for at least the duration and was renamed *Monarch Sun*. The *Veendam*, the former *Argentina*, became the *Monarch Star*. They cruised in the Caribbean and Alaskan waters, and were not returned to full Holland America operations until early 1978, although both ships retained their Panamanian registry.

Reverting to their Dutch names, the two ships cruised again for the Dutch until 1983-84, when they were replaced by a brand new pair, the 33,900-ton sisterships *Nieuw Amsterdam* and *Noordam*. After some time laid-up, the *Volendam* was used briefly as an accommodation ship in the St Lawrence and then sent out to Japan for a full refit for her new owners, American Hawaii Cruises, which is part of the huge C. Y. Tung Group of Hong Kong. She returned to cruise service, in December 1985, sailing on weekly voyages in the South Pacific from Papeete, Tahiti, as the *Liberte*. The *Veendam*, also sold to the C. Y.

Tung Group, has been placed on long-term charter to the British-owned Bahama Cruise Lines and cruises in North American waters as their *Bermuda Star*.

Undoubtedly, there is more to be written in the story of the beautiful *Brasil*.

Gross tonnage: 22,770 (1958); 23,395 (1973); 23,858 (1983)
Length overall: 617 feet
Width: 86 feet
Machinery: Steam turbines, twin screw
Speed: 21 knots
Capacity: 553 First as built
Built: Ingalls Shipbuilding Corporation, Pascagoula, Mississippi, 1958

Right *A new upper deck was added to give her more earning powr and the nude sunbathing idea was quietly dropped.*

Below *She is shown here as the* Volendam *for Holland America Line, while her sister became the* Veendam.

Savannah

She was a dream ship, a ship of dreamers, who went wrong on two counts. The dreamers thought she would show the world that the United States wished to use atoms for peace. The dreamers were sure that she would herald the new atomic age in shipping. As for being an 'Ambassador of Goodwill', the poor *Savannah* was very quickly demoted to attempting to earn her way as a cargo ship. And as for showing America's intentions were peaceful, this too was quickly forgotten when, as President Eisenhower had warned would happen, the military-industrial complex took over the nation. And one more failure must be recorded in the story of the *Savannah*. Her proponents failed to understand that nuclear power would not be safe until a sure means of protecting future generations from the hazards of nuclear waste was found. With this sad prologue, let us tell the story of the ship herself, a story which is remarkably like that of her namesake, the original *Savannah*, of 1819.

Your author [FOB] played a part in this story at the outset. When proposed, the first atomic merchant ship was to have been named *Atom Queen* or something of that ilk. I thought she should be named in honour of the first vessel with a steam engine to cross any ocean and campaigned successfully for her to be called *Savannah*. The day the contract was announced I suggested to her builders that she should have her keel laid on National Maritime Day, May 22, which in 1933 had been designated by President Franklin D. Roosevelt to honour the departure of the original *Savannah* on her historic Atlantic voyage. This was done. I attended the keel laying, the launching, and sailed on her first voyage out of the yard and made many visits to her and trips aboard her.

The *Savannah* was the brain child of President Eisenhower. He proposed her in a speech on April 25, 1955. She was intended to show the world that America as a nation wished to use atoms for peaceful purposes. She was designed to carry 60 passengers in luxury and to be able to move 746,200 cubic feet of cargo at a sea speed of 20 knots. Much attention was devoted to the fact that the thimble-sized pellets of enriched uranium oxide which she used would provide full power steaming for 3½ years. Only rarely was there mention of what would be done with the highly dangerous radioactive nuclear waste she generated.

The keel was laid at Camden, New Jersey, by the New York Shipbuilding Corporation, on May 22 1958, with Mrs Richard Nixon officiating. Mrs Eisenhower was sponsor when the ship was launched July 2 1959. In the spring of 1961 the ship was completed. Thousands of press releases, tens of

Above right *Yard officials help Mrs Eisenhower, wife of the President, to break the traditional bottle on* Savannah's *bow at her launching ceremony.*

Below right *A cutaway drawing showing the nuclear power plant.*

Above Savannah *at the fitting out berth.*

Above right *Her maiden arrival at Savannah, Georgia.*

Left *Captain De Groote and the engineers inspect her control panels.*

Fifty Famous Liners

thousands of magazine and newspaper articles and many films later, the *Savannah* was retired. The year was 1970. Her 'five important missions' trumpeted so proudly by the Maritime Commission when she was new had only partially been achieved. The two other nuclear merchant ships built in the world, one in Germany and one in Japan, had been retired in an atmosphere of failure. Since then there have been no other nuclear merchant ships. Slowly over this period the world public has become aware of the danger to life on earth from the nuclear waste of the many hundreds of atomic plants and naval craft, not to mention the many thousands of nuclear warheads so assiduously being created by misguided zealots in the military.

At the beginning the glowing press releases about the ship casually alluded to what would happen to her radioactive waste. The matter was brushed off with phrases such as 'liquid radioactive wastes are collected for disposal at sea under rigidly controlled conditions', or are collected for 'ultimate disposal ashore by a licensed contractor'. Although very few references to the disposal of such waste matter ever reached the press, near the end of her active life a few instances were recorded in reports and documents. On April 19 1968, for example, 130 cubic feet of solid waste was taken ashore. It was delivered 'to a licensed waste disposal contractor'. Again, in April 1969, 2,310 gallons of liquid waste 'and an estimated 21.1 curies of tritium' were transferred to a 'licensed contractor' for disposal.

Back to the actual story of the ship in her brief and harried career. The States Marine Corporation was named as the operator in July 1958, and teams of deck and engine officers were trained in reactor theory, engineering and operation. The ship was declared ready for operation early in 1962. In August of that year she made her first voyage to a commercial port, sailing from Yorktown, Virginia, to her home port of Savannah, Georgia. She made one cruise touching at 11 American ports and being toured by 340,000 persons and was then berthed at Galveston, Texas. It was here that her luck ran out. She was the victim of a series of jurisdiction strikes between deck and engine officers that not only put her out of commission for nearly a year but ended up with a different union and a new company as her operator. The new operator was American Export-Isbrandtsen Lines. The single union that provided all her crew was the Brotherhood of Marine Officers.

In February 1964, the *Savannah* finally set sail on a tour of 11 European nations. She still had her passenger facilities intact and fares ranged from $550 for each of two persons in a three-berth cabin from the 'last US port to ports in Europe'. A voyager could go from Antwerp to Le Havre for $60 or from Barcelona to Naples for $125. Passengers could carry their own automobiles at from $425 for the transatlantic crossing to $140 for the run from Copenhagen to Goteborg. The operators published a wide variety of domestic passenger rates, the like of which had never before been offered by any one ship. The fare from New York to Providence, Rhode Island, was $40 for each of two in a three-berth cabin. A similar berth from New York to Mobile, Alabama, cost $190. The price of an overnight ride between New York and Philadelphia, one of the trips the author took, was $50.

The *Savannah*'s passenger facilities had been an integral part of the original plan by which she would serve as an ambassador of good will. It had been hoped that foreign citizens, from diplomats to tourists, would use her elegant public rooms and cabins. However, American Export lost so much money in her operation that it was decided to eliminate passengers altogether. This alteration took six months to do and then the ship set out again but strictly as a freighter.

By no means all the publicity was favourable to the *Savannah* at this point in her career. *The Economist* had an editorial entitled 'Atoms Unseaworthy', concluding that the ship had not been a stimulant to the development of more genuinely commercial designs. The editorial concluded: 'Even the Americans have now grown tired of footing the subsidy bill for this great white sacred sea-cow'.

In mid-1968 there was a move to lay her up, but some public agitation to 'save her' saw this overruled and she was sent on a voyage to a number of Far East ports. She completed this trip on July 25 1970, and was sent to Galvaston to be shut down. On November 9 she was returned by American Export to the Maritime Administration. The *Savannah*'s active life was over. In the five years after the year-long labour strike she had performed reliably and without untoward incident. Her first atomic core had powered her 332,405 nautical miles from the time she was built until August 1968. When it was decided to operate her a little longer four spare fuel elements were loaded into her reactor and the others re-arranged. After that she voyaged 122,270 more miles. Her core contained sufficient fuel for about 50,000 more miles when she was finally laid up for good. In her total steaming of nearly half a million miles she had used 163 pounds of nuclear fuel uranium. She had visited 77 ports in the United States and 25 foreign countries. She had been visited by about 1¼ million people and had carried 154,000 tons of cargo.

After several years in Galveston the *Savannah* was turned over to the Georgian port after which she and her eqully unfortunate pioneer predecessor were named (see *Fifty Famous Liners 2*). It was hoped that she would become a maritime museum. A combination of local squabbling and disinterested city officials resulted in a decision that shocked citizens of Savannah almost as much as the laying up of their beautiful white liner. She was taken away from them and given to the Patriots Point Naval and Maritime Museum at Charleston, South Carolina, the arch rival of the Port of Savannah. Here she remains at the time of writing.

Gross tonnage: 13,599
Length overall: 595 feet 6 inches
Width: 78 feet
Machinery: Babcock & Wilcox atomic power using pressurised water as a coolant; single screw
Speed: 21½ knots
Capacity: 60 passengers, 9,900 tons cargo
Built: New York Shipbuilding Corporation, Camden, New Jersey, 1959-62

Eugenio C

It was a very productive, very exciting, even very glamorous period in Italian passenger shipping. In all, seven large and important liners sailed away from Italian shipyards in a six-year period, between 1960 and 1966. It began with the exquisite *Leonardo da Vinci*, completed at Genoa in 1960 as a replacement for the ill-fated *Andrea Doria*. A pair of sisterships followed, closely based upon the *Leonardo da Vinci*'s fine exterior design, for Lloyd Triestino in 1963 and which were named *Galileo Galilei* and *Guglielmo Marconi*. Two years later, in 1965, the superliners *Michelangelo* and *Raffaello*, with their novel lattice-cage funnels and low superstructures, were delivered and as was the engines-aft *Oceanic*, a superbly designed and decorated liner that was then the largest liner to be used for year-round cruising. The final statement for that period was another engines-aft design, in fact a ship closely following the *Oceanic* both in design and arrangement, the Costa Line's new flagship *Eugenio C*. She entered service in the late summer of 1966.

When commissioned, *The New York Times* even recorded the new liner's maiden sailing, on the South Atlantic run to Latin America. 'The $24.5 million Costa Line flagship *Eugenio C*, the largest post-war liner to be built for a private Italian steamship company, sailed yesterday [August 31 1966] from Genoa on her maiden voyage. Larger Italian-flag liners have been constructed for Government-owned lines. Gleaming in fresh coats of white paint, she represented the great success of the Costa Company, which had entered passenger shipping only after the Second World War, in 1948. Then, they used the converted former Furness liner *Southern Prince* in mostly migrant service as the *Anna C*. Secondhand ships were their mainstay for a decade, until 1958, when the Company added its first brand new liner, the 20,400-ton *Federico C*. The *Eugenio C* was the Company's second brand new liner.

A three-class ship, which remained almost unique to the East Coast of South America run from Europe, the *Eugenio C* was designed to spend most of her year in this service, sailing from Naples, Genoa, Cannes, Barcelona and Lisbon to Rio de Janeiro, Santos, Montevideo and Buenos Aires. In tourist class, she carried capacity numbers of westbound migrants; homebound, in the same spaces, were tourists and students as well as 'reverse immigrants', who were seeking resettlement in Europe. The ship was also schemed for cruising, mostly as a one-class liner. In her first year, this was rather limited—an 11-day

Christmas cruise around the Mediterranean, and then a mid-winter 35-day cruise around continental Africa. In later years, as her cruise schedules would be expanded, she would cruise around South America, to North America (including visits to such ports as New York, Montreal, Miami, New Orleans and San Francisco) and on several around-the-world cruises (begun in 1977). She has also cruised to West Africa, East Africa, Scandinavia, the Northern cities and throughout the Mediterranean. She was the last liner to run class-divided sailings to South America, but these were halted almost completely by the time of the Falklands conflict in 1982. Presently, she cruises almost full time and most often on 11-day trips in the Mediterranean, to Alexandria, Port Said, Ashdod, Haifa and Heraklion on Crete.

The *Eugenio C* has a sleek external appearance, a creation resulting in ideas from a number of other ships. Assuredly, the greatest influences came from Home Lines' innovative *Oceanic* (see *Fifty Famous Liners 1*), but with some modifications. Instead of a funnel, she has the twin uptakes inspired by the likes of the Dutch *Rotterdam* and Britain's *Canberra*. A midships pool, placed before the funnel area, was also derived from the *Canberra* and then used on the *Oceanic* as well. Her flair bow is copied from the *Galileo* and *Marconi*, and then the *Oceanic* once

Fifty Famous Liners

Right *A postcard view.*

Left *An aerial view of* Eugenio C *when new. Her twin stacks were copied from those on* Canberra.

Below left *An advertisement featuring an aerial view of* Eugenio C.

Below right *The cover of a daily programme issued aboard* Eugenio C *on August 20, 1981.*

again; the well-rounded stern is a duplicate of those found on the *Michelangelo* and *Raffaello*.

In the early eighties, as the Costa success continued, the *Eugenio C* was, for a time, the flagship of the largest cruise operator apart from the Soviets. However, there has been some rethinking on this position and a number of ships were sold off, including the aforementioned *Federico C*, which is now cruising for American-owned interests as the *Royale*. In reorganising the company as Costa Cruises, there was some thought given to rebuilding the *Eugenio C*, possibly for the three and four day overnight trade between Florida and the Bahamas or, in a fleet reshuffling, reassigning her to year-round cruises from Sydney, Australia. None of these plans have yet materialised.

Still a splendid liner, now engaged in the cruise trades, more is to be written on the history of the flagship of the Costa Line.

Gross tonnage: 30,567
Length overall: 712 feet
Width: 96 feet
Machinery: Steam turbines, twin screw
Speed: 27 knots
Capacity: 178 First, 356 Cabin, 1,102 Tourist
Built: Cantieri Riuniti dell'Adriatico, Monfalcone, Italy, 1966

Eugenio C

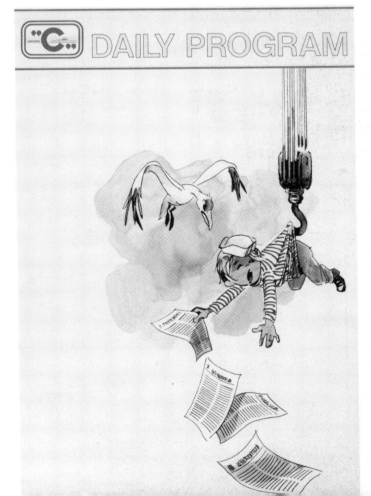

Sea Venture

Even the Norwegians could not have predicted the level of success of the North American cruise industry. In the late sixties, the business was still rather seasonal, still handled by aged transatlantic liners that were seeking alternate employment. More specifically, in Florida, which geographically is ideally suited to the ever-appealing Caribbean, there were but a handful of very old, mostly ill-equipped passenger ships. In 1966, Norway's Klosters Rederi boldy placed their brand new *Sunward* in cruise service out of Miami. It was not just a success, but a huge success. In quick time, three larger sisters were ordered and led, by 1980, to the addition of the world's largest cruiseship, the 70,200-ton *Norway*, converted from the transatlantic *France* of 1962. At the time of writing (1986), the Norwegian Caribbean Lines was reportedly planning a 30,000 tonner, for its subsidiary, the Royal Viking Line, at $150 million; a 90,000 tonner for 3,000 passengers, priced at $250 million; and still reviewing the 'Phoenix project', a Caribbean cruiseship of catamaran style that would be some 250,000 tons, carry 5,000 or more passengers and cost in excess of $500 million. NCL, as the company is commonly called, had just reached its 20th birthday. The cruise business, particularly in North America, has boomed.

Soon after Norwegian Caribbean's original success, in the late sixties, other Norwegians decided to follow in their path. Among these were two well-known cargo and tanker owners, Oivind Lorentzen and Fearnley & Eger. They decided, in 1969, to enter the American cruise trades with not one but two 20,000-tonners. More specifically, they saw potential in the weekly run between New York and Bermuda, which had been abandoned by the well-known Furness Bermuda Line in 1966 and then was followed by the Cunard Line. The highly important Bermuda Government contract, which included the essential ingredient of a guaranteed berth along Front Street in Hamilton, Bermuda, was obtained and would begin in 1971. The stage seemed to be set. The two shippers then created a US operational arm, which was named Flagship Cruises.

The two liners, with space for 646 one-class passengers using all of the lower berths and 750 maximum berths, were ordered from a firm that was comparatively inexperienced in building deep-sea passenger ships, the Nordseewerke Shipyard at Rheinstahl in West Germany. The keel for the first of the pair was laid in place; her launching took place on May 9 1970 and she was completed a year later. Her sister was launched on March 6 1971 and finished that December. Handsome vessels with all-white hulls, rather high superstructures and a single funnel placed aft, they were named the *Sea Venture* and *Island Venture* respectively. The *Sea Venture* was planned as the Bermuda ship, the *Island Venture* intended for long, luxurious trips, but then assigned mostly to seven to 18-day Caribbean sailings as well as relief service on the Bermuda run. The *Sea Venture*, sailing each Saturday at 4.00 pm and then returning a week later, at eight in the morning, quickly became a familiar fixture to the Port of New York.

The new Norwegian liner Sea Venture *being docked in Manhattan* (courtesy of Moran Towing).

The accommodation as arranged on eight passenger decks—observation, sun, bridge, boat, lounge, Atlantic, foyer and coral. Fully air-conditioned and stabiliser-equipped, both of which had become essential ingredients to any new passenger ship, their amenities also included a closed circuit television system, two outdoor swimming pools (one of which was covered if the situation warranted by a retractable glass covering known as the Solardome), a gymnasium, sauna, theatre facilities, a gift shop, beauty salon and barber shop. Their de luxe accommodation included numerous interchangeable arrangements, known variously as suites, de luxe cabins, townhouses, penthouses and apartments. These arrangements could sleep from one to nine passengers and might include as many as three bedrooms, three sitting rooms and three bathrooms. The remaining cabins, located on the Atlantic, foyer and coral decks, included one to three berth rooms and all were equipped with private bathroom facilities. The public rooms were most attractively decorated and spacious, and included the Galaxy Lounge, Terrace Room, Bermuda Lounge, Rainbow Bar, the auditorium, Bridge Lounge, International Lounge, Skal Bar, music room, club room, the lounge and, of course, the dining room.

By September 1972, as the full ownership was

taken over by the Lorentzen Company, the two ships seemed to be another encouraging success story. However, within a year, especially as the cost of fuel oil so radically increased, the picture seemed to change. There was talk of using the ships in charter service, sailing them on other routes or selling them off completely. Within another year, by October 1974, the latter became a reality. Both ships were sold to Britain's giant P&O Group for its US cruise subsidiary, Princess Cruises of Los Angeles. The transfers would be almost immediate. (Flagship decided to continue in service, however, and at first planned to charter Holland America's laid-up *Veendam* and sail her as the *Sea Venture II*, but, at the end of 1975, purchased Swedish American's impeccable *Kungsholm* (of 1966). Retaining her well-known name, but under Liberian colours, the *Kungsholm* was not as successful as had been hoped and was sold off, rather ironically, to the P&O Group, who refitted her as their *Sea Princess*. Flagship Cruises ceased to exist after 1978.)

Princess Cruises had developed a very strong presence in US cruising, particularly along the lucrative West Coast (California was, in the mid-eighties, the most active state for cruise clientele). Even P&O's name was not quite as strong to US travellers and the all-important travel agents. Consequently, while thought had been given to naming the two new acquisitions as the *Spirit of Southampton* and *Spirit of Liverpool*, P&O directors wisely decided instead to use the Princess nomenclature. The *Sea Venture* became the *Pacific Princess*, the *Island Venture* changed to *Island Princess*. Both ships hoisted the British colours as well.

Based at Los Angeles for their seven to 14-day Mexican Riviera, Trans-Panama Canal and Caribbean cruises, and at San Francisco and/or Vancouver for their summer trips to scenic Alaska, the two ships—joined by the *Spirit of London*, which was thoughtfully renamed *Sun Princess*—soon became very successful. But, ever greater acclaim was ahead, especially for the *Pacific Princess*.

In the mid-seventies, a television 'pilot' (a sample production) was ordered with a storyline that centered around a cruiseship. There were to be no disasters, no murders, no slapstick comedy, but instead at least three themes that were built around love and romance. Aptly, the production was entitled 'The Love Boat.' At first thought, especially by the cruise companies themselves, to have little if any merit, its initial success caused considerable notice. Once again, few could have predicted its far-reaching success and impact.

By the early eighties, as the US cruise industry passed a $4 billion annual level, 'The Love Boat' was cited as one of the three most important contributing factors. The others were the offerings of air-sea packages and the well-rounded, very appealing range of entertainments and diversions to be found aboard these modern, highly equipped 'floating hotels'.

In a stroke of tremendous good fortune, 'The Love Boat' with its familiar cast of characters was filmed mostly aboard the *Pacific Princess*. Quickly, she became synonymous with the television series. She was, perhaps, even better known as 'The Love Boat' in some circles than for her actual name. P&O and Princess capitalised on the situations by, among other additions, having the television catchy theme song played onboard and particularly on deck in tropic ports on seemingly endless occasions. While the series was filmed mostly in a Hollywood studio, in mock-ups of a cruiseship's outer decks, lounges and cabins, the actors and film crews went to sea about six times a year, mostly for outdoor and special effects. Princess Cruises was, at times, overwhelmed with requests from cruise travellers wanting to be on board for these particular voyages. Later, as the series' popularity increased further still, the standard voyage pattern to the Mexican Riviera from Los

Renamed Pacific Princess *for Princess Cruises, she is famous as the 'Love Boat' of the American television series.*

Pacific Princess *at Bora Bora*.

Angeles was extended to include the Caribbean, the Panama Canal, Alaska and, farther still (but then on other cruiseships) to Australia, the Far East, Scandinavia, Northern Euorpe and even along the Nile River.

Specifically, this television series—broadcast mostly on Saturday nights, which was considered peak viewing time in the United States—reached households in Middle America. It portrayed cruising as a wonderfully exciting, fun-filled, romantic and largely informal way of travel. Most of the viewers thought of cruising as being only for the rich, the privileged and always quite formal in tone. Often the viewers became 'converts' and soon sailed off on their first vacation voyage. As one Princess captain later reported, 'Assuredly, ''The Love Boat'' has been a stroke of genius for us, but it has also served our competitors to a large extent'. However, even as recently as 1985, only four in every one-hundred potential cruise passengers has yet to take an actual voyage.

Within a decade of their acquisition, Princess was able to add the 44,300-ton *Royal Princess*, the most expensive British passenger liner built to date (1984), which cost some $165 million. While the television series was, in spring 1986, cancelled of its weekly format, it will continue as a series of periodic special productions. No doubt, the *Pacific Princess* will again be a featured star. She is surely one of the most important cruise liners of our times.

Sea Venture

Gross tonnage: 19,903
Length overall: 550 feet
Width: 80 feet
Machinery: Fiat diesels, twin screw
Speed: 20 knots
Capacity: 750 maximum berths
Built: Nordseewerke Shipyard, Rheinstahl, West Germany, 1971

The 'sun dome' deck on Pacific Princess.

Mikhail Lermontov

In 1986, the Soviet Union had the largest passenger fleet on earth: over forty passenger ships, in services ranging from the Danube and Volga Rivers to voyages around the world. While many of the deep-sea ships are thought to have military undertones, including side loading doors and an excess of antennae on their top decks, the ships used on international cruises serve an important financial purpose—they are used as a source of foreign currencies, which are eventually sent home to Moscow. These cruises on the larger liners are run mostly under charter or by a Soviet affiliate, the CTC Lines, which operates from London and Sydney.

In the late fifties, after being content mostly with secondhand passenger tonnage, namely salvaged ex-German ships of pre-war and even pre-First World War vintage, the Soviets embarked on a programme of building new passenger ships. Most of these came from an East German yard, Mathias-Thesen Werft at Wismar. It all began rather gently with a series of no less than 19 3,300-tonners. However, a major increase in size took place by 1961, when the first of a series of 19,800-tonners was ordered. She was launched, in June 1963, as the *Ivan Franko* and then delivered in November 1964. She was followed by several twin sisters and near-sisters, the *Alexandr Pushkin* in June 1965, the *Taras Schevchenko* in April 1967, the *Shota Rustavelli* in May 1968 and finally, the *Mikhail Lermontov*, almost as an after-thought, in April 1972. These ships, with as many as 700 one-class berths each, were so designed as to trade almost anywhere—on cruises, to Australia, transatlantic, even in Soviet service such as along the local Black Sea route out of Odessa.

The *Alexandr Pushkin* was most notable when, in April 1966, she reopened Soviet service on the North Atlantic, dormant since the era of Cold War in the late forties. She sailed between Leningrad, Bremerhaven, London, Le Havre and Montreal. This attracted considerable attention and became quite popular, especially as many travellers saw it as a great novelty to travel in a Soviet passenger ship. Years later, in 1972, and soon after being commissioned, the *Mikhail Lermontov* made several crossings to Eastern Canada as well. A year later, however, she inaugurated another service not offered since the forties, the run to New York. Once again, and combined with the disappearance of many of the more traditional, well-known liner firms on the Atlantic, the novelty of a Soviet passenger ship led to considerable popularity (and profit) for her owners.

Above Mikhail Lermontov, *the first regularly scheduled Soviet passenger ship to sail out of New York. She operated during the brief period when the 'Cold War' warmed up a little in the 1970s.*

Below *Steaming under the Verrazano Bridge, her lovely sheer forward is evident.*

Mikhail Lermontov

Docked at a port in the mountainous West Indies, Mikhail Lermontov *dwarfs everything around her.*

She was also used for cruising, most of which was deliberately inexpensively priced, to Bermuda, Nassau, the Caribbean and even on summer trips to the St Lawrence. Co-author Miller recalls being aboard one of her trips, in August 1975, from New York to Boston, Halifax, Gaspe, Saguenay, Quebec City and Prince Edward Island. The cost was a mere $310 for the 11-day voyage! The food was superb, the entertainment colourful and ethnically different, and the ship spotlessly clean. Almost all of us were intrigued, especially when it was discovered that two-thirds of the staff were women including the ship's doctor, head chef and third officer. While on the overnight visit to Quebec City, at Wolfe's Cove, I especially remember that she looked deliciously lovely—glowing in strand of lighted 'pearls' that were strung from stem to stern and, as it seemed, her

hammer and sickle were electrically illuminated. Another special recollection was the return to New York, which had already declined tremendously in activity, particularly as a passenger ship port, where we were berthed stern-in, bow-out. We were moored at the far end of Berth 1, resting stern-to-stern with another Soviet liner, the *Maxim Gorky*, ex-*Hamburg*.

Political difficulties spelled the end for Soviet passenger service from both the United States and Canada in 1980. While those continually popular transatlantic crossings had to be eliminated, it was decided, at least for the *Mikhail Lermontov*, to upgrade her as a cruiseship. She was refitted at the Hapag-Lloyd Shipyards at Bremerhaven, which had just completed the mammoth transformation of the liner *France* into the tropical cruiseship *Norway*. The

Fifty Famous Liners

A baggage label from Mikhail Lermontov.

Lermontov re-emerged with some structural changes, an all-white hull and vastly improved accommodation.

She began to cruise full time, first from European ports and then from Sydney. It was during one of the cruises from that latter-named port when she tragically met her end. Newspapers were filled with tales of her sad sinking. 'Passengers aboard the Soviet cruiseship *Mikhail Lermontov* said that there was no panic when the vessel hit a reef in Cook Strait [New Zealand] last night [February 16 1986] and some even continued dancing until ordered to evacuate. The order to evacuate the ship was given about 2½ hrs after the vessel struck the reef off New Zealand's South Island. She sank at about 11.00 pm. There were 400 passengers aboard, most of them elderly Australians and New Zealanders, and some 300 Soviet crew members. Officials said only one person, a Soviet crewman, was missing and presumed drowned. Evacuees were picked up from lifeboats by rescue craft and taken to Wellington, about 35 miles across the Cook Strait from where the ship sank. Despite the ordeal, most passengers were cheerful and happy to talk. One said that the moment of impact on the reef was terrifying. ''I thought it was an earthquake—the ship listed straight away.'''

Inquiries revealed that the loss of the ship was due to the New Zealand pilot, who was in command at the time. He had consulted the proper charts yet brought the ship into an area with insufficient water. At the time of writing, a salvage company was contracted to remove fuel oil from the wreck. Removal of the wreck itself seems unlikely, especially as the waters are rarely used and that the entire operation would be both costly and time-consuming. No doubt, the *Mikhail Lermontov* will remain in her underwater grave.

Gross tonnage: 19,872
Length overall: 578 feet
Width: 77 feet
Machinery: Sulzer diesels, twin screw
Speed: 20 knots
Capacity: 700 one-class passengers
Built: Mathias Thesen Werft Shipyards, Wismar, East Germany, 1972
Demise: Rammed a reef and later sunk in Cook Strait, New Zealand, on February 16 1986

Mikhail Lermontov

Royal Viking Star

It appeared, at least by the yearly 1970s, that the Norwegians saw no limits in US cruise potential. The Norwegian Caribbean Lines had four liners either in service or on the ways, the Royal Caribbean Cruise Lines began with a trio of identical sisterships and the aforementioned Flagship Cruises introduced a pair of sisters. All of these were, however, geared for the all-tropic markets, on mostly one-week runs to the likes of San Juan and St Thomas, Nassau and Bermuda. With the exception of Flagship, which used New York, they confidently saw Miami as the new international 'capital of cruiseships'. (By the mid-seventies, that latter-named port—then in the throes of rapid expansion—was proclaimed the busiest ocean liner port in the world.) One exception—and seemingly exceptional—firm

among these farsighted Norwegians was the Royal Viking Line. It too was created in the late sixties, but for a different trade—long and luxurious trips.

Organised by three further well-known Norwegian shippers, the Bergen Line, Nordenfjeldske D/S and A F Klaveness & Co, they planned three highly specialised, highly luxurious liners. The Company then selected what was then fast-becoming the master ocean liner builders of the world, the Finns, at their Wartsila Shipyards of Helsinki. At nearly 22,000 tons each, the three sisters were named as the *Royal Viking Star, Royal Viking Sky* and *Royal Viking Sea*. The first was launched in May 1971 and commissioned in the following June; the second was launched in May 1972 and delivered in June 1973; and the last, launched in January 1973, was commissioned eleven months afterward.

Carrying as few as 539 passengers that were looked after by 326 crew members, the design concept of these ships was even more than 'floating hotel' and instead more akin to a 'floating country club'. The Royal Viking directors saw an inheritance, of sorts, of the older, well-heeled passengers that had been loyal to the likes of Cunard's fabled *Caronia* and, more recently, to the Norwegian America and Swedish American lines. This new Norwegian firm wanted to create an ambiance and consequently a loyalty and following that prompted passengers to book passage with them for months at a time or on at least one long cruise each year. In many of the earlier instances, this came about. On Royal Viking world cruises, there were passengers who booked continuously and who had been passengers on board ships such as the *Caronia, Kungsholm, Gripsholm* and *Bergensfjord*. There were other recorded instances wherein passengers moved on board for several months at time, and included amidst their baggage some sentimental pieces of objects d'art and even furniture. There were even some celebrities who joined the lists of the loyalists and these included actress Merle Oberon.

The handsomely styled, art-filled passenger quarters on board the *Royal Viking Star* were arranged on seven decks; Sky, Promenade, Scandinavia, Atlantic, Pacific, Mediterranean and Sauna. The amenities included complete air-conditioning, stabilizers, closed circuit television, an outdoor pool,

Royal Viking Star at sea before she was lengthened.

gymnasium, sauna, theatre, chapel, gift shop, beauty salon and barber shop. The cabin accommodation included four suites, all two-berth, located on the Promenade and Atlantic decks. Each consisted of a bedroom, sitting room and bathroom. There were also 32 de luxe bedrooms, all two or three berth, and consisting of a bedroom, sitting area and bathroom. The remaining cabins, in one, two and three berth configurations, were located on three decks, Atlantic, Pacific and Mediterranean. All have private bathrooms. The public rooms included the Sky Bar, the Night Club, Lido Bar, main lounge and the dining room.

The *Royal Viking Star* and her two sisters were designed and have been used ever since in a continuously roving pattern of cruises, from seven to 107-days. (Most recently, in 1985, a special book entitled *Voyages of the Royal Vikings* has been published by the Royal Viking Line and its seemingly endless number of flawless colour photos are grouped according to geographic cruise areas.) Each year, the most spectacular voyage would be the full circumnavigation of the globe. This trip, priced from as much as $18,000 (in the mid-eighties), might travel westabout, leaving Port Everglades, Florida, touching in the Caribbean and then passing through the Panama Canal. Following calls along the Mexican Riviera and California, the ship will travel to Hawaii and then to some of the islands in the South Seas such as Fiji and Tahiti. Afterward, she might continue to New Zealand, and then Australia, even remote Tasmania. The trip continues to Hong Kong and Singapore possibly, then to Ceylon, India and the Seychelles. The homeward leg would begin in South Africa, then across the southern Atlantic and put into Latin American ports before concluding in the Caribbean and finally at Florida. The same ship would then make something of a nostalgic 'crossing', a positioning trip as most cruise companies now

Royal Viking star

call them, eastbound on the Atlantic, to the Mediterranean or to Southampton. In 'the Med', she would offer springtime cruises from Piraeus or from Venice to the Greek isles, North Africa, the Holy Land and into the Black Sea (and including calls at Soviet ports such as Odessa and Yalta). Leaving the Mediterranean by early summer, she might call at Southampton for a cruise 'around the British Isles', calling in Ireland, Wales and even some remote ports in Scotland. Afterward, she would cross the North Sea for summer season positioning at Copenhagen for mostly two-week long cruises to the Norwegian fjords and into the Baltic for the Northern Cities. At summer's end, she might return to the Mediterranean by offering a West European cruise that included stopovers in the wine regions of France and historic cities in Spain and Portugal. Once in the Mediterranean, there would be additional cruises from Piraeus and Venice. In December, she might recross the mid-Atlantic and return to Florida, usually just in time for a two or three week Christmas-New Year's cruise, possibly as far south as Rio de Janeiro. By early January, she would again be on schedule position for another around-the-world cruise.

Of course, Royal Viking has other varied offerings; New York to Eastern Canada, Trans-Panama Canal cruises, California to the Mexican Riviera, Vancouver to Alaska, transpacific crossings, cruises from Japanese as well as Australian ports and such periodic

long voyages as trips around continental Africa and South America. The Company's shortest voyage of all seems to have been a two-day cruise 'to nowhere', offered from New York in September 1984 and which included a large group of passenger ship enthusiasts of the Ocean Liner Museum Project, a museum scheme based at New York.

The 'long cruise' market had changed in a decade, by the early eighties, however. Disappearing slowly was that older, loyalist set from the age of the *Caronia*. Gradually, a new and different generation of passengers were emerging, younger, perhaps more vibrant, but who could only afford (in terms of both time and money) to spend two, three or four weeks on board. This is the 'air-sea cruise passenger', who flies out to meet the ship at a specific port, such as Athens, Rio, Kobe or Sydney, and then cruises to a specific region. Realising that they had to appeal to a changing, quite different market within the highly competitive cruise industry, Royal Viking first thought of acquiring the rival Norwegian America Line and its two de luxe cruiseships, the *Sagafjord* and *Vistafjord*. Rumours were brisk that they would become the *Royal Viking Saga* and the *Royal Viking Vista*, before the project collapsed. Then, Royal Viking—following in the steps of the innovative Royal Caribbean Cruise Lines—signed a $100 million contract with the Hapag-Lloyd Shipyards of Bremerhaven for the lengthening of its three cruiseships. The *Royal Viking Star* was the first to be

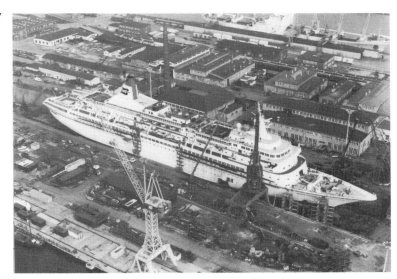

treated, entering the yard on August 28 1981 and returning to service in December. She was enlarged to over 28,000 tons and to 674 feet, and her capacity was increased by nearly 200 berths, to 700 passengers.

The Company, which was acquired by the Norwegian Caribbean Lines in 1984, but which has kept its own, quite distinctive identity, remains as one of the most prestigious in the world. Their praises are frequently sung. At the time of writing, and while there had been brief reports that one of this Royal Viking trio was to be transferred to Norwegian Caribbean for weekly Caribbean sailings with over 1,000 berths, more contemporary news is that there

is to be a fourth Royal Viking liner, bigger still, at 30,000 tons, and no doubt just as luxurious and well appointed.

Because of Royal Viking and several others, the heritage of Norwegian passenger shipping has remained among the most colourful.

Gross tonnage: 21,847 (1972); 28,221 (1981)
Length overall: 581 feet, lengthened to 647 feet in 1981
Width: 83 feet
Machinery: Wartsila-Sulzer diesels, twin screw
Speed: 21 knots
Passengers: 539 First (1972); 758 passengers (1981)
Built: Wartsila Shipyards, Helsinki, Finland, 1972

Royal Viking star

Finnjet

'The revolutionary Finnish vehicle-passenger ferry *Finnjet* is one of the most progressive ships of the present era', according to Philip Dawson, an expert journalist on passenger ship design and propulsion. Completed in the spring of 1977, the 25,000-ton *Finnjet* was assuredly then the largest ferry yet built. She was also the fastest.

Passenger ferries began to increase in size, speed and style of amenities since the 1960s, as the tourist and accompanying auto numbers began to increase. From the little 5,000-tonners that plied the English Channel and the more notable 10,000 tonners on the North Sea, there came the age, in the early seventies, of 12,000-ton, then 15,000-ton and finally 20,000-ton ferries. As a class of ship, they had reached the proportions of major deep-sea liners. Furthermore, in terms of design and comfort, they were also on an equal scale with their trans-ocean sisters.

The *Finnjet* came from the Wartsila Shipyards of Helsinki, which had become one of the world's master shipbuilders by the seventies. Their background in passenger ship construction was already considerable—numerous ferries, a series of liners for the Soviets and a trio of superb cruiseships each for the Royal Caribbean Cruise and Royal Viking lines. For the Finns themselves, the creation of the 692 foot *Finnjet* was a bold and innovative undertaking. She would be, of course, the largest passenger ship ever to fly the Finnish colours and, at the time, the largest ferry in Baltic waters.

The *Finnjet* was used on a steady relay of 22 hour passages between Travemunde in West Germany and Helsinki. Soon after she was commissioned in April 1977, there had been some investigation toward using her in an off-season, winter cruise service, possibly between New York and the Caribbean, but this never came to pass. She has remained in the Baltic ever since.

In her maiden season, she received enormous attention. She was the world's first gas-turbine powered passenger ship. Philip Dawson added, 'This type of machinery has only ever been used on some specialised naval vessels and a few fast freighters and tankers. The *Finnjet*'s aviation-type Pratt & Whitney turbines are a special marine version of the JT9D engines, which power Boeing 747 aircraft. Consequently, she can make the 600 nautical miles trip between Helsinki and Travemunde in only 22 hours at a speed of over 30 knots or the same speed as the illustrious French liner *Normandie* achieved on her record breaking maiden voyage in 1935.'

There are ten passenger decks aboard the *Finnjet* and these include such passenger facilities as the Lighthouse Bar, Sky Bar, passenger viewing bridge, conference centre, cinema, children's playroom, a night club, Jet-Snack Shop, shopping centre, a grill restaurant, aperitif bar, dance hall, beer bar, restaurant, the Gambling Den and a full health complex with an indoor pool, fitness centre, solarium, saunas and with adjacent sausage grill and bar. Philip Dawson added, 'The *Finnjet* also has the distinction of being the first of the really large vehicle-passenger ferries offering cruise liner

Below *Compare her amazing outline with the more traditional liner moored ahead of her.*

standards of comfort and service. She was also the first to introduce a permanent onboard conference centre, complete with audio-visual equipment and simultaneous language translation facilities. The idea caught on with business people and such amenities are now fairly standard aboard most large Europ-Scandinavian ferries.

'No doubt the most influential feature of the *Finnjet* has proven to be the layout of her accommodations. This is based on an absolute vertical division amidships, between the cabins and the public rooms. All sleeping accommodations are in the quieter forward half of the ship. The public rooms are aft of the cabins and above the ship's machinery and catering facilities. Services in the two parts of the ship are thus arranged around efficient vertical "cores" as is normally done in high-rise hotels ashore. This layout has become very popular and has been used for many jumbo passenger ferries built since the *Finnjet*'s debut. A number of highly successful contemporary cruiseships, including the *Berlin*, *Europa* and *Song of America*, have adopted the same plan.

'The *Finnjet* is something of a floating ambas-

Finnjet

This aerial view clearly shows her rounded bow (courtesy of Wartsila Shipyards).

sador to Finland. She became an instant success with the travelling public, carrying more than 200,000 passengers every year. However, since entering service a number of modifications have been made such as to her machinery so as to allow less expensive low-grade fuels to be used in the interest of economy. In early 1982 [during an extended refit at Amsterdam], a complete alternative set of engines were installed so that she could operate economically at lower speed under diesel-electric power during the winter and while retaining her powerful turbines for fast peak-season summer operation. In 1986, her accommodations were upgraded to the latest standards, with the addition of luxury suites on the upper-most decks. These changes have served to keep the *Finnjet* abreast of the times and in the favor of her clientele.'

A unique, large and powerful vessel, the *Finnjet* is the appropriate selection as the first ferry to feature in this series—others might be included in future volumes of *Fifty Famous Liners*.

Gross tonnage: 24,605 (1977); 25,042 (1981)
Length overall: 692 feet
Width: 83 feet
Machinery: Gas turbines, twin screw (diesel-electric drive in winter months)
Speed: 30.5 knots
Capacity: 1,532 passengers
Built: Wartsila Shipyards, Helsinki, Finland, 1977

She seems huge beside the harbour excursion craft, which is by no means small (courtesy of Theodore W. Scull).

Index

232

Biggest Ship
CRUISING NORWAY

Empress of Australia
OIL BURNER.
22,000 TONS

9 DAYS – 14 GUINEAS
14 DAYS – 20 GUINEAS

The Dream Ship of Cruises

CANADIAN PACIFIC

CANADIAN PACIFIC
WANTED

CHRISTMAS CRUISE TO THE WEST INDIES

LLOYD SABAUDO

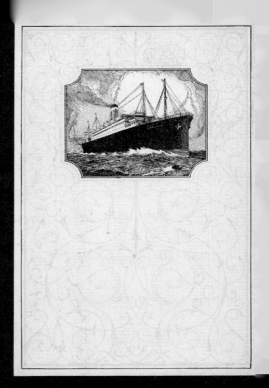

I
M

Launching Program
SS BRASIL

CROCIERE
FRANCA C.
estate 1965

"C."

mediterraneo
oriente
mar nero
atlantico

GO Canadian Pacific
EMPRESS
TO EUROPE

EMPRESS OF BRITAIN   EMPRESS OF ENGLAND
EMPRESS OF FRANCE   EMPRESS OF SCOTLAND